ALSO BY ANGELO M. CODEVILLA

Modern France
Open Court, 1974

The Arms Control Delusion
ICS Press, 1987

While Others Build: The Commonsense Approach to the Strategic
Defense Initiative
Free Press, 1988

War: Ends and Means
Basic Books, 1989

Informing Statecraft: Intelligence for a New Century
Free Press, 1992

American Security: Back to Basics
Hoover Institution Press, 1994

Principe [*The Prince*]
Translated and edited by Angelo M. Codevilla
Yale University Press, 1997

Between the Alps and a Hard Place: Switzerland in World War II and
Moral Blackmail Today
Regnery Publishing, 2000

No Victory, No Peace
Rowman & Littlefield, 2005

Seriousness and Character: The Intellectual History of American
Foreign Policy
Yale University Press, 2006

Advice to War Presidents: A Remedial Course in Statecraft
Basic Books, 2009

*The Character of Nations: How Politics Makes and Breaks
Prosperity, Family, and Civility*
Basic Books, 2009

*The Ruling Class: How They Corrupted America and What We Can
Do About It*
Beaufort Books, 2010

A Student's Guide to International Relations
ISI Books, 2010

To Make and Keep Peace Among Ourselves and with All Nations
Hoover Institution Press, 2014

Informing Statecraft: Intelligence for a New Century

The fruit of many years' experience of intelligence service, this is a masterful exploration of the field, its critical role in statecraft, and the principles underlying its use and misuse ... [a] closely reasoned, authoritative study.

PUBLISHERS WEEKLY

Codevilla's *Informing Statecraft* is an excellent work. It reads like a novel, yet it is sure to become one of the most useful reference books in the library of anyone who works with or benefits from intelligence. I will return to it again and again. Read it at your first opportunity.

JULIE NEUMANN
Naval War College Review

*The Character of Nations: How Politics
Makes and Breaks Prosperity, Family, and Civility*

Codevilla does a good job of demonstrating the social effects of policy.

FRANCIS FUKUYAMA, *Foreign Affairs*

[T]he thesis is simply a sturdy framework on which Codevilla mounts his contention that America today is rotting because its government lacks a basic belief in the rule of law and morality.

PUBLISHERS WEEKLY

Mr. Codevilla's two arguments—against government activism and for government retrenchment—are eloquently presented in this book, and they are eminently plausible.... *The Character of Nations* helps us to think about recent, and, it seems, ever-widening fissures in the conservative movement.

WALL STREET JOURNAL

An impressive catalog of how regimes in different nations have shaped the character of their citizens and a sobering alarm about what America is doing to itself.

ROBERT L. BARTLEY, Pulitzer Prize winner,
Wall Street Journal

A powerfully articulated essay of discontent with the status quo.

BOOKLIST

Advice to War Presidents:
A Remedial Course in Statecraft

Accessible ... Codevilla writes intelligently on topics as diverse as the affect of economic sanctions on Iraq in the 1990s and contemporary relations between Russia and Georgia.

PUBLISHERS WEEKLY

Compelling reading .... There is no shortage of wisdom and wit in Codevilla's book ... bracing and intelligent.

BRET STEPHENS, *Claremont Review of Books*

Advice to War Presidents proffers a bracing tonic for dealing with the world as it is and how to more effectively match means to ends in foreign policy.

JOHN COFFEY, *U.S. Army War College Quarterly: Parameters*

Veteran international relations author Codevilla ... questions basic assumptions that have guided U.S. foreign policy since Woodrow Wilson tried to make the world safe for democracy.... Recommended for academic and larger public libraries.

LIBRARY JOURNAL

Machiavelli could not have written a better book to give advice to "war presidents."

AMERICAN SPECTATOR

Angelo Codevilla teaches as one having authority. The new book by the former Foreign Service officer and professor emeritus of international relations at Boston University, *A Student's Guide to International Relations* delivers the same kind of wisdom and brilliant analysis that filled his earlier books, *War: Ends and Means* and *The Character of Nations*.

CALEB NELSON, *WORLD* Magazine

[T]hese slim volumes come close to constituting mini-great books in themselves.

WALL STREET JOURNAL

*To Make and Keep Peace Among Ourselves
and with All Nations*

Angelo Codevilla makes clear that peace is not preordained. There once was a popular advertisement "When E. F. Hutton speaks we listen." When Angelo Codevilla writes *To Make and Keep Peace*, we listen.

J. WILLIAM MIDDENDORF II
Secretary of the Navy, 1974–1977

To Make and Keep Peace is an eloquent and deeply thoughtful reflection upon the greatest issue of statecraft, war and peace. It is distilled from a career in academia and high levels of government service. Angelo Codevilla has the breadth and depth of experience combined with the intellectual horsepower to understand the dynamics of international power and politics and to see clearly what must be done to avoid repeating the tragic blunders of history. Most importantly he has a precise yet fluid style that engages specialist and nonspecialist alike.

JOHN LEHMAN, Secretary of the Navy, 1981–1987,
and member of the 9/11 Commission

AMERICA'S RISE AND FALL AMONG NATIONS

*Lessons in Statecraft
from John Quincy Adams*

ANGELO M. CODEVILLA

NEW YORK · LONDON

First American edition published in 2022 by Encounter Books,
an activity of Encounter for Culture and Education, Inc.,
a nonprofit, tax-exempt corporation.
Encounter Books website address: www.encounterbooks.com

Manufactured in the United States and printed on
acid-free paper. The paper used in this publication meets
the minimum requirements of ANSI/NISO Z39.48—1992
(R 1997) (*Permanence of Paper*).

FIRST AMERICAN EDITION

LIBRARY OF CONGRESS CATALOGING-IN-PUBLICATION DATA

Names: Codevilla, Angelo, 1943–2021, author.
Title: America's Rise and Fall among Nations: Lessons in Statecraft from
John Quincy Adams / by Angelo M. Codevilla.
Description: First American edition. | New York, New York : Encounter Books,
2022. | Includes bibliographical references and index. |
Identifiers: LCCN 2021048433 (print) | LCCN 2021048434 (ebook) |
ISBN 9781641772723 (hardcover) | ISBN 9781641772730 (ebook)
Subjects: LCSH: Adams, John Quincy, 1767–1848—Influence. | National
security—United States--History. | Nationalism--United States—History. |
United States—Foreign relations.
Classification: LCC E183.7 .C597 2022 (print) | LCC E183.7 (ebook) |
DDC 973.5/5092—dc23/eng/20211116
LC record available at https://lccn.loc.gov/2021048433
LC ebook record available at https://lccn.loc.gov/2021048434

1 2 3 4 5 6 7 8 9 20 22

CONTENTS

This book contrasts America's successful foreign relations under presidents from George Washington to Theodore Roosevelt with the disarray resulting from Progressive management ever since. It shows how the principles that inform these two approaches have had such different consequences. It bids us reenter the minds of America's founding generation to consider how their principles might be applicable in our time.

Differences with regard to the notion of "America First" is not the least of these principles. Presidents George Washington through Theodore Roosevelt would not have used the term to describe United States policy toward other nations—because they would have deemed any other priority to be mad or criminal. By contrast, the Progressive movement that conquered the hearts and minds of American elites a hundred years ago argued precisely that U.S. policy must concern itself primarily with world issues, and with American priorities only secondarily. Because of this, Progressives use the term "America First" to accuse other Americans of neglect of duty, stupidity, or selfishness.

Catchphrases such as "Our strength as a nation is inextricably linked to the strength of our alliances" and "Binding ourselves to international rules enhances our security" assume that peoples and regimes *can* mind each other's business as well as their own, and that they do not mind having their own business minded by foreigners. This is fantasy on so many levels. The reality is that allies—like bank loans—are available in reverse to the need for them, and that nobody likes to be anybody else's tool. Minding one's own business is reality.

In fact, America First, namely pursuing what benefits our American character and advances our legitimate interests—in short, fully minding our own business while leaving other people to mind theirs—was the basis of the United States' successful foreign policy from 1815 to 1910, as best described by John Quincy Adams and carried out by his successors. It is the foreign policy by which America grew great in peace. It fulfills the Declaration of Independence's promise to take up our "separate and equal place among the powers of the earth." It is common sense.

This book looks at the original America-centered foreign policy and compares it to the results of the subsequent century's Progressive policy. Then, it examines our twenty-first century's international environment and asks how our original foreign policy's principles may be applied to it.

That policy sought to secure peace while affirming America's distinctive character. It worked by distinguishing between our business and that of others, and by calibrating our interest in foreign matters according to their importance to America.

By contrast, Progressive policy has sought to create a "better" world by confusing America's interest with mankind's "improvement," by assuming that other governments would or could do the same, and by substituting "progress" for peace. Now that Progressive policy's involvement in other nations' affairs has led to America's own insecurity, Americans are turning once more to America First.

This is necessary because U.S. foreign policy wonks have failed to reconcile what they imagine to be the requirements of successful foreign policy with reality—and with the American people's common sense about it. There is broad agreement within the foreign policy establishment that U.S. foreign policy cannot continue as it has. But its members, stuck in their ways, only offer options that differ in quantity: more or less U.S. "leadership" (read: one kind or another of intervention); or more or less military action. Their suggestions don't lead to confidence that those in power understand what they are doing. Mostly, they don't.

Case in point: Henry Kissinger writes that "the structure of the twenty-first-century world order has been revealed as lacking in four important dimensions." First, nation-states are ever less relevant. Second, pressures for protectionism imperil the world's prosperity. Third, the multiplicity of international "joint declarations" does not reflect any underlying "common conviction."

Fourth, and most importantly for him, the United States is not doing enough to foster world order. Kissinger's analysis (now the U.S. foreign policy establishment's standard), however, is irrelevant to North Korea or Turkey, Russia, China, or Japan. Foreign nations are no longer impressed by our establishment's degrees and pedigrees. They now look to themselves. Our foreign policy establishment gurus haven't noticed their own lack of international standing. Because they imagine a universal culture that mirrors their own outlook, they gave up studying real peoples from the perspective of those peoples' own languages and cultures. Obsessed with themselves, they also came to despise America's unique culture and history. In short, the world's publics, above all Americans, have lost confidence in the people and ideas that have been ruling them for generations.

And for good reason. Since World War II, U.S. political and military leaders have gotten more than twice as many Americans killed in Korea, Vietnam, the Middle East, etc., as in all of World War I—and multiples of that number injured. The U.S. government supported allies and enemies—real and imagined—in its quarrels around the globe and spent trillions of dollars on behalf of those judged best fit to uphold "world order." But after all this, foreigners' disrespect of Americans is higher than ever, endangering our safety abroad and even at home. Each generation of leaders left America worse off than they found it. Nobody respects serial losers. A taste for violent nation-building abroad has kindled the violent desire to do the same at home. America's ruling class has proved itself ignorant, impotent, and corrupt. Yet its members seem to think that the American people's desires are foolish and not in our own "best interests."

On the contrary: the American people's hunger for peace, our sharp distinction between Americans and foreigners, our rejection of no-win wars, our demands for defensive military superiority for crushing terrorists, and for hostility if not outright aggressiveness toward America's enemies—in short, our preference for an America First policy—are not incompatible. Understanding the reasonableness and compatibility of these demands requires only openness to the history of America's past success and failures. It also requires attention to the changes that have occurred and are occurring in the world around us and in our country as well.

Another reason for revisiting early American foreign policy is that refocusing on America itself, and the name of John Quincy Adams, has become attractive to many—as has the label "America First." Yet some have attempted to use these sentiments to justify their longstanding preference for diminishing and disarming America. Such attempts are intellectually illegitimate because they are contrary to fact. Adams, who followed George Washington, as well as the statesmen who followed him into the twentieth century's first decade, were proud advocates of American greatness. And even the most peace-loving among them would fight for America's honor even more readily than for U.S. interests—of which peace is foremost.

This book, then, is written to provide its reader with a factual basis by which to contrast how America's role among nations has been mismanaged during the past one hundred years.

This author realizes that any country's foreign policy is less a choice between alternative courses of action than it is another expression of the character of the nation itself and of the persons who set its tone. Any country's relationship with others depends on and changes with these. Ancient Sparta, an armed camp without walls, behaved moderately and cautiously with regard to its neighbors, because the ruling class of Spartans was all about forestalling revolt by Helot slaves. The Athenian polity of Miltiades and Themistocles that defeated the Persians at Marathon and Salamis "in a manner not to be forgotten" had aided Ionian cities. But imperial Athens, under Pericles, Cleon, and Alcibiades, had become accustomed to living off them. Caesar Augustus's desire to keep his newly founded empire within peaceful limits proved powerless against the Roman people's continual passion for war. What kind of peace is America capable of today?

In America, as everywhere else, a people's choices and priorities reflect who they are. For a people to settle on who they are collectively is essential for its existence as a nation even more than for its relations with other nations. Today, we Americans are divided about who we are. The most influential among us despise their fellow citizens, America as a nation, and our civilization itself. Other Western peoples suffer the same weakness.

Lately, non-Western governments have sought to represent their peoples to themselves as completely different from—if not hostile to—a Western Civilization they see as failing. Thus we see the government of Turkey Islamizing the Hagia Sophia cathedral to pretend kinship with the Ottoman Empire; India's prime minister building a Hindu temple on a Mughal mosque as if Hindu gods could cancel castes rather than conform them; China's Communist Party presenting itself as the legitimate heir of Confucius; and Vladimir Putin wearing the Russian Orthodox Church's cross.

In spite of the limited extent to which these attempts are rooted in fact, and the scarce relevance of their content to what gives these nations whatever importance they have today, these actions answer the vital need to rally their peoples behind symbols of identities that, whatever else may be said of them, at least are uninfected by what they perceive as the sociopolitical disease that debilitates America and Europe.

In Part Two we will see the extent to which Americans' increasing conflicts regarding values and priorities have weakened the United States among nations. But we begin by noting that the statesmanship that turned small settlements into a great nation flowed from the American people's character.

American foreign policy's successes from George Washington's time to Theodore Roosevelt's must be understood less as the result of wise choices—though they were mostly wise—than as reflections of the American people's and their leaders' character in those years. Unfortunately, these traits have changed in the last hundred years. As a result, peace at home and abroad such as Americans enjoyed back then may come less by imitation of yesteryear's policies than by a return to our ancestors' principles and character.

What follows is not a list of recipes. The text invites us to reenter the minds of the statesmen who made America; to understand the character, beliefs, and qualities in their America that they sought to encourage as they dealt with the realities of international affairs; to consider the radicality of the Progressive movement's shift from these realities to a statecraft based on an imaginative view of America and the world; and to review how this shift's consequences have made the United States government both over-armed and impotent, over-allied and at odds with much of mankind—even with its own people. Then, we try to recapture our foreign policy's relationship with reality by looking at today's world from within the minds of America's founding generation.

*PART I—THE FOUNDATIONS OF
AMERICAN FOREIGN POLICY*

THEME

What were America's founders and their followers trying to foster and preserve by their conduct among nations? What were they trying to put first? Why did the Progressives turn away from these concerns? What did they put first? How dismissive were they of reality? What have been Progressivism's effects on how America has fared among nations? How have changes in the world and in America itself made it impossible to continue on the Progressive course? How would John Quincy and those following his principles manage America's present international situation? By what principles might today's statesmen put America First?

In America, as everywhere else, a people's choices and priorities reflect who they are. From the earliest settlements, Americans have thought themselves fortunate that they or their ancestors had distanced themselves from the rest of European civilization— and not just geographically. America was their final destination. They had not come on the way to anywhere else. Few went back. They left old quarrels and did not come to start new ones. They came because they expected America to be different, a nearly empty land where they would have peace, freedom, and the bread that their hands earned. And that is why Americans' relations with foreigners were always premised on appreciation for what made America different. Putting America First meant more than natural self-interest. It meant putting a better, describably different way of life first.

The Americans

The Europeans who had come to America had not been great men—actual or would-be contenders in Europe's partisan or national struggles. Although the Puritans were unusually concerned with spiritual perfection, most early arrivals were ordinary but adventuresome Brits and Germans, old-fashioned about their Christianity and morals. They had left the Old Country to escape its troubles, as well as to run their own affairs, and had become happily accustomed to running their own lives with a minimum of trouble from without. The Puritan strain has played a considerable role in America's foreign as well as domestic affairs. But for most Americans, the overriding objective of American foreign policy has ever been, first of all, protecting a decent, autonomous way of life for our citizens.

Putting America First always meant defending that way of life. Until 1765, frontier life in New England and New York also meant serving in militias to fight the Indian tribes that slaughtered, enslaved, and retreated behind France's protection. In 1812, the local militia was not enough to prevent Indians armed by Britain from massacring the inhabitants of the Chicago settlement. So long as Spain held Florida, it enabled deadly Indian raids into the southern United States. In west-central Texas, the Comanche held up the frontier for a half century. President Lyndon Johnson's mother narrowly escaped being murdered by them as a baby. Neither the British nor the French, nor the Spaniards who controlled the exit from the Mississippi, nor the Barbary pirates who ruled the Mediterranean, were going to be nice to impotent Americans. The founders had won America's independence by cruel war and were perfectly willing to make war for its honor and for the safety of Americans. Peace-loving Americans had no pacifist illusions.

Neither did they mean to "isolate" themselves. Americans may have been more dependent on international commerce than any other people in history, and at least as eager as any to explore the globe. Americans' relations with peoples who differed from themselves in every way, whether ancient civilizations or modern despotisms, were easy and peaceful because Americans' focus on their own business made them uninterested in others' affairs. George Washington never lost an opportunity to urge his fellow citizens to view their concerns through the prism of their identities as Americans.

The Founders

In the first six of the *Federalist Papers*, Alexander Hamilton, James Madison, and John Jay summarized the opinions about foreign affairs common in the mass media of the day—sermons and newspapers. Foremost, Americans wanted peace. In No. 3, Jay wrote that peace being Americans' objective, we must neither insult nor injure foreigners. That means minding our own business. And in No. 4, he wrote that peace would also depend on readiness to punish foreigners' interference in our affairs. In No. 6, Hamilton pointed out that since wars arise from ubiquitous, unpredictable causes and circumstances, Americans must be ever ready to fight. The founders also knew that, as other nations were surely going to fight among themselves, Americans had better be careful lest they be drawn into others' quarrels. More than a century later, Theodore Roosevelt summed all this up in homespun terms: "Speak softly and carry a big stick."

No sooner had the Constitution come into being than the quarter century of the French Revolution's wars became the crucible in which the American people's international character was forged. George Washington's 1793 proclamation of neutrality in those wars, seconded by Alexander Hamilton's *Pacificus* and *Americanus* essays, and young John Quincy Adams's *Marcellus*, laid the theoretical base. Washington's 1796 farewell address warned against the domestic temptations that entice us to set aside our geographic good fortune and common sense. "Why quit our own to stand on foreign ground?" Washington asked. "Observe good faith and justice toward all nations," he adjured. He argued that neutrality with regard to others' business is the other side of intense focus on our own. By contrast, confusing other nations' interests with our own, he said, sets us against one another.

Since Washington's statecraft aimed foremost at uniting Americans, he was careful—even when waging a war in which a significant part of the population sided with the enemy—to treat all as if they were loyal citizens.

Washington never tired of urging his fellow citizens to have arm's length relationships with foreign nations and to back them up with a respectable army. His successor, John Adams, fathered the U.S. Navy. The lead ship thereof, the *U.S.S. Constitution*, is still in commission.

In 1777, John Adams took his son, ten-year-old John Quincy, on his diplomatic mission to secure military aid from France and loans from Holland. The boy grew up fast—mastering perfect French and Dutch, helping his father, and conversing with statesmen. In 1781, when Charles Francis Dana was appointed to represent the United States in Saint Petersburg, fourteen-year-old J. Q. Adams accompanied him as his secretary. Since Dana spoke no French—the language of Russia's elites—J. Q. effectively transacted the embassy's business for two years. In 1784, when John Adams became America's representative to King George III, seventeen-year-old John Quincy functioned as his father's deputy. That was before entering Harvard, and then studying law. In 1794, George Washington appointed John Quincy Adams minister to the Netherlands. Successive presidents then sent him to represent the United States in Prussia, Russia, and Great Britain. In the course of these duties, he also became fluent in German, Russian, Italian, and Spanish. Since earliest youth, he had read the Latin and Greek classics.

As secretary of state (1817–1825), J. Q. Adams summed up and personified what America's unique people would have to do to live peacefully among diverse nations. As we will see, although J. Q. Adams did not invent any principles of statecraft, neither adding to nor subtracting from what Washington, Hamilton, and his father had prescribed, his dispatches, diary, and memoirs specified and applied their principles in a way that constitutes a comprehensive course of instruction for international relations in general, and for American statecraft in particular.

Adams shared, specified, and conveyed to his successors the founding generation's fundamental interest in preserving and enhancing America's own character. He sought occasions for reminding other nations—but especially our own—of the principles that make America what it is. Doing this encourages us to carefully consider how any decision we make in international affairs affects what is most important to ourselves as well as to others.

Adams is the fount of American geopolitical thought. The reader should pay particular attention to Adams's primordial distinction between America's own interests—hence the "causes" for which Americans might fight—as well as to the (largely geographic) bases for evaluating the extent to which any cause or interest may be our own. The peoples on our borders and on the islands around us concern us most, followed by the oceans, then the rest of the world. Diplomatic experience had also taught Adams that, where the interests of nations coincide, negotiated agreements are scarcely necessary, and that when interests do not coincide, agreements are not worth the paper they are written on. That is why Adams practiced and taught a meticulous sort of diplomacy that aims at the mutual clarification of objectives.

John Quincy Adams considered the treaty that extended the United States' border to the Pacific Ocean to have been his great achievement, alongside having established good relations with the governments of Britain, Russia, and so forth, in full acknowledgment of the radical differences between their regimes and ours. Adams had not invented the principle of mutual non-interference. That principle is, after all, the essence of the 1648 treaties of Westphalia. But Adams's formulation of the Monroe Doctrine established non-interference as American foreign policy's operational core.

The Legacy

Perhaps nothing shows how thoroughly Adams's ways had conquered American statesmen's minds as does his successor Andrew Jackson's conduct. Jackson had beaten Adams in a bitter election. No two Americans could have been more different. Nevertheless, like Adams, Jackson combined commitment to peace and harmony with near-reflexive retaliation to physical attacks on Americans and on America's honor. Like Adams, Jackson was about enhancing America. But despite being a man of the sword, his attempts to gain additional territory from Mexico were limited to offers of purchase, just as Adams's had been. And though President Jackson owned slaves, his refusal to admit Texas as a slave state and his forceful stand against South Carolina's attempt to nullify federal law were as forceful as Adams's would have been. America's greatness had been Adams's great objective—a greatness that could not be purchased by unjust war or by any sacrifice of its principles.

In short, John Quincy Adams had codified the founding generation's principles in foreign affairs into a set of practices by statesmen and expectations on the part of the public. That is why even the far-lesser statesmen in the years preceding the Civil War adhered to the Adams Paradigm, if—as in the case of the Mexican War (1846–48)—only ineptly and hypocritically. To wit: President Polk *did not intend* to start the Mexican War; he *resisted pressures* to take over Mexico for nation-building, and *paid Mexico* the price he would have paid to purchase what he conquered. Meanwhile, presidents between Jackson and Lincoln delivered peaceful adjustment of interests with the rest of mankind.

Abraham Lincoln's first major speech expressed his quintessentially American approach to international affairs: "All the armies in the world led by a Bonaparte, disposing of the earth's treasure, our own excepted, could not take a drink from the Ohio or make a track on the Blue Ridge in a trial of a thousand years." Only Americans, he said, can truly hurt America. And they can do that only by putting their own passions and interests against America itself. That is why, as discord led to secession, Lincoln adjured the South not to start the war. Both Northerners and Southerners, he said, must think of themselves as Americans, first.

Because Lincoln kept in mind Washington's commitment to treating fellow Americans as citizens, he aimed his conduct of the Civil War at reconciliation from start to finish. All manner of war aroused Lincoln's deepest fears. "Peace among ourselves and with all nations" was the star by which he steered.

Following that star and the American people's sentiments, William Seward, secretary of state and Lincoln's closest adviser, helped return America to a path of peaceful, righteous greatness. Having eulogized John Quincy Adams, Seward showed what the Monroe Doctrine can mean by helping drive French imperialism out of Mexico. Like Jefferson and Adams, Seward built up America

by purchasing a big chunk of territory (Alaska). He grew it also by
recruiting immigrants who could contribute talent and effort. His
frank, generous diplomacy with China laid bases of friendship
that more than a century's vicissitudes have never wholly erased.

Temptations

As Seward and the statesmen of the following half
century tried to practice the founders' statecraft, they had to deal
with the new temptations that stemmed from America's growing
power. Principle, not national weakness, had led George Washington, John Quincy Adams, and Andrew Jackson, the American lion,
to practice "good faith and justice" to all nations. Nevertheless,
temptation to throw America's weight around had not presented
itself to them. Starting about 1880, it did.

The temptations of big-country status first presented themselves in the Western Hemisphere. In the 1880s, the U.S. government's attempt to mediate a border dispute between Guatemala
and Mexico produced only trouble with Mexico. Peru and Chile
sought U.S. influence against one another. What were the limits
of U.S. concern with foreign lands? Geography always meant that
it would be dangerous for Hawaii to come into a hostile power's
possession. By the late nineteenth century, American sugar plant-
ers had come to dominate there and wanted to be annexed. But
Hawaii had a native government that prized independence. Justice was on one side, interest on the other. Meanwhile, either or
both France and Britain considered digging a canal across Nicaragua or Colombia as they had at Suez. Surely, this would impact
America's security. But what right had Americans to prevent such
a thing? As these things were happening, Germany was building
coaling stations on South Pacific islands where similar U.S. facilities were located. How could Americans secure themselves
against being denied trans-Pacific coaling?

To roughly sum it up, U.S. foreign policy in the two decades
between the 1877 withdrawal of Union troops from the South and
the imperialist fever that briefly infected America at the turn of
the century, resulted from the countervailing influences of radical

Republican James G. Blaine and conservative Democrat Grover Cleveland—the first more active and intrusive than the second. As presidents and secretaries of state alternated, U.S. policy swayed gently from one side to the other of the Adams Paradigm, never exceeding its bounds. In the South Pacific, Americans reached an "understanding" with German Chancellor Otto von Bismarck. Quietly but surely, America let the world know that any canal across the Americas could only be part of the U.S. coastline. Inevitably, Hawaii was becoming part of the United States. Americans reciprocated Japan's friendship. American missionaries flowed to China, as U.S. policy tried to limit European powers' exploitation of it. U.S. policy for Latin America focused on J. Q. Adams's original concern: limiting European influence. In short, as the century was closing, America reaped peace from a foreign policy of peaceful benevolence.

Imperialism

Few could imagine that peace would turn into war from an excess of benevolence. But that is what happened.

The European virus of imperialism struck America's upper classes, whose hearts and minds had already been infected with Progressivism. That social–moral disease had been present among the Northerners and Southerners who had integrated their contrasting sentiments regarding slavery into their own narratives about human progress. Those conflations of politics, morality, and pseudoscientific millennialism, that self-identification with the "greater good," explain to a large extent the willingness of both sides to fight in a way that killed some two percent of the entire population. Progressivism and the sense of duty to spread some kind of progress made nineteenth-century European imperialism different from that of previous centuries. The imperialism that so thoroughly infected some Americans was the altruistic kind depicted in Rudyard Kipling's poem "The White Man's Burden."

Just about nobody in America fought the 1898–1903 Spanish–American War to end up managing an empire. The war's efficient cause was the American people's desire, fueled by the press, to

stop Spain's maltreatment of the rebellious Cuban people. The
most powerful argument for stopping it, the argument that President McKinley cited, was none other than the question raised by
Christ's parable of the Good Samaritan: what if that good man had
come by as the mugging was happening? Is it right to stand by as
evil is being perpetrated? As we shall see, American statesmen in
1898 had no intention of transcending the founders' foreign policy. But, because war has its own logic, transcend it they did.

In 1900, as Senator Albert Beveridge (R–IN) was arguing for
fighting harder to subdue resistance to U.S. rule in the Philippines, he said: "The Declaration of Independence does not forbid
us to do our part in the regeneration of the world. If it did, the
Declaration would be wrong." Though that statement appealed to
many, it would have had no traction two years earlier, as Americans were debating intervention in Cuba. Nobody wanted to rule
it, never mind to regenerate it.

By the following year, Andrew Carnegie's quip about "having
substantially civilized and sent to heaven" some eight thousand
Filipinos struck President McKinley deeply. Within another two
years, the crest of empire's glories had passed over the U.S. population. Thereafter, some of the 1890s' most vocal imperialists,
notably Theodore Roosevelt and Sen. Henry Cabot Lodge (R–MA),
had refocused soberly and forcefully on peace, national power,
and balancing ends with means.

Power, Peace, and Policy

President Theodore Roosevelt relished the United
States' power and shared the founders' commitment to peace as
well as their understanding that peace is to be earned by focusing
on America's own business. He personified the fact that great
power wielded strictly on America's own behalf and measured to
its purpose is likeliest to secure peace.

Roosevelt had always despised most imperialists for being
concerned with foreign nations as if these were their own. Rudyard
Kipling had written "The White Man's Burden" as if to sober TR
about imperialism. Empire, said Kipling, means to "send your

sons to exile, to serve your captives' need" and "to seek another's profit and work another's gain." It means ending up with "the blame of those ye better, the hate of those ye guard." America's experience in the Philippines was confirming these warnings; thus, TR's steadfast love for America First, and his experience dealing with other nations at the highest levels, led him back to the founders' fundamentals.

As a patriot and a scholar of naval history, TR had always advocated for the biggest, most modern navy possible and was dismayed to see Progressives, including many imperialists, advocate for foreign commitments while holding back money for the U.S. Navy. Solvency—squaring ends and means—is common sense, he said. Like Washington and the Adamses, TR saw no contradiction between armed force and peaceful intentions. He proved the diplomatic truth of this with his orders to the Great White Fleet that circled the globe: to be battle ready and practice gunnery at all times, but to conduct themselves as eager tourists and grateful guests in a grand traveling show of friendship. Enlistment in the Navy soared.

TR's conflict with President Woodrow Wilson was prototypical of mutually exclusive paradigms of statecraft. TR supported the efforts of Progressives, such as his own secretary of war (and then of state), Elihu Root, to arrange for the arbitration of international disputes and treaties to reduce the horrors of war. But, as a disciple of John Quincy Adams, TR always warned that such arrangements could not possibly bind nations against their own wishes. For this reason, he said, no one ought to count on such agreements to have any effect on matters involving what governments consider their vital interests. Wilson spoke as if he believed that treaties *could* do just that, even as the Great War that they were supposed to have forestalled was raging.

Wilson said and believed that America exists for no other purpose than to serve mankind. TR thought this was nonsense because no nation can decide for any other what serves it; he considered it a lie because it denied that the founders had committed their lives, fortunes, and sacred honor to serve only Americans, and because the American people never voted to change that

primary commitment. For Wilson, humanity's good was primary
and America's secondary. For TR, it was the other way around.
Because Wilson's inversion of priorities was divorced from reality,
he was able to talk about grand objectives without explaining,
even to himself, what those priorities entailed by way of actions,
costs, and consequences. TR insisted that seriousness means
doing precisely that accounting. For Wilson, foreign policy was
about reshaping the world. For TR, it was about shielding the
Republic.

Precisely why did Wilson and his followers step off the solid
ground of America First? They talked a lot about humanity. But no
genie of humanity had ever whispered in their ears. No, they had
deserted the priorities of ordinary Americans, not for those of other
nations, but for their very own priorities, which they thought
more noble—just as they thought themselves more noble than
ordinary Americans. Because Wilson led America into the Great
War on behalf of his private abstractions, and because his admirer
Franklin Delano Roosevelt led America into an even greater war
on similar bases, the American people have known little peace
ever since.

From Hope to Pretense

Minds obsessed with abstractions ignore concerns
with concrete matters. To defend against truth, lies call forth
more lies. But lies discredit liars.

Wilson had wanted to take America into the Great War for reasons that the American people did not share. That is why he
engaged in undeclared co-belligerency with Britain: to invite German reactions that would serve as excuses for open war. But why
did Americans fight Germans in 1917? Wilson fed hopes of the
perpetual peace that he promised would follow naturally from
Germany's utter defeat. He branded as traitors whoever questioned that. He then told Americans that his League of Nations
would make it unnecessary ever to fight again, *and* that it would
require fighting to destroy any and all challenges to world peace.
When voters rejected that as the proverbial three-dollar bill and

concluded that Wilson's war had been a deadly fraud, Wilson and his followers blamed Americans for "isolationism"!

Meanwhile, Wilson's followers of both parties continued to pursue gauzy goals, only formally following the public's determination never again to be fooled into bloodshed for anything but for America itself. What could have been the point, for example, of the bipartisan praise heaped on the Washington Treaties of 1921 that guaranteed China's territorial integrity while reducing the U.S. Navy's size and promising not to fortify U.S. bases in the Far East? What effect on America's maintenance of its own peace might any reasonable person have expected to result from FDR's secretary of state, the Wilson-worshiping Cordell Hull's 1937 circular to the world's powers impotently preaching good behavior?

In sum, Wilson's Democrat and Republican followers did just enough to put the U.S. in the middle of wars in Europe and Asia. Meanwhile, they starved the U.S. armed forces. Statesmen from George Washington to TR would have warned that they were blundering into the middle of a second world war even more incompetently than Wilson had blundered into the first. What, they would have asked, are you doing to limit our exposure and to strengthen our capacity to keep our peace?

When the shooting started, FDR did what Wilson had done: he substituted hate for the enemy and promises of a new world for concrete plans to serve and secure America. Charles de Gaulle, who visited FDR in 1944, noted that the president's "broad brush strokes" showed estrangement from the war's practical issues, an estrangement guarded by the demand for unconditional surrender.

Cold War Eclipse

FDR's inattention to international issues was due at least in part to his attention to his domestic political coalition's varying demands. Not the least part of that coalition dreamed of exercising a Progressive world co-dominion with Stalin's communist regime under the United Nations' formalities. Other Progressives, whose ranks grew as America's power spread over the globe

throughout the war, came to think of themselves as humanity's
teachers, vanguard, etc.

After World War II, the now swollen U.S. foreign policy establishment split into roughly three groups. One group confused
America's interest strictly with "defeating communism." Another
confused it with "getting along" with this most Progressive of
forces. But the establishment's biggest part confused it simply
with "exercising global leadership." All together, they overlooked
concrete concerns with America itself.

The FDR administration radically expanded the number of
official and unofficial persons involved in formulating and exe-
cuting foreign policy. The president's own reluctance to deal with
details, along with the complexities of world war, meant that the
government's decisions were becoming the geometric result of
countervailing establishment pressures, more or less arbitrated
by the president. After the war, the number of persons involved
grew into yet another arm of the administrative state that decides
internally, non-responsibly. No longer focused by and on the president's understanding of America First, U.S. foreign policy fused
with the fancies and interests of individuals and groups.

During the Cold War's forty years, America's foreign policy
evolved with the changes in this establishment. Unanimously
and completely, it rejected the intellectual/moral compass by
which statesmen from Washington to TR had steered. As the
establishment matured into solipsism, it loosed the remainder of
what had bound it to reality. Members of the establishment practiced a foreign policy aimed less at affirming America than at
denying reality.

International Leadership and War

In the postwar world, being an American was an
enviable lot. The war left America the world's only undamaged,
bountiful producer of all good things. Because all manner of foreigners were seeking some help from Americans, U.S. civil and military officials and businessmen could be forgiven for taking too
seriously the flattery and offers that came their way apparently to

take a hand in their affairs. It was seductive to believe that the foreigners were following America, rather than asking Americans to fuel vehicles that only the locals could steer. American Progressives, imagining the golden chance had arrived to realize the dreams that had animated their movement since the 1880s, the chance to really *do* what Wilson had hinted and FDR had promised, set about what they imagined to be re-creating the world in their own image.

They produced a caricature, in large part because they were not trying to replicate America—unrealistic as even that would have been. Rather, they were trying to bring into reality their own imagination. In what had been Europe's African, Asian, and Middle Eastern colonies, this resulted in a set of corrupt, oppressive, anti-American regimes that we now know as the Third World. In the developed world, American statesmen fostered economic arrangements that—behind high tariff walls and enjoying low tariff access to America and in league with U.S. multinational corporations— went on to substantially de-industrialize America.

No one should be surprised that, wherever and whenever the U.S. Progressive ruling class used America's money and influence, it thereby advanced the fortunes of persons they believed to be of the same intellectual, moral, and political stamp as themselves. Because they succeeded in this, the relationship between rulers and ruled in much of today's Western world—as in America itself—is one of mutual contempt.

Keeping foreign lands out of Soviet hands was merely the international background of and the domestic justification for the U.S. establishment's deep involvement in other nations' affairs. Its members acted as they did because it gave them no small professional satisfaction and personal gain.

The Progressive ruling class's seriousness about transformative global leadership came intertwined with and at the expense of growing unseriousness about military matters. This has its recent roots in the FDR administration's recycling of Woodrow Wilson's fraud that the victory by a league of peace-loving nations would banish war forever. Hard to comprehend nowadays, but not so long ago America's ruling class really did believe this, and went on believing it, even in the UN. Hence, reality be damned, they started to deny the reality of the real wars that came their way.

They also believed that the invention of nuclear weapons had made it impossible for nations—especially the U.S. and the Soviet Union—to fight real wars. But since military threats big and small could not be imagined away, Progressive American academics and officials tried to make sense of what they were doing by working and reworking Progressivism's false premises into any number of theories about deterrence and limited war. Between about 1959 and 1975, these theories came to dominate America's (but only America's) highest venues.

The intellectual and practical development of this flight from reality matured in how the U.S. government fought military campaigns in Korea and Vietnam. No doubt, keeping communist enemies at bay was part of the reason—and the entire rationale—for the U.S. government sacrificing over a hundred thousand American lives in these so-called "small wars," in the same way that the so-called War on Terror was wholly justified in terms of safeguarding Americans from terrorists but had little to do with terrorism. Rather, these commitments and the way the government carried them out has had less to do with their ostensible purposes than with Progressive ideology's negations of reality and with the corporate interests of the establishment's several factions. In 1961, Henry Kissinger had written that the United States should engage in the sort of wars that "a great nation can afford to lose." America lost the wars. But many made their fortunes in them.

From the first, detachment from reality and the common good characterized the manner in which the establishment has dealt with nuclear weaponry. Abstruse language has not totally obscured the dread fact that the U.S. government, officially and for real, has consistently refused to place any barriers to Russian and Chinese nuclear-tipped missiles striking American soil. The government's expensive refusal to safeguard the country against such missiles, even from North Korea, has stripped naked its incompetence.

The War on Terror, against no one in particular and with no concrete objective, became a vehicle by which persons in power advanced personal, corporate, and partisan interests. Advantage over domestic competitors was high among these. Quickly, they applied the label "terrorist" to their domestic competitors, and increasingly turned that war's extraordinary powers against other Americans. No more thorough negation of the Washington/Adams approach to war can be imagined.

In short, the American people, having experienced foreign policy as an endless drain of blood, treasure, and honor detached from and even opposed to the common good, have withdrawn support, even respect, for their government's role among nations.

America's Real Circumstances

The American people and international circumstances of today could hardly have been imagined only a few decades ago. They have come about in no small part due to how America's Progressive ruling class has thought and ruled. Surely, the pitiful results should prevent this ruling class from continuing as it has.

During the twentieth century's second half, U.S. statesmen made excuses for and deflected criticism of their meddling in other nations' affairs, and of making wars that they refused to try to win, by citing the need to prudently protect against the deadly Soviet monster. By 1991, when that monster had died of its congenital diseases, they had already gone a long way toward earning for America the reputation of an overweight, intrusive, unserious, and incompetent paper tiger. The end of the long Cold War emergency should have led them to reset foreign policy onto solid, timeless grounds. Instead, freed from the last vestiges of responsibility, they gave free rein to their Progressive tendencies which, over the past thirty years, have neutered the United States of America among nations.

In the Gulf War of 1990–91, they showed once again how incompetence can negate power and options. Saddam Hussein's conquest of Kuwait had not disadvantaged America. Saddam made neither more nor less difference to America after his conquest than he had before. But the Bush 41 administration struck at him on behalf of Saudi Arabia and of its own notion of a "new world order." Then, according to those priorities and earlier Progressive doctrines, it decided (as Machiavelli used to say) neither to caress nor to extinguish Saddam, but merely to diminish him— a huge mistake.

This combination of recklessness and fecklessness unleashed three decades of Muslim terrorism against America, to which the U.S. ruling class reacted with inconceivably counterproductive measures. Instead of holding foreign leaders accountable with their lives for incitement and troubles that came from their jurisdictions, they sent American troops to try to bring democracy to their peoples. Instead of reducing contact with Muslim countries and mobilizing the American people to guard against the Muslims already among us, they imported a million immigrants from the Muslim world; imposed demoralizing, useless security measures on the entire U.S. population; and accused their fellow Americans of racism. Who'd have thought that some Americans would do such things to other Americans?

During the past three decades, the international environment has become ever more hostile to America. In Russia, Communism's collapse had been followed by a wave of pro-Western, pro-American sentiment. But U.S. statesmen's impotent preaching combined with incompetent involvement with the former Communist party bosses that were privatizing the country into their own pockets quickly made Russians anti-American for the first time in history.

In 1990, China had loomed small. Its economy was worth $367 billion while America's was about $6 trillion. Neither was China a military threat. By 2020, China was a major power. Its economy was worth some $15 trillion to America's roughly $25 trillion. But China had become the world's premier manufacturing power, so much so that America depended on it for basic goods. By going into business with major U.S. companies, China had become a major power within America itself. Its military had de facto control of East Asia. Its semi-official anti-U.S. alliance with Russia bid for all manner of alliances, convergences, etc., against America around the globe. As China scared and seduced South Korea, Japan found it increasingly difficult to regard America as its insurance against being encompassed within China's greater East Asia co-prosperity sphere. In sum, most of the security Americans had earned in the Pacific War of 1941–45 was gone.

By 2020, Europe had long since ceased to be America's ally. Anti-Americanism had been growing among Europe's ruling classes since the 1960s. That continued growth, along with the Muslim world's post-1990 virulence against America, combined with increasing Muslim migration into Europe, had made Old Europe into a political deadweight for America, if not into politically hostile territory. Yes, relations between its ruling classes and America's continued to be close. But, increasingly, as the ruling classes on both sides of the Atlantic were beset by challenges from their own people—as neither set of elites could nor would marshal popular support for their transatlantic partners—they related to each other on ever-narrower bases.

In the new century, as America's Progressive statesmen lost war after endless war, *as the reservoir of respect for America dried up*, it seems that no petty dictator has passed up the chance to inflict harm or humiliation on Americans. This recalls Montesquieu's description of the Romans in the Western Empire's last years: "There was no people group so small that it could not do them [the Romans] harm."

The biggest changes occurred within America itself. In short, the U.S. ruling classes ceased to respect the American people who, in turn, have ceased to respect their rulers. More fundamentally, both rulers and ruled have become very different from the Americans who bestrode the globe in the mid-twentieth century.

All measures of personal and social power show the American people's diminished capacities. Today's Americans read, count, and comprehend less well than their parents, and much less well than their grandparents. Their knowledge of basic science and history is inferior. That is because today's Americans spend less time studying. A majority of young adults report having cheated on exams and papers. Fewer score at the highest levels of standardized tests. And as objective performance declines, the level of grades continues to rise, especially at prestigious universities. American elites describe themselves as a meritocracy. But for decades, under a variety of pretexts—especially non-discrimination—America's elites have raised up successors who excel principally at pleasing their superiors. Round after round, the negative selection of elites degraded America.

Nearly all the Americans who fought in World War II had grown to adulthood with two married parents. But today, the most basic measure of social irresponsibility—data on births outside of families, combined with data on divorces—shows that only a minority of today's Americans grow to adulthood with two married parents. Nor does a majority of today's Americans grow up as part of any church or synagogue. Americans who grow without allegiance to family or God don't learn allegiance to the country in school. Often, schools teach the contrary. Political allegiances are most likely to be to ideas and groups juxtaposed to those of other Americans. Increasingly, Americans experience their government as partisan and capricious. The experience of three generations has taught them that their government plays global chess with their sacrifices. It loses, moves on, and does it again.

Progressives practiced their brand of foreign policy, drawing on the American people's reservoir of competence, initiative, and patriotism. They also drew on the reservoir of respect that Americans had built up among nations. These reservoirs have never been lower. It remains to be seen whether any foreign policy for today's America is possible. But to be credible in today's domestic and international reality, any such policy must be highly focused on what little today's diminished Americans have in common. Dispensing with Progressivism's fancies, foreign policy must return to the role of fiduciary for America, as well as to the founding generation's principles and practices.

Old Wine in New Bottles

No task is more important, or more difficult to accomplish, than recovering respect. But attempting to recover it by abruptly jettisoning unwise commitments or by simply withdrawing from foolish positions would merely continue to squander it by ignoring any reasonable definition of policy.

Redirection of efforts or redeployment of any kind of force

necessarily contains some element of retreat. But any retreat is most dangerous because it tends to confuse and discourage those who practice it while emboldening adversaries. That is why redeployments, however useful, must be part of that reasonable connection between actions taken and things desired that aim at success and deserve names like "policy" and "strategy." "America First" is the most concise description possible of the studied complex of objectives, reasoning, and actions by which America's founders related to other nations.

Fully and safely returning to the principles and practices that built the once-great but now-depleted reservoir of respect for America requires disposing of current problems in a manner that enhances America. That means leaving enemies either dead or sorry that they ever troubled America, and eager to avoid giving Americans cause for reengaging against them. And that means using our unrivaled economic position and naval power seriously and unforgettably to hurt enemies in areas from which we withdraw.

It means counter-fortifying against the military deployments that allowed China to dominate the eastern Pacific Rim, and it means making economic war on China to compensate for the economic war it has waged on us, until China decides to act in strategically peaceful ways. With regard to Russia, it means coming to terms of geopolitical reciprocity with it—demanding that it reverse its support of anti-American regimes in the Western Hemisphere on pain of U.S. economic warfare, while Americans cease to abet anti-Russian activities in Russia's front yard.

Simple to conceive, the principles by which early Americans earned respect have always been hard to practice. "*Shut up about other people's business!*" has *always* been the bedrock principle of international communication. John Jay did not make it so in *Federalist* No. 3; nor did George Washington in his farewell address; nor John Quincy Adams's instructions with regard to South America's and Greece's struggles for independence; nor Theodore Roosevelt's rebukes to imperialists. For these statesmen, minding their own business was second nature.

These leaders recalled Americans to that principle precisely because many in their time were paying insufficient attention to it while others violated it to showcase their pretenses to virtue. In our time—Progressives having made loose talk a virtue—the beginning of international seriousness must consist of restricting official comments strictly to America's own business, speaking unadorned truth insofar as it concerns ourselves, saying what you mean and meaning what you say. Alas, only serious people can do that.

John Quincy Adams did not install peace as international relations' primary goal or discover that mutual non-interference is the foundation of peace. That primacy and that principle happen to be the foundation of the modern (post-1648) international system. J. Q. Adams's formulation of the Monroe Doctrine simply made that principle into a system of priorities adapted to the United States of America's peculiar regime and geographic circumstances. Since these peculiarities have not changed, the order of those priorities remains intact: America First, then everything else in decreasing order of its influence on America.

But just as two hundred years ago even statesmen of Thomas Jefferson's and James Monroe's caliber were attracted to the mirage of greatness through alliances, so today lesser men find it difficult to grasp John Quincy Adams's teaching that alignment of interests among nations can only be creatures of time and circumstance. This means that although alliances are often keys to events, any people may pursue with any level of confidence only such objectives as they can achieve unilaterally.

The men who made America great, the men on Mount Rushmore, would counsel us strongly to decide unilaterally on our international affairs, and to do so by deliberation through our elected representatives—by their votes and by ours. The importance of doing so, they would tell us, transcends the matters at hand because it reaffirms and reminds us of the most basic of all political facts: our independence—meaning our collective liberty and responsibility for being what we were and should be again: different from other peoples, fortunate for that difference, grateful for it, and committed to maintaining it.

Never has it been so important to remember and reaffirm that our autonomy depends on our unity as Americans.

ADAMS'S STATECRAFT

John Quincy Adams did not invent American statecraft. For that matter, neither did his father as he negotiated
France's alliance in the Revolutionary War, nor did Thomas Jefferson in the Declaration of Independence, nor Alexander Hamilton
and John Jay in the *Federalist Papers*, nor even George Washington
in his Neutrality Proclamation and his masterly Farewell Address.
That statecraft stemmed from early American statesmen's attitudes toward the rest of the world. It expressed who Americans
were, where they were, and why they and their forefathers had
crossed the Atlantic.

For Americans high and low, the priorities were axiomatic: liberty and peace, eating the bread that their own labor earned, and
living Christian lives as they understood them. Such things do not
depend on foreigners. None suggested that caution with regard to
foreigners, virtue, or commitment to justice, were expedients dic-
tated by their present status as small communities, to be discarded as soon as growing power permitted. On the contrary,
adherence to history's hard-earned lessons about honorable character, both personal and national, was part of the basis on which
early Americans hoped for the continuation of God's blessings.

As the founding generation's statesmen dealt with the challenges before them, each formulated some of the common sentiments that became American statesmanship's essential principles.
John Adams and Benjamin Franklin provided the guidance and
Thomas Jefferson the words by which the United States declared
itself into existence, "separate and equal" among the powers of
the earth. John Adams tested and acknowledged the requirements
of alliances as he solicited France's arms and Holland's money.
John Jay wrote on how America might minimize its exposure to
war by giving no offense and suffering none, while Alexander
Hamilton warned that, no matter how hard America tried to avoid

wars, mankind's multiple depravities made war an ever-present danger.

George Washington gave practical as well as theoretical substance to foreign policy based on mutual non-interference, and focused Americans on America itself. Arguably his most important legacy is his prayer that his successors might treasure "the name AMERICAN" above all others, and that they will look at all matters from America's standpoint. Washington's army and Adams's navy provided effective reasons for foreigners' respect. As these statesmen wrote and acted, they expressed the American people's common sense about who they were in relation to others.

But it was left to John Quincy Adams, American history's premier diplomat and secretary of state (1817–25) to sum up that common sense into a coherent whole—a paradigm that guided U.S. foreign policy for nearly a century, and that offers guidance in our time as well.

Declaration and Shield

J. Q. Adams's statecraft is founded on the Declaration of Independence. His father's and his generation had fought the Revolutionary War "to assume among the powers of the earth, the separate and equal station to which the Laws of Nature and of Nature's God entitle [Americans]." Independence, they said, had been necessary to secure the enjoyment of the "unalienable rights" with which the Creator endows all men, among which "are Life, Liberty and the pursuit of Happiness." These, said Adams, are "the truths of the Christian religion": God gives to all peoples the right to rule themselves, just as He gives to each human the right to life, liberty, and the pursuit of happiness. As it happens, few peoples manage to rule themselves. Fewer do so while leaving others to do the same. Fewer yet manage to use self-rule to secure civil and religious liberty for themselves. Only Americans had grasped, declared, and practiced to some extent the connection between civil liberty, self-rule, and reciprocal respect among nations.

The Declaration's commitment to *nations' collective* rights and to *individuals' civil liberties* is the kernel, the seed, from which the whole tree of American statecraft has grown. Adams understood the exercise of collective liberty to be statesmanship's root. That is how the generation of those who planted and nurtured it understood it.

For them, although the Declaration also serves as "a beacon on the summit of the mountain, to which all the inhabitants of the earth may turn their eyes for a genial and saving light," it was first and foremost by, of, and for the American people. It was uttered by one people, Americans, to assert their own collective liberty. Of these Americans, J. Q. Adams wrote:

> The people … were associated bodies of civilized men and Christians, in a state of nature, but not of anarchy. They were bound by the laws of God, which they all, and by the laws of the gospel, which they nearly all, acknowledged as the rules of their conduct. They were bound by the principles which they themselves had proclaimed in the declaration … by all the beneficent laws and institutions, which their forefathers had brought with them from their mother country, by habits of hardy industry, by frugal and hospitable manners, by the general sentiments of social equality, by pure and virtuous morals.

These were American peculiarities. Other peoples would and should take note of Americans' peculiarities. Adams even invited them to "do likewise." But Americans could behave as they did only because they were none other than the people he had described. Peoples with other habits of heart and mind did not have it in them to "do likewise."

Americans, he said, were to cultivate and show forth character, commitment, and cohesion, distinct and separate from that of other nations:

> It is a common government that constitutes our country. But in THAT association, all the sympathies of domestic life and kindred blood, all the moral ligatures of friendship and of neighborhood, are combined with that instinctive and mysterious connection between man and physical nature, which binds

the first perceptions of childhood in a chain of sympathy with
the last gasp of expiring age, to the spot of our nativity, and the
natural objects by which it is surrounded. These sympathies
belong and are indispensable to the relations ordained by
nature between the individual and his country.... These are
the feelings under which the children of Israel "sat down by
the rivers of Babylon, and wept when they remembered Zion."

Like the inhabitants of ancient Israel, Americans were not
merely adherents to a set of commands or ideas. They were a distinct set of human beings in a God-given land.

The entire absence in early America's history of pronouncements, from any quarter, of desires or designs to reform, to dominate, much less to conquer any other people makes it superfluous
to repeat the multiple instances in which theologians and politicians alike condemned the example of empires, especially of Rome.
The most influential piece of writing ever published in America,
Thomas Paine's 1776 *Common Sense*, scoffed at the notion that
Americans might seek international power. Whoever might be
interested in such power, wrote Paine, would stick with Britain.
But to independence-minded Americans, he wrote: "What have
we to do with setting the world at defiance? Our plan is commerce." Accordingly, early America abounded with talk of contacts
with peoples as far as "the Indus and the Ganges," with ancient
despotisms as well as modern monarchies. All contacts were to
be, and could be, politically neutral and friendly because Americans so thoroughly identified with America that other nations' differences among themselves or with us concerned only them.

Combining virtuous living at home with political neutrality
abroad was Christian politics in the most fundamental sense:
Christians believe that Christ's birth ended the history of nations
and that, thenceforth, God's relations have been with individual
souls, not with nations. For this reason, Christian politics is inevitably about providing the context within which individuals might
worship God and show His glory. That means that government is
surely meant to provide peace—and perhaps to foster honorable
character. But no more.

From the beginning, American preachers had stressed Deuteronomy's command to exemplary obedience of God's laws. John Winthrop's 1630 speech before the founding of Boston had echoed: "Do justly, love mercy, and walk humbly with our God ... The Lord will be our God and delight to dwell among us ... But if we deal falsely with our God ...," Moses' litany of woes would befall Americans.

This is Old Testament Judeo–Christianity. During the Revolutionary era, preachers—the mass media of the day—described the Republic's purpose, as did Samuel Cooper in 1780 at the inauguration of the Massachusetts constitution, by quoting Timothy 2: Americans are to seek "a quiet and peaceable life in all godliness and honesty." In 1839, John O'Sullivan's ardent advocacy of "manifest destiny" envisaged America as "the noblest temple ever dedicated to the Most High .... Its floor shall be a hemisphere—its roof the firmament of the star-studded heavens, and its congregation an Union of many Republics, comprising hundreds of happy millions." This would not be an empire of domination, but a super-congregation that would manifest God's glory to other nations—not interfere with them.

America's business is America itself. Christianity assumes that the world is made up of peoples, of nations, different from one another. Christendom is not universal. Deuteronomy had warned Israel to "meddle not" with other nations. Bible-reading Americans took that to heart. This notion of a nation limited to its own concerns by its very calling—be that calling ever so grand—happened to fit perfectly with Westphalian international law's assumption of "separate and equal" sovereignties.

For this reason, the foreign policy of such a people, ordained to respect one another as well as other peoples, committed to showing forth God's glory, would be to manage its own survival and growth among peoples legally identical but possessing habits and objectives quite contrary to its own. No one needed to use the words "America First." The opposite notion (that Americans are to show their own exceptionality by doing things for or to other nations), is one that Adams and his generation would have judged insane. For them, foreign policy was to protect America's independence—

the people's sole temporal right to do right for themselves, by themselves. Foreign policy was to be what, as late as 1943, Walter Lippmann still called "the shield of the Republic"—not the sword.

Identity, Righteousness, and Greatness

Accordingly, John Quincy Adams said, "The most important paper that ever went from my hand" was the November 27, 1823, draft of his reply to Russia's envoy, Baron de Tuyll. Adams thought it of supreme importance because he had taken Russia's communication as the occasion for stating America's identity among nations: what that identity implies and what it does not.

In the course of ordinary discussions about plans for Russia's colonies that then stretched south from Alaska, Tuyll had conveyed a message from the tsar, soliciting the continuation of America's neutrality in the wars that had been raging between Spain and its American colonies and informing Washington that Russia, in accord with its own political principles, would not recognize these colonies' independence nor receive diplomats from them. A second message from the tsar gratuitously stated his belief in the superiority of monarchic, divine-right rule.

Adams wanted his reply to be part of "a combined system of policy" (to be expressed in President Monroe's December 2, 1823, annual message to Congress) that would also address Great Britain's offer to cooperate with the United States in dealing with possible attempts by France, Russia, and Spain to reconquer the newly freed South American states. Adams would use an ordinary diplomatic occasion to set current affairs in the context of America's very identity.

In a draft written before receipt of the second message, Adams had described America's and Russia's obligations to one another in general terms, as duties "to independent *Christian nations* of *Christians*." By this Adams implied that Russia and America had identical perspectives. Now, Adams confronted the differences between them. He wrote:

The United States is *republican*. The principles of this form of polity are 1. That the Institution of Government to be lawful, must be pacific, that is founded upon consent, and by the agreement of those who are governed; and 2. That each Nation is exclusively the judge of the government best suited to itself, and that no other Nation may justly interfere by force to impose a different Government upon it …. They are both principles of peace and good will. (emphasis in original)

Because of these republican principles, he continued, Americans have sought honest friendship with all peoples and governments, and they have taken no part in any other peoples' quarrels. The United States had recognized the South Americans' independence only after they had established it, exchanged diplomats, and would continue to do so. The United States would continue to be neutral in any wars between them and Spain—so long as others so remained as well. This was a broad hint that if Russia wanted neutrality from the United States, it should itself practice neutrality.

Adams went out of his way to express, sincerely, that America cherished its excellent relations with Russia, and wanted them to remain that way. The tsar had avowed his government's principles and wished by them "to guaranty the tranquility of all the states of which the civilized world is composed." Of this, Adams wrote: "The President wishes to perceive sentiments, the application of which is limited … to the affairs of Europe." So long as Russia would continue that limitation, so long as its promotion of monarchy did not touch the Western Hemisphere, so could continue the harmony that had characterized U.S./Russian relations.

And finally:

The United States and their government could not see with indifference the forcible interposition of any European power other than Spain either to restore the dominion of Spain over the emancipated colonies in America or to establish Monarchical Governments in those countries, or to transfer any of the possessions heretofore or yet subject to Spain in the American Hemisphere to any other European Power.

Note well, however, that Adams said nothing (nor did President Monroe's message) about any plans that Russia might have had to expand its colonies on the Northwest coast of America. Why? As Adams explained to Monroe: first, Russia had not raised the subject. The fact that Russia had sold Peter the Great's battleships to Holland, and that Tsar Alexander was fully occupied on land in the West, guaranteed that whatever anyone in Russia might have had in mind about Alaska would come to nothing. Practically, principles notwithstanding, Russia was not going to make trouble for America in the Americas. There was no need to talk about troubles that were not going to materialize.

Adams's point was, in short: because we Americans are who we are and where we are, we want peace with everyone, and will deal amicably with whomever does so with us, regardless of what they might think or do elsewhere. But, to maintain ourselves as we are, we will guard the political character of the hemisphere in which we live against such intrusion as we might find dangerous.

Like George Washington, Adams took for granted that the United States would become very powerful. In 1819, as he negotiated the treaty that set a U.S. border on the Pacific Ocean (then known as the South Sea), he took some satisfaction in confiding to his diary his disdain for Europeans who looked down on America: "[who] after vilifying us twenty years as a mean low minded peddling people having no generous ambitions and no God but gold,... were endeavoring to alarm the world at the gigantic grasp of our ambition." Such people are going to have to accustom themselves to realize "our proper dominion to be the continent of North America.... Europe shall find it a settled geographical element." In short, America's greatness depends on Americans, regardless of what any other nation might think or do.

But, as Lincoln would later say dramatically, only we ourselves could author our ruin.

America's founders, steeped as they were in Livy and Montesquieu, never forgot that republicanism rests on virtue. Washington had written that "virtue or morality is a necessary spring of popular government .... Can it be, that Providence has not connected the permanent felicity of a nation with its virtue?"

Although the founding generation rejected Rome's imperialism, they were nothing short of devotees of Roman virtues.

Power's Temptations

For Adams, the existence of slavery was an inherent negation of republican virtue. But virtue and vice were far from coterminous with the issue of slavery. Adams said that "the *virtue* which had been infused into the Constitution of the United States ... was no other than the concretion of those abstract principles which had been first proclaimed in the Declaration of Independence" (italics in the original). For the most part, that "concretion" involved a host of homey practices, such as paying one's debts, honest labor, frugality, political moderation, truth, adherence to law, and peace. George Washington had summed up virtue's political meaning in the term *national character*. On the fiftieth anniversary of Washington's inauguration as president of the United States, Adams reminded Americans that the first statute passed by the first Congress had been a tax to pay the debts overdue to veterans of the Revolutionary War. Fulfilling oaths and keeping one's word is as fundamental to a nation's integrity as it is to an individual's.

Sacrificing virtue to the prospect for greatness was an everpresent temptation. How Adams dealt with it further defined what he meant by American greatness, and what it was about America that he wanted to put first. Though Adams rejoiced at the Louisiana Purchase's doubling of American territory, he trembled that it had been done without clear constitutional authority, and that neither party was interested in regularizing such authority through constitutional amendment.

Later, Adams opposed the admission of Texas as a slave state because he believed that power that decreases the nation's moral integrity makes for domestic strife, which precludes greatness as he understood it. Adams had wanted California before James Polk ever thought of it. But Adams opposed taking it by war against Mexico because doing so was aggression on a weak neighbor and because he believed that what is now our Southwest would become American inevitably because it was being peopled by Americans. In this he was joined by a young Abraham Lincoln as well as by Lincoln's friend Alexander Stephens, a principled defender of Negro slavery who would become the Confederacy's vice president. For Adams, greatness and righteousness would have to be sides of the same American coin.

It was left to Lincoln, in his debates with Stephen Douglas, to clarify the issue. Douglas had supported the admission of Texas and the War on Mexico on what we might call a value-free basis: he was for whatever made America bigger and more powerful, regardless of how. Each of greater America's parts would worry about the moral worth of what it was doing. This was different from John O'Sullivan's original formulation of "manifest destiny," which had envisioned diverse congregations united in God's service. By contrast, Douglas left no doubt that he did *not care* about the character of whatever might make America greater, whether that be slavery or dominion over Latin America, or anything else. Lincoln pointed out that this approach to greatness, devaluing as it did human equality as the only proper basis for government, devalued America's own claim to independence.

Adams had said that Americans, like Themistocles, "knew how to make a great city of a small one." The greatness that he and his followers pursued was to be like that of Athens under Themistocles, requiring adherence to ancient virtues—the opposite of Periclean Athens's morally ambiguous imperialism.

Early American statesmen were mindful that the very biblical passages that promise exceptional blessings to those showing exemplarily obedience to God's commandments also warn that God imposes dire consequences for disobedience. As well, they could not have helped but notice that Livy's history of Rome, which had inspired their own age's iconic texts—Edward Gibbon's *Decline and Fall of the Roman Empire*, as well as Montesquieu's *Spirit of the Laws* and *The Greatness of the Romans and Their Decadence*—recount secular versions of the Old Testament story, and of Greek tragedy: Nemesis follows hubris. Pride goeth before the fall.

George Washington's injunction to "observe good faith and justice towards all nations; cultivate peace and harmony with all" was no innovation. America's founders stressed peace in general because peace is Christian politics' primary purpose. *Defensor pacis*, defender of the peace, had been the classic definition of good government ever since St. Augustine's fifth-century explanation of Jesus's command to separate that which is due to God and that which is due to Caesar.

Specifically, peace was especially essential to maintaining the American people's way of life. Washington's injunction told Americans that we have no *substantive* objective regarding foreign countries—none. What we want from foreigners above all is to have no trouble with them. That is also justice. To want to direct another nation's course, to take sides in any of its quarrels, said Washington, is to court giving what John Jay (*Federalist* No. 3) had called "just causes" for war. Interference in their affairs would make their causes against us *just* because Americans have no more right to interfere in others' business than others have to interfere in ours.

Washington, writing in 1796 from bitter experience, noted that involvement, even vicarious, in foreigners' quarrels brings foreign quarrels home by leading some Americans to take sides against other Americans. All too easily, warriors discover that their tools are even more useful against domestic competitors. To make sure that even mere commercial relations do not lead to political antagonisms foreign and domestic, he said, Americans must "hold an equal and impartial hand: neither seeking nor granting exclusive favors or preferences; consulting the natural course of things; diffusing and diversifying by gentle means the streams of commerce but forcing nothing." That meant seeking only "most favored nation" treatment and practicing strict reciprocity. While at peace, America must practice neutrality along with reciprocity—not economic warfare or power politics of any kind.

In 1793, young John Quincy Adams, subsequent to Washington's declaration of neutrality in the wars between France and

Marcellus:

> The rights of nations are ... all mediately or immediately derived
> from the fundamental position which the author of Christian-
> ity has taught us as an article of religion ... "Whatsoever," says
> the Saviour of mankind, "you would that men should do to
> you, do ye even so to them." Let us therefore ... do as we should
> choose others might do to us, and we shall deserve the favors
> of Heaven ... an impartial and unequivocal neutrality between
> the contending parties is prescribed to us as a duty, unless we
> are bound by some existing contract or stipulation, to make a
> common cause with one of them .... The natural state of all
> nations, with respect to one another, is a state of peace—
> *damus petimusque vicissim*: It is what we have a right to expect
> from them, and for the same reason it is our duty to observe it
> towards them.

For Adams, reciprocity is to be U.S. foreign policy's proximate
end as well as its principal means. In 1821, he wrote:

> America, in the assembly of nations, since her admission
> among them, has invariably, though often fruitlessly, held
> forth to them the hand of honest friendship, of equal freedom,
> of generous reciprocity ... in the lapse of nearly half a century,
> without a single exception, [she has] respected the indepen-
> dence of other nations, while asserting and maintaining
> her own.

For him, as for Washington, neutrality is neither timidity nor
agnosticism. Neutrality with regard to others is the other side of
the America First coin. America, he writes, "is the well-wisher to
the freedom and independence of all. She is the champion and
vindicator only of her own." To what he judged a duty of principle
("Who has appointed us a judge in their case?"), Adams added the
practical impossibility that Americans might untangle, never
mind control, the intentions, passions, and possibilities of foreign

contending parties. Because America can neither know nor control them, "once enlisting under banners other than her own, she would involve herself, beyond the power of extrication, in all the wars of interest and intrigue, of individual avarice, envy, and ambition, which assume the colors and usurp the standard of freedom." An America thus engaged, while unlikely to do any good abroad, must surely become disoriented in "the murky radiance of dominion and power." She would lose her proper perspective and "be no longer the ruler of her own spirit."

Autonomy, ruling one's own spirit, deciding for one's self, is not just good policy; it is a great good to be sought in and for itself. It is also the essence of international law, which is based on an even more inescapable law—self-interest.

International Law, Diplomacy, and Will

The scholars who elaborated international law following the 1648 treaties of Westphalia—Hugo Grotius, Emmerich de Vattel, and Samuel von Pufendorf—translated as much as they could of what had been intra-Christian diplomatic practice into an environment now dominated by the wholly secular principle of sovereignty—namely the unfettered will of sovereigns. While peace was to remain the system's end, and reason and comity the means, sovereign nations would inevitably counterpose their self-interest. Adams had no doubt about what that meant for his job as a diplomat. He wrote:

The Declaration of Independence recognized the European law of nations, as practiced among Christian nations, to be that by which they considered themselves bound, and of which they claimed the rights. This system is founded upon the principle, that the state of nature between men and between nations, is a state of peace. But there was a Mahometan law of nations, which considered the state of nature as a state of war—an Asiatic law of nations, which excluded all foreigners from admission within the territories of the state—a colonial law of nations, which excluded all foreigners from

For this reason, Adams recognized that, in practice, Westphalian international relations, just as much as any other kind, is based on will.

Sovereignty, then, reduces international law to a few basics: *pacta sunt servanda*, "agreements are to be kept," is Westphalian international law's bedrock, taken bodily from intra-Christian practice, as well as from the Roman *Jus Gentium*, or "law of nations." Adams believed that America, like all nations, is bound only by whatever explicit treaty commitments it makes. But he knew, practically even more than theoretically, that all governments behave as they think suits them at any given time whether or not a treaty exists to enjoin or to forbid. He knew that the reality of will, of real agreement or disagreement, supersedes documents. For this reason, Adams's diplomacy was about clearly, carefully, defining all sides' interests, aiming less at formal agreements than at maximizing real, reciprocal understanding and forbearance.

Since one country's diplomat could seldom if ever change what another government deems to be its interest, the best he can do is to understand what that interest really is, to leave no doubt as to what America's own is, and to emphasize where interests coincide—all in a clear, dispassionate, businesslike manner.

For Adams, diplomacy was the verbal representation of reality. For this reason, as Adams negotiated the end of the War of 1812, he felt confident in rejecting the British side's demand for a military presence in the Great Lakes because, in the long run, Britain could not maintain it against the American people's growth. Reality would convince the Brits of that. In 1818, Adams dealt with Spain's ambassador, Luis de Onis, over Florida by the same principle. Spain's diplomatic positions notwithstanding, the fundamental reality was Spain's inability to control Florida. As a result, Adams's communications respectfully combined America's offers of purchase with confidence that Spain would come around to accepting them.

America's long-term interests determined Adams's diplomatic objectives—not the least being expansion over the North American continent. Let us note here that Adams's understanding of expansion was identical to that of Thomas Jefferson, under which he had made the 1803 Louisiana Purchase. Jefferson had been among the authors of the 1787 Northwest Ordinance which, re-passed by Congress under the Constitution, embodied the principle that new states would come into the Union on the same basis as the old. Jefferson had quipped that America was the only empire that conquered new states to be ruled by them! That is the understanding that Adams shared and conveyed to his successors. Adams wanted our empire of liberty to border the Pacific Ocean. For this reason, he considered the Transcontinental Treaty of 1819 to be his biggest achievement.

As Spain sold Florida, it wanted to give up as little as possible of what would become Texas, and it was eager enough to accept Adams's concession on the Gulf Coast in exchange for agreeing to extend what, for Spain, was a meaningless line across the northern end of its claim, westward to the Pacific at northern California's border. Many Americans blamed Adams for trading a piece of ground for a line on a map. But Adams knew that that line, which became America's internationally recognized border on the Pacific alongside British settlements, was more important than a bit of land on the Gulf of Mexico.

By contrast with this great American interest, Adams thought that concerns with what was happening in other countries mattered nothing. In 1817–19, Adams had rebuked Henry Clay and John C. Calhoun's proposals to issue declarations with regard to the independence of Latin America and of Greece. What good do such words accomplish? Adams argued that they could have no effect on the outcome of the struggles in their respective regions, but would surely make trouble between America, Spain, and Turkey respectively. When Calhoun wanted to send frigates to help the Greeks, Adams asked if he had thought what war with Turkey would mean. It could do nothing but diminish America. "I have not much esteem for the enthusiasm which evaporates in words," said Adams.

Adams noted the unalterable nature of all nations' fundamental focus on their particular interests as a reason why America should not fear, indeed why it was obliged, to assert its own particular interests in the Western Hemisphere, and preferably to do so unilaterally. Since the point of acting unilaterally is to minimize entanglements with other governments that have a stake in the matter, it requires special care to ensure that they do not feel unnecessarily threatened.

The diplomacy associated with the Monroe Doctrine is a prime example. In 1823, the United States and Russia were in agreement on the major practical question with regard to South America: non-interference. But they were at opposite poles about matters of principle. Adams's 1823 dealings with Russia's ambassador, Baron de Tuyll, are a prototypical example of the care he took to circumscribe differences on principles alongside agreement on practical matters.

Spain's South American colonies had gained independence de facto during the Napoleonic Wars as Spain itself was undergoing something of a liberal revolution. At the 1815 Congress of Vienna, the nations of Russia, Prussia, Austria, and remonarchized France had formed what they called a "Holy Alliance" to help each other oppose liberal movements. Britain, which had vanquished Napoleon at Waterloo, abstained. The Allies, with France at their head, invaded Spain to restore its king. They spoke of reconquering its South American colonies for her. Britain did not like the idea and quietly asked Richard Rush, the U.S. minister in London, if America might wish to join in discouraging such a venture—which venture also worried the Monroe administration. This happened just as Russia's minister, Tuyll, delivered the tsar's aforementioned note to Adams.

President James Monroe so wanted to commit to defending South American independence alongside the British that in an October 17, 1823, letter to his mentor, former president Thomas Jefferson, he suggested it might be a good idea if the two governments jointly declared they would regard any attack on the South Americans as an attack on themselves—language that foreshadowed what would become NATO's Article 5. Secretary of State

Adams sought to say No. In his previous assignment as minister to Britain, Adams had established the best possible relations with its leaders, and he intended not to spoil them by involvement in details. He counted on the partial alignment of British and U.S. interests with regard to South America to maintain them. His diplomacy set about defining that partial agreement—sorting who wanted what from whom—in the most advantageous manner for the United States. The Monroe Doctrine would be the result.

Adams began by reassuring Monroe and Calhoun that a multilateral European invasion of South America was beyond the Allies' *political* capacity. Five years earlier, he had noted that governments so unsure of their standing with their own peoples as to require each other's support to stay in power could not risk sending their armies across the ocean to secure a nonmember's colonies. Even were such an invasion to take place, he said, the Allies' contrasting interests would doom it quickly. For this reason, as the United States was doing with regard to Russia, the only one of the Allies that had contacted the United States about South America and one without a navy, the U.S. should stress to the rest America's interest in continuing cordiality, while being as forthright about its own principles as the tsar had been about his.

Britain, mistress of the oceans, was the real question—potentially part of the problem and of the solution. France was the only one of the Holy Allies with a good navy. As Adams soon learned, the mere prospect of British opposition had convinced France not to hazard a transatlantic invasion. In the absence of an invasion, Britain's intentions with regard to weak Spain and its even weaker ex-colonies posed challenges to the United States. Would Britain try to monopolize commerce with South America? Would it try to purchase any of Spain's remaining colonies, especially Cuba? U.S. diplomacy's principal job at the end of 1823 was to safeguard its southern flank from the one country that already controlled the northern one and that could do America geopolitical harm—Britain.

That is the context in which Adams shaped President Monroe's annual message to Congress, in the course of which he elaborated a lasting framework of American geopolitical priorities.

Wisdom of Geopolitical Necessity

By the time the occasion arose for the Monroe Doctrine, its framework's elements were already in existence. Adams added the principle of "no colonization" to deal with the problematic possibility of Britain's reach for Cuba and to strengthen his negotiator's hand with Russia regarding the Northwest.

Adams had written the classic statement of American geopolitical policy in his April 28, 1823, instructions to U.S. Minister in Madrid Hugh Nelson. Its principle is straightforward: the avenues by which both good and ill may come to America are the peoples on our borders, the nearby islands, and the oceans, "the common possession of all." As a result, U.S. foreign policy must begin with a defensive focus on them. What is nearest is of dearest concern.

> It has been the policy of these United States from the time when their independence was achieved, to hold themselves aloof from the political system and contentions of Europe .... *The first and paramount duty of the government is to maintain peace amidst the convulsions of foreign wars and to enter the lists as parties to no cause, other than our own .... In the maritime wars of Europe, we have, indeed, a direct and important interest of our own; as they are waged upon an element which is the common property of all .... To all maritime wars Great Britain can scarcely fail of becoming a party; and from that moment arises a collision between her and these states .... This cause is peculiarly our own; and we have already been once compelled to vindicate our rights by war.* (emphasis added)

Though Spain had lost power over nearly all her possessions, "the islands of Cuba and of Porto Rico still remain nominally, and so far really, dependent upon her, that she yet possesses the power of transferring her own dominion over them, together with the possession of them, to others."

> [Cuba] has become an object of transcendent importance to the political and economic interests of our Union. Its

commanding position with reference to the Gulf of Mexico and the West India Seas; the character of its population; its situation between our southern coast and the island of Santo Domingo; its safe and capacious harbor of the Havana, fronting a long line of our shores destitute of the same advantage; the nature of its production and of its wants ... give it an importance in the sum of our national interests scarcely inferior to that which binds the members of our Union together.

It would be good if Cuba could become part of the Union, Adams thought. But there were countless reasons why it could not. And yet, were Cuba to be cut off from Spain, "the laws of political as well as of physical gravitation" would dictate that it could only gravitate toward the North American Union.

Cuba could declare its independence. But, because it was incapable of upholding it, "the wishes of this government have been that the connection between Cuba and Spain should continue." The rumors that Britain might have designs on Cuba worried the U.S. government. "The transfer of Cuba to Great Britain would be an event unpropitious to the interests of this Union .... The question both of our right and our power to prevent it, if necessary by force, already obtrudes itself upon our councils." Adams told Nelson to tell the Spanish government of "the repugnance of the United States to the transfer of the island." Should Spain try to transfer Cuba, and should the inhabitants declare independence, the United States would consider itself in its rights in supporting the Cubans to resist such transfer.

What Adams had chiefly in mind as he guided the Monroe administration in formulating and adopting the Doctrine was not the Holy Alliance's hordes descending on South America, but keeping Cuba out of Great Britain's hands. That would require a general statement of policy crafted as much as possible—but not totally—in alignment with British Foreign Secretary George Canning's proposals.

On July 18, 1823, Adams had written to U.S. Minister to London Richard Rush to reaffirm America's recognition of the South American republics' independence and opposition to Europe's further colonization. Then, in August and September, Canning proposed to Rush that America agree on five "principles": (1) Spain's recovery of its colonies is hopeless. Adams had been saying that for a year; (2) Recognition of their independence depends on time and circumstance. For America, these had come a year earlier. Now, Adams hoped that Britain would realize that they existed; (3) None should object to arrangements between Spain and its colonies by amicable negotiation. America would not object, and it would seek "most favored nation" status with any and all; (4) "We aim not at the possession of any portion of them ourselves"; and (5) "We could not see any portion of them transferred to any other power, with indifference." Adams fully concurred with 4 and 5, and he added: America "could not see with indifference any attempt by one or more powers of Europe to dispose of the freedom or Independence of those States without their consent or against their will."

Insistence on respecting the locals' will allowed America to join any eventual Cuban rejection of being transferred to Britain. That is why Adams made respecting the locals' will a condition for joining Britain in the declaration that Canning was soliciting.

After securing the president's and cabinet's approval on November 30, 1823, Adams instructed Rush to tell Canning that, while America agreed with his government's five stipulations, it realized that Britain's reference to "time and place" with regard to South America referred to Britain's necessary relationships with the world of European states—a world in which America had no part. America valued the present alignment of British and American interests. But it realized that this alignment was indeed one of circumstance, of time and place, rather than of principle. Therefore America and Britain should continue to foster their happy concurrence by continuing to proceed on parallel courses. *Adams sought no treaty, no agreement, not even an unwritten one. There was something more concrete than these: a real, solid, though partial, alignment of interest.*

This message to Canning, along with the one to Tuyll, laid a basis for President Monroe's statement of U.S. foreign policy that was clear, frank, friendly, principled, and entirely unilateral. It showed succeeding generations how to put America First while peacefully accounting for other peoples' interests.

The Monroe Doctrine

President Monroe had already agreed that Adams should formulate a statement that should answer both Russia and Britain and would "dissent from the principles avowed in [the British and Russian] communications ... assert those upon which our government is founded, and, all the while disclaiming all intention of attempting to propagate them by force; and all interference in the affairs of Europe, to declare our expectation and hope that the European powers will equally abstain from the attempt to spread their principles in the American hemisphere, or to subjugate by force any part of these continents to their will." But Monroe's own draft was full of condemnations of European policies with regard to Greece and Spain. Adams thought that these were none of America's business. "The ground I wished to take," wrote Adams, "is that of earnest remonstrance against the interference of the European powers by force with South America, but to make an American cause, and adhere inflexibly to that."

Accordingly, Monroe's 1823 message defined America's cause. The first paragraph on foreign affairs softly mentions that the U.S. minister in St. Petersburg had been given full powers amicably to discuss "the respective rights and interests of the two nations" regarding the Northwest Coast (which led to the 1824 agreement on Alaska's southern boundary). This occasion, Monroe continued, "has been judged proper for asserting, as a principle in which the rights of the United States are involved that the American Continents ... are no longer to be considered as subjects for future colonization by any European powers." Note the statement's passive verbs, as well as its lack of specificities and of subject.

Then, after several pages of comments on domestic matters, Monroe's message took up foreign policy again. Concerning events in Europe, it said, Americans "have always been anxious and interested spectators." American spectators have "sentiments the most friendly" toward Europe. Because America's friendship applies to all, "in the wars of the European powers in matters relating to themselves we have never taken any part, nor does it comport with our policy to do so. It is only when our rights are invaded or seriously menaced that we resent injuries or make preparations for our defense.... With the existing Colonies or dependencies of any European Power we have not interfered and shall not interfere.... With the movements in this hemisphere we are of necessity more intimately connected.... The political system of the allied powers is essentially different."

Note the sentences' clarity and active verbs. But the final sentence, "We should consider any attempt on their part to extend their system to any portion of this hemisphere as dangerous to our peace and safety," returns to vagueness, leaving to Americans' judgment what we would consider dangerous.

One thing is obvious: the Monroe Doctrine is *a principle of geopolitical priorities that concerns Latin America only because of its proximity*. Its essential concern is to reiterate George Washington's formula for America's relationship with extra-hemispheric powers: mutual non-interference, and to extend that formula to the rest of the hemisphere.

Nothing shows that the Monroe Doctrine does not imply any grab of Latin America as well as does John C. Calhoun's May 15, 1848, successful opposition to President James Polk's proposal that America accept the invitation of Yucatan's white population to cede themselves to U.S. sovereignty. The Yucatanese wanted help to avoid slaughter by Maya Indians. Polk was arguing, on the basis of the Monroe Doctrine, that Americans should give that help lest Britain do so and thereby gain a colony in our hemisphere.

Adams had just died. Calhoun might have been expected to favor annexing a prospective slave state. But Calhoun, having been Adams's vice president, stood on the fundamentals of American foreign policy. The Monroe Doctrine, he said, did not state that "the attempt of any European state to extend its system of government to this continent, the smallest as well as the greatest would endanger the peace and safety of our country." If we were to admit that the existence of strife in any country in our hemisphere that might lead to foreign interference should oblige us to intervene first, it would put it "in the power of other countries to make us a party to all their wars."

Following Adams, Calhoun was not for intervention or for non-intervention, but for judging each case on its merits. As for Yucatan, he said, Britain would be welcome to it because he considered it "most worthless." He acknowledged the humanitarian calamity there, made no mention of the racial factor, noting instead that all the countries of the region seem to be afflicted with maladies. Curing them is beyond us. "We should do all that humanity requires." But securing the fate of that people or any other is not our government's job.

For the rest of the nineteenth century, any number of Latin American states tried to secure U.S. interference in their affairs, mostly to no avail.

Interference and Non-Interference

Ensuring the American people's safety and welfare is the U.S. government's primary business. It is also the criterion by which to judge whether the U.S. government should intervene in the business of others. Adams was unequivocal that Americans are bound to respect other nations by the very right by which we assert respect for ourselves. He often observed, "Who has appointed us judges in their case?" But just as others' business, others' quarrels, and others' objectives are rightfully and inescapably their own, America is the sole, sovereign judge of its own business, of what our own safety and welfare require. This, Adams argued, is international law as well as common sense.

General Andrew Jackson's 1818 incursion into Spanish Florida occasioned Adams's fullest argumentation of this theme. After the War of 1812, British officers, followed by British soldiers of fortune, had continued to lead mixed bands of Indians and escaped Black slaves to attack American southern settlements from forts in Spanish Florida. Some of these attacks had wreaked atrocities. Spanish authorities had turned a blind eye and shared in the profits. General Andrew Jackson had led a U.S. regiment in pursuit, killed all the raiders it could find, captured their fort, court-martialed the two British organizers, and hanged them ceremoniously. Britain and Spain demanded Jackson be punished. The Monroe cabinet wavered. Adams convinced it to praise Jackson and to authorize his own November 28, 1818, instruction to the U.S. minister in Madrid.

Adams wrote that America had not invaded Spanish territory. Britain had done that in 1814, when it sent a detachment of Marines to Florida to make war on the United States. Spain had not protested. The fort, thus established, continued in operation after the end of the war, with the Spanish authorities' complaisance. Adams continued,

> The firebrand by whose touch this negro-Indian war had been re-kindled was found an intimate of the [Spanish] commandant's family… storehouses had been appropriated for their use; that it was an open market for cattle known to have been robbed by them from citizens of the United States.

Also, Spain's governor at Pensacola "had permitted free ingress and egress to the avowed savage enemies of the United States." Therefore General Jackson "took possession of Pensacola and of the fort of Barrancas, as he had done of St. Marks not in a spirit of hostility to Spain but as a necessary means of self-defense; giving notice that they should be restored whenever Spain should place commanders and a force there able and willing to fulfill the engagements of Spain to the United States or of restraining by force the Florida Indians from hostilities against their citizens."

Spain, not the United States, had interfered unlawfully in another country's affairs. Spain's obligation to prevent harm to others from coming out of its sovereign territory, said Adams, "is explicit, is positive, is unqualified." Therefore, "Spain must immediately make her election, either to place a force in Florida at once to the protection of her territory and to the fulfillment of her engagements, or cede to the United States a province of which she retains nothing but the nominal possession." General Jackson's invasion of Spanish territory had taken care of the U.S. government's responsibility to its own people. Incidentally, that invasion had fulfilled a responsibility of the Spanish government as well, which it had chosen to evade. Spain's claim to sovereignty was no excuse for evading its duty to exercise that sovereignty to curb international crime.

The concept of failure to try to perform an international duty casts some light on the negotiations between the United States (Adams) and Britain in 1823–24 on suppression of the slave trade. Passionately committed as Adams was to this goal—in 1820 he had sponsored the imposition of hanging as the penalty for attempts to import slaves into the United States—he supported the rest of the U.S. government in resisting Britain's request to search U.S. flagged ships at sea for slaves. America would do its best to suppress the slave trade within its sovereign sphere. But the harsh legacy of British impressment of American sailors prevented Americans from countenancing British ships searching American ships. The logic of sovereignty prevailed over antislavery policy.

Force and War

J. Q. Adams wrote that Thomas Hobbes had been wrong in believing that human beings exist in a state of war of all against all, that governments are essentially despotic to their subjects and warlike to each other. But, as a Christian who accepted the existence of original sin, he had no problem integrating the belief that peace is mankind's natural state with the occasional necessity of war. His policy regarding pirates and slave traders was physically to exterminate them as vermin. His father, John Adams, considered the father of the U.S. Navy, had used it to good account in 1799–1800 to prevent the quasi-war with France from turning into the full-blown thing. The Adamses agreed with Alexander Hamilton's exposition in *Federalist* No. 6 of war's multiple, ineradicable causes, and of the foolishness of trying to avoid them through economic incentives alone. They shared George Washington's appreciation of military power's essentiality, and of the necessity of being able to win wars. They watched as Jefferson and Madison learned this the hard way by blundering into the War of 1812.

J. Q. Adams watched the War of 1812 from Russia and, as Napoleon encroached on Russia, he had no doubt that the French emperor's military defeat was peace's prerequisite. As the British burned Washington, he hoped Americans would follow Russia's example. When negotiating the Peace of Ghent, he was willing enough to let the war go on rather than agree to intolerable terms. By fighting that war (albeit badly) rather than continuing to suffer indignities, America had secured for itself Europe's respect for its independence.

He argued that war is inherently despotic because it brings to the fore man's inescapable concern for survival. Thus does war cancel existing law and makes new law by force of arms. In this regard, as the Southern states were threatening forcible resistance to federal legislation in 1836, Adams warned them not to court civil war because its very outset would remove all constitutional protection from the institution of slavery.

President Adams

President John Quincy Adams's inaugural address expected that America would continue its wondrous growth with peace at home and with all nations. To Latin America in particular, he offered "disinterestedness ... cordial good will ... fair and equal reciprocity." He continued to try to minimize European influence in the Western Hemisphere as well as to expand the Louisiana Purchase's boundaries westward.

As secretary of state in 1819, Adams had pressed to set the Transcontinental Treaty's southwestern boundary at the Brazos river, if not the Rio Grande, rather than at the more easterly Sabine. When reconfirming that treaty with newly independent Mexico, he sought to move the boundary westward by presenting its government with the same prospects by which he had negotiated with Spain. He had paid Spain to purchase territory that it could not hold in the long run against the inevitability of American settlements. The Mexicans, however, refused to bargain on that basis, believing that the American immigrants they were inviting into their empty Tejas (Texas) province would obey Mexican laws.

Adams would not antagonize Mexico over Texas or encourage Americans to colonize it. But neither could he stop them even if he wanted to. Though he would have preferred to have the transfer happen in an amicable transaction, he was content to let demographic nature aggrandize America. During his presidency, the prospect of Texas troubling the Union by joining as a slave state was beyond the horizon.

Cuba's future troubled U.S. relations with the rest of Latin America as well as with Britain. The most potent of the newly independent Spanish colonies, Mexico and especially Colombia (then the huge state of Gran Colombia governed by the Liberator Simon Bolivar), were openly considering invading the remaining Spanish colonies of Cuba and Puerto Rico. Fearing that an unstable Cuba would draw British or/and French influence, Adams sought to discourage these countries from expanding their war with Spain. Believing that these islands were incapable of stable self-government and that neither Mexico nor Colombia could provide it, Adams let Mexico and Colombia know that the United States would not let an independent Cuba become their colony either. If Cuba were to be loosed from Spain, its destiny would have to be with the United States, which really did not want to deal with it. He sought to convince the Spanish government directly, as well as through Russia, to make peace with its former colonies so as more easily to hold on to the islands. By so doing, Adams was pursuing U.S. foreign policy's primary purpose: to keep powerful Europeans away from the Western Hemisphere and to avoid foreign troubles in general.

Simon Bolivar offered a more proactive path to that end. Since his last campaign's end in 1822, Bolivar had promoted his own, far more muscular version of the Monroe Doctrine: an alliance, perhaps a confederation, of all American republics to keep European monarchies at bay. In 1824, he proposed that all American republics, including the United States, send delegates to a congress to be held in Panama in October 1825 to discuss how to cooperate.

This was an offer that the United States could not afford categorically to refuse. But such a permanent alliance would contravene U.S. foreign policy's most basic commitment to unilateralism, while any kind of confederation would negate our independence outright. Still, since some sort of cooperation with other hemispheric republics made undeniably good sense, Adams agreed to send U.S. representatives and convinced Congress to authorize and fund the mission.

The vagaries of personnel, of Panama's pestilential climate, and of the era's means of travel having prevented the conference from ever fully assembling, the justification for it that Secretary of State Henry Clay drafted under Adams's guidance turned out to be its most enduring result. In a nutshell, Adams and Clay aimed to induce Latin American countries individually to redouble their commitment to republicanism, to hold European influences at bay, and to act as good neighbors while privileging commercial contact with one another—in short, to adopt what Adams and Clay called the American System: the Monroe Doctrine's U.S. version rather than Bolivar's.

THE PARADIGM

Andrew Jackson

John Quincy Adams's defeat in the 1828 election did not diminish his legacy in foreign affairs because his understanding of what defending and promoting America among nations requires had become common sense.

Although Andrew Jackson was a Southern frontiersman, his foreign policy was hardly distinguishable from the Northern aristocrat's. Both wanted America to be among the world's great nations. Adams had extended U.S. borders to the Pacific. In 1833 Jackson laid claim to its unfettered use by signing a treaty with Thailand, whose coasts straddle the British-dominated Straits of Malacca.

Though both were deeply committed to international peace, both were ready to make war rather than suffer injury to America's honor. In 1831, Jackson had received word that Malaysian pirates under the protection of the potentate of Quallah Battoo had robbed an American trading ship and murdered two crewmen. Jackson sent a U.S. frigate under the command of Captain John Downes to demand redress, or else. Downes, perhaps following Jackson's own example from 1818, skipped the demanding. The "else" erased the town, its potentate, and about a hundred others. Jackson's opponents grumbled. But Jackson backed his commander-on-the-scene just as J. Q. Adams had led the Monroe administration to back him.

In 1835, former President John Quincy Adams rose in the House of Representatives to back President Jackson's bellicose confrontation with France just as he, as secretary of state, had backed General Jackson's 1818 armed incursion into Spanish Florida. France was merely refusing to pay an indemnity awarded by arbitration. The money was not the point. But being publicly stiffed was as insufferable for Adams as for Jackson.

Jackson's vision of foreign policy, as he outlined it in his first annual message to Congress, is hardly distinguishable from that of his predecessors: confidence that America is mistress of her own future, rejoicing at peace, and determination neither to do nor to suffer wrong. He committed to resolve boundary issues with Britain in a spirit of cooperation. He praised our ancient ally France and our ancient friend Russia, wished Spain peace, and remarked that the existing peace with the Barbary powers and Turkey was due to the U.S. Navy. He congratulated Mexico for maintaining its independence and wished well for Latin America's future.

Jackson dwelt at length on having been forced to recall Joel Poinsett, the U.S. diplomat whom Mexico had declared *persona non grata*. But he did not explain that Poinsett was expelled because he had continued to try purchasing Texas on Jackson's behalf—as he had on Adams's—and refused to take no for an answer. Jackson wanted Texas neither more nor less than Adams. But because both were righteous men committed to peace, both wanted it by fair purchase and were content with diplomatic rebuff.

As Sam Houston led American settlers in Texas's fight for autonomy and then independence, Jackson, a personal friend of Houston's, combined personal affection for the Texans' cause with strict official neutrality. Some, then and since, questioned that neutrality's sincerity, especially after Jackson extended de facto recognition to the Texas republic just before leaving office in 1837. But by then, Texas had established its own independence without doubt. De facto recognition was as much an Adamsian principle as neutrality. Jackson had not fostered the Texas revolution any more than Adams had. Jackson had thought the Texas revolution inevitable, as had Adams. Neither had intervened on its behalf. Jackson did not then advocate admitting Texas to the Union any more than did Adams.

Any doubts about Jackson's sincerity should have vanished when his successor and dutiful follower, Martin Van Buren, refused even to consider Texas's application to join the Union because doing so would mean war with Mexico, as well as because the admission of a new, big, slave state would destabilize the

Union. That is also why, in 1838, Van Buren resisted pressures to support Canadians' drive for independence from Britain despite much support from Americans along the border.

Surely, President Andrew Jackson's greatest success was to have preserved the Union against South Carolina's 1835–36 attempt to nullify federal tariff law. In this, he had no firmer, more prestigious support than from Adams, whom he had defeated for the presidency. The Union and peace, peace and the Union, what Lincoln would later call "peace among ourselves and with all nations" was the hallmark of Jackson's foreign policy as it had been of Adams's, eclipsing all lesser concerns. In sum, until 1840, presidents and congresses put America itself first, clearly and unambiguously. Had the modern understanding of the adjective "nationalist" existed, neither Jackson nor Adams would have minded the label.

Antebellum: the 1840s and '50s

President William Henry Harrison's untimely death ushered in a period in U.S. foreign policy during which a host of personal and partisan considerations, conflicts, and insufficiencies overshadowed concern for America itself. This period's major personages—John Tyler, accidental president; Daniel Webster, old-fashioned Adamsian statesman; James K. Polk, who tried to imitate Jackson; and President James Buchanan, with a small man's view of American greatness—were so absorbed by the pressures of the moment that America's primary interest slipped from the top of their priorities. That led first to war with Mexico, then to disunion, and finally to civil war.

John C. Calhoun, who was vice president to J. Q. Adams as well as to Andrew Jackson in his first term, and Stephen Douglas, the Democratic Party's post-Jackson giant, contributed their considerable intellectual leadership to America's disorientation. We begin with that.

South Carolina's Calhoun, the only American whom J. Q. Adams considered a peer in intellect and education, had become prominent in 1812 as an ardent nationalist. Early on, his political support for slavery had not lessened his devotion to a Jeffersonian view of the Declaration and of the Constitution. Calhoun, however, was very much an intellectual in tune with the changing biological science of the nineteenth century's first half, by which evolution replaced creation in millions of minds, and the degrees thereof made nonsense of human equality. What came to be known as Darwinism fit too well with the immediate interests of Southern aristocracy and spawned the doctrine that Negro slavery was not a necessary evil but a *positive good*. This was the basis for this class's moral secession from the Union long before 1861.

No one should be surprised that those most fascinated by genetics and evolution would see themselves as the most advanced of specimen, with corresponding rights over those in line below, and that the belief of entitlement by their scientific superiority would energize all manner of presumption of authority. As the century advanced, any number of Americans, including abolitionists, came to believe that *they* had the scientific right to dictate to lesser beings for their own good. Indeed, that is how the most advanced slave owners thought of their relationship with their slaves. The Civil War's run up and aftermath was full of such sentiments.

Stephen Douglas, "the little giant," was the master politician who, out of the sense of biological necessity, nearly forged a North–South consensus to discard what had made America America, by putting greatness itself first. On August 27, 1858, facing Lincoln at Freeport, Illinois, this was the most seductive of his arguments:

> I tell you, increase and multiply, and expand is the law of this nation's existence .... Any one of you gentlemen might as well say to a son twelve years old that he is big enough, and must not grow any larger, and in order to prevent his growth put a hoop around him to keep him to his present size .... Either the hoop must burst or the child must die ... our interests and our destiny require additional territory in the north, in the south, or in the islands of the ocean. I am for it and when we acquire it will leave the people, according to the Nebraska bill, free to do as they please on the subject of slavery and every other question.

This version of nature's laws took no account of what neighboring peoples to the north or south might want, nor of the substance of what was to be done there. For Douglas, right was the dominant will of the dominant people, period. Far from novel, this is the oldest of political philosophies best articulated by Plato's character Thrasymachus. Left behind was the original, Adamsian version of Manifest Destiny such as the *New York Morning News* had editorialized even in 1845: "Rapacity and spoliation cannot be features of this magnificent enterprise. We take from no man."

All too quickly, all sides of American life became so convinced of their beliefs' correctness and of their duty to act accordingly that they became more or less parties to taking and to war.

We cannot know whether Harrison, a Whig, a learned man and an admirer of J. Q. Adams, would have succeeded in continued commitment to peace at home and abroad. He had been ambassador to Gran Colombia and was committed to Henry Clay's vision of the United States somehow at the head of an "American System." He intended to let another of Adams's admirers, Secretary of State Daniel Webster (1841–43), run foreign policy. It seems that Harrison and Webster meant to keep the federal government officially neutral regarding both slavery and American emigrants' demographic appropriation of Mexican territory. But John Tyler, who succeeded Harrison after his death thirty-one days after taking office, was a lesser man. Though he retained Webster, courtship of the Democratic Party defined his presidency.

The Democratic Party's Southern wing focused increasingly on protecting and expanding slavery. Its foreign policy priority had become to expand—mostly at Mexico's expense. Webster, for his part, was willing enough to help tamp down the Northern abolitionist sentiment that fueled Southern ire, and he did what he could to maintain relations with Mexico in a spirit of respect and friendship despite the intrusion of American citizens along the Santa Fe Trail. But more and more, the U.S. government was caught in the middle between its official neutrality and good neighbor policy, and the reality of private American settlement. Outside of that quandary, Webster completed Adams's extension of U.S. borders to the Pacific, and started, albeit awkwardly, establishing friendly relations with China on the basis of equality, resulting in the Treaty of Wangxia, which admitted U.S. shipping to China's ports. Yet the increased trade with China fueled further interest in acquiring California or at least San Francisco.

Whatever good President Tyler had done through Webster he undid massively by finagling the admission of Texas to the Union right before leaving office in 1845. Since Mexico was still at war with Texas, its disputes over borders further inflamed tensions with the United States. By taking on Texas's quarrel, Tyler wrecked Adams's, Jackson's, and others' domestic and foreign balancing act. Perhaps it had merely run its course.

That is why President James K. Polk's inept attempt to resume that balancing act was foredoomed. Westward-bound Americans had also branched off the Oregon Trail to settle California. The Mexicans had every reason to expect a replay in California and New Mexico of what had happened in Texas, and they saw Polk's repeated offers to purchase these territories as insincere and as insults added to injury, a thin cloak for naked aggression. They threatened war and moved troops to the disputed Texas border. Neither side had clear objectives. Polk and the Mexican government backed themselves and each other into the proverbial corner by publicly threatening war if their demands regarding the Texas boundary were not met. But of course, the real issue was bigger: American appetite that had become urgent as well as insatiable, and Mexico's unwillingness to make the best of an irremediable problem.

Polk proved his incompetence by falling for exiled Mexican dictator Antonio López de Santa Anna's promise that if U.S. military operations facilitated his return to power in Mexico, he would agree to sell California and New Mexico as well as to set the Texas border on the Rio Grande. Then Santa Anna proved his own incompetence by reneging and fighting a war that he could not win.

Meanwhile, when Mexico's commander in California proclaimed that foreigners could no longer own land, the American settlers revolted, chased him out, raised the bear flag, and declared independence. Polk had sent the U.S. Navy's Pacific squadron to seize Monterey and San Francisco in case war broke out in Texas.

They got there in July 1846, incorporated the Bear Flaggers, and conquered California against token opposition.

Mexico lost the war as well as New Mexico and California. But the winners paid the losers $15 million and also paid U.S. citizens' claims against Mexico. The money paid allowed Polk and company to imagine that they had purchased the territories, not stolen them. Reality was somewhere in the middle, and as ever, hypocrisy was the price that vice pays to virtue.

James Buchanan, Polk's secretary of state and the last president before the Civil War, typified the Democratic Party's attitude to American greatness best explained by Stephen Douglas in his debates with Abraham Lincoln, namely the bigger and stronger the better, regardless of how achieved. Polk had resisted Buchanan's advice to take more of Mexico. Buchanan and others, including Douglas, had wanted Cuba as well, citing geopolitics as Adams had, but casting aside the ethical and political considerations that had prevented Americans from governing others. So single-minded was Buchanan about taking pieces of Latin America that, in the interval between service with Polk and his own presidency, he had organized the Ostend Manifesto that called for wresting Cuba from Spain and attaching it to "our family of states" by purchase if possible but by force if necessary—as a slave state, of course.

In those years, a lively but tiny minority of Americans took these sentiments, such as those of Douglas and the Ostend Manifesto, to their logical conclusion. Taking up arms, they mounted private invasions to conquer Latin American countries. What thousands of farmers had done peacefully, hundreds of what came to be known as "filibusterers" tried to accomplish violently in violation of the 1818 Neutrality Act that John Quincy Adams had authored. To its credit, the U.S. government left them to their fates abroad and jailed them when they got home.

Meanwhile, a not-so-tiny minority of prominent citizens—such as journalist Walt Whitman and commodore Robert Stockton—advocated a more sophisticated version of the filibuster to high-end audiences. Their call to take forceful stewardship over Mexico, Cuba, etc., to teach and help them drag themselves up the evolutionary ladder even if it took a hundred years, foreshadowed the turn of the twentieth-century imperialist call to "take up the white man's burden," Woodrow Wilson's paternalistic invasions, and our own time's passion for "nation building." In all cases, the words are nearly identical.

In sum, during those years, more Americans put America itself behind countless other concerns. Abraham Lincoln was a rare exception.

Abraham Lincoln

On January 12, 1848, freshman congressman Abraham Lincoln delivered a speech showing that President Polk's explanation for the start of the Mexican War was more rationalization than reason. A month later, he was on the House of Representatives' committee that arranged J. Q. Adams's funeral. Like Adams, Lincoln had always seen America's essence, as well as its origin, in the Declaration of Independence. Already in 1838, having noted that America had little to fear or hope from other nations, he had warned against letting any concern interfere with the country's ancient "political religion."

He explained his understanding of it in his 1858 debates with Stephen Douglas. The Declaration's recognition of the equality that follows from God's creation of man in His image commands us equally to respect all human beings among ourselves as well as those in other nations. On October 15 at Alton, Illinois, Lincoln argued that whoever supports Americans' sovereignty over America must also support the Mexican people's sovereignty over Mexico. Whatever man or whichever nation wishes to be respected must also respect others. That is the only basis for peace, said Lincoln.

Candidate Lincoln offered a peaceful vision of growth. America's empty lands, he said, had been made for immigrants like "Hans, Patrick, and Baptiste," farmers who would freely raise families. As president, he sponsored the Homestead Act that gave title to land to whomever would improve it.

Like George Washington, Lincoln fought his war without ever losing sight of its peaceful objective. The memory of Lincoln's military conduct of the Civil War improperly overshadows the essence of the statesmanship by which he conducted the conflict; from first to last, Lincoln aimed at reconciliation. The Civil War's character—and its *relatively* non-disastrous ending—depended on Lincoln's constant insistence that the Union had not been broken and of the need to reestablish friendship. Lincoln never spoke ill of Southerners. From his perspective, there had never been any need for shooting. He had begged South Carolina not to fire on Fort Sumter. What if it had not? Lincoln was sure that, eventually, there would have been deals, as there had been between Jackson and Calhoun in 1836. Just doing nothing would have given all non-violent alternatives their chance.

Throughout the conflict, focused as he was on minimizing intersectional hate, Lincoln remained willing to pursue whatever deals anyone on the other side might be willing to make. As the South's defeat loomed, and even with the Emancipation Proclamation in effect, Lincoln proposed purchasing all the South's slaves at fair market value. Despite this proposal's rejection from all sides, and despite the passage of the Thirteenth Amendment, Lincoln's second inauguration ended the Civil War very much in the spirit in which he had watched it begin—blaming no one but focusing all on the practical tasks of national unity. The words he spoke in 1865, "peace among ourselves and with all nations," were neither more nor less than what his public life had been about: America First.

William Henry Seward

In 1849, William Henry Seward, newly installed governor of New York, delivered a eulogy of John Quincy Adams to his legislature and published a laudatory biography of him. As secretary of state for Presidents Lincoln and Johnson from 1861 to '69, Seward became, next to Adams, the nineteenth century's most consequential influence on foreign affairs. Temperamentally more high-spirited, and hence more in tune with the feeling of power and entitlement to primacy that pervaded America after the Civil War, nevertheless his sincere adherence to Adams's priorities helped ensure that U.S. foreign policy remained mostly old fashioned until at least 1898.

It is not too much of an exaggeration that, with regard to war and slavery, Seward was a more passionate, less thoughtful, version of Lincoln. He had denounced the Mexican War more vehemently, and he'd advocated the abolition of slavery earlier than Lincoln. When the prospect of foreign intervention arose at the Civil War's outset, Seward tried to force Lincoln to issue ultimata to Britain and France as much to rouse domestic public opinion as to warn off the Europeans. As he learned from Lincoln's greatness, and was aided in London by J. Q.'s son, U.S. Minister Charles Francis Adams, he framed Europe's choice as one between the uncertain possibility of gains from Southern independence and the absolute certainty of enmity from a far stronger North. Following the war, he helped to push France out of Mexico, never threatening but warning France of the realities that doomed its adventure there, including the fact that a million American ex-soldiers were volunteering for a military expedition to chase it out—a textbook application of the Monroe Doctrine.

Seward wanted America to become greater and more exemplar. For him as well as for many others, the Civil War's end opened vistas. He took to reciting the following rhyme:

Our nation with united interests blest
Not content to poise shall sway the rest
Abroad our empire shall no limits know
But like the sea in boundless circles flow.

He traveled the country, talking up visions of American merchants bringing the flag to the world's farthest corners, of feats of innovation and productivity such as the world had never known. Far from being bellicose, or even political, this vision recalled that of colonial era preachers who gloried in the notion of American ships in the "Indus and the Ganges." It was a view of greatness entirely consistent with the book of Deuteronomy.

Fulfilling this vision required no changes in attitude. It did require more people, for sure, and maybe more territory. Under

Lincoln, Seward sponsored the Immigration Act of 1864, which paid the voyages of persons who would work in American factories and farms. But he also sought to grow America by large-scale purchases. Like Adams, he recoiled at the prospect of taking in thickly populated Caribbean islands that would import more racial/cultural problems than we already had. Since he did not see Alaska as posing such problems, he was so eager to have it that he ended up paying more than the original asking price. He also held out the possibility of assimilation and voluntary annexation of Canadian and Mexican provinces.

Seward's diplomacy toward China, executed by his ambassador, Anson Burlingame, so impressed the Chinese with America's intention of treating China as a sovereign power that they commissioned Burlingame himself as China's own ambassador to the Western world. The ensuing 1868 U.S.–China Treaty, written in Washington by Seward and Burlingame, based as it was on reciprocity in trade and movement of people, succeeded too well. The extensive immigration that it allowed brought on anti-Chinese riots in California, and eventually was responsible for the Chinese Exclusion Act.

1869–1885

Post–Civil War America, the world's superpower of food and of railroads, a nation that had wielded a modern army of millions, now reconsidered its rank among the nations of the earth. Prussia had united with Germany. France and Britain had built the Suez Canal and were carving up the planet. European powers were gobbling up trade concessions in China and Korea and were colonizing remote Pacific islands. Where was America in all that?

Ulysses S. Grant did not spend much time on this question. Grant so yearned for calm in foreign affairs that he considered Seward's diplomacy excessively adventuresome. He devoted his two presidential terms to trying to return the country to the path of internal peace that Lincoln had indicated and that he himself had begun by the manner in which he had accepted Robert E.

Lee's surrender—and that Lincoln's assassination and the Reconstruction policy had wrecked. Despite Grant's best efforts, all sides' bitterness prevented the withdrawal of federal troops from the South until the next presidency.

Nevertheless, under President Grant, U.S. diplomacy continued to compete for influence in the Pacific, reaffirmed America's preponderant interest in Hawaii, and established a coaling station in Samoa. Moreover, it was Grant who first ordered a technical survey of a canal route across the Isthmus of Panama. It was Grant who turned official Washington's attention to the Pacific and who, albeit after his presidency, arguably did most to lead Japan to becoming America's pupil for two generations.

When the Cuban people revolted against Spain, some Americans wanted to promote their struggle for independence, just as their fathers had sought to promote South America's independence, or even to annex the island. Grant reasserted the classic American policy of neutrality regarding other people's quarrels—the other side of primary concern for America itself.

As some Americans grew impatient at Britain's slow pace of settling Americans' claims for damages that the Confederate ships built in British shipyards had inflicted on American commerce, Grant consistently valued over mere money the peace in the Atlantic that only friendship with Britain could secure. Nor did Grant ever consider supporting those Americans who wanted to help Canada's self-rule struggle against Britain.

As Grant left office, he congratulated himself on turning over to his successor Lincoln's promised peace among ourselves and with all nations.

As Rutherford B. Hayes withdrew troops from the South, he sent them to the Mexican border to pursue cross-border bandits. The Mexican government first protested, then cooperated. His biggest international challenge was to rescue the country from the Burlingame Treaty's unintended consequence of Chinese immigration that had grown to levels that Californians had found intolerable, without wrecking relations with China.

In 1880, when Ferdinand de Lesseps, who had built the Suez Canal and had formed a massive private company to build one across Panama, came to the U.S. to raise money, he raised fears that such a canal might be controlled by other than Americans. Hayes responded by stating that such a canal "would be the great ocean thoroughfare between our Atlantic and our Pacific shores, and virtually a part of the coastline of the United States. Our merely commercial interest in it is greater than that of all other countries, while its relations to our power and prosperity as a nation, to our means of defense, our unity, peace, and safety, are matters of paramount concern to the people of the United States." In short, while no one could be sure that a canal across Central America could be built, Hayes reassured all that regardless of who built it, the United States would control it.

Having made that clear, Hayes set off on a camping trip into the Yellowstone country, pitching base camp in the trout-filled meadow at the confluence of Wyoming's Wind and Dunoir Rivers that still bears his name.

But America in the 1880s, though by no means aggressively hostile, was ever more conscious of its power, more eager than ever to have its status recognized abroad, and to reap the rewards of bigger trade networks. Popular demand for international prestige and profit brought forth politicians who turned their ambitions to supplying them. President James Garfield's secretary of state, James G. Blaine, was the most prominent of these. Serving during Garfield's brief life in office, and though failing to accomplish his objectives, Blaine is noteworthy for how he tried to wield U.S. influence without overstepping the bounds of traditional policy.

Blaine's diplomacy was unsuccessful in mediating the 1881 War of the Pacific between Chile and Peru because his ambassador, Hugh Judson Kilpatrick, simply took Chile's side. Nor was Blaine successful in mediating a border dispute between Mexico and Guatemala because the stronger party, Mexico, did not want mediation, while the weaker party was using it as a lever against the stronger. Blaine learned that good intentions neither imply good results nor redound to the mediator's credit. All sides were the worse for it. His efforts however, inspired by the hopes that J. Q. Adams had placed on the Panama conference of 1826, led him to call for just such a conference which, not incidentally, would compensate for the failure of his specific ventures. But his time ran out. He would be back.

Chester A. Arthur, having become president after Garfield's death, continued Blaine's ambitious agenda in Latin America along with Secretary of State Arthur Frelinghuysen. They tried to bind the region to the United States by mutual reductions of tariffs, as well as by committing initial capital for the construction of an inter-ocean canal through Nicaragua. In both cases they got ahead of public opinion.

They also learned the hard way that cooperation in what appears to be humanitarian and/or scientific enterprises are fraught with the intrigue of lobbyists. Such was America's participation in the Congo Conference of 1884.

This is what happened: as Britain and France were painting the maps of Africa and Asia in blue and red, the minor powers scrambled for the leftovers. Such was Belgium and such was the Congo basin, then almost as unexplored as the moon. Prominent among the explorers was the Welsh American Henry M. Stanley. Belgium's King Leopold II recruited him for something he called the African International Association—a front for the Belgian government, formed in 1876 ostensibly for philanthropic and scientific purposes. Thereafter, Stanley organized trading stations on the Congo coast under the association's flag as other lobbyists of Leopold's worked to secure U.S. recognition of the association.

They plied Secretary Frelinghuysen with offers of free trade and Senator John Morgan of Louisiana with the prospects of a place that might lure U.S. Negroes to emigrate. After the U.S. extended formal recognition to the association, German Chancellor Bismarck extended and the U.S. accepted an invitation to a conference in Berlin where the powers present—the United States included—recognized Belgian sovereignty over the Congo and approved the last details of Europe's carve-up of Africa.

Thus did America, having slipped down the hierarchy of its own statesmen's priorities, end up an unwitting partner in one of the more sordid episodes of European imperialism.

Democrat Grover Cleveland, winner of the 1884 election, thought the foregoing episode appalling and committed the country to a "policy of peace suitable to our interests. It is the policy of neutrality, rejecting any share in foreign broils and ambitions upon other continents and repelling their intrusion here. It is the policy of Monroe and of Washington and Jefferson—Peace, commerce, and honest friendship with all nations; entangling alliance with none." For him, pursuing peace meant not exposing the United States to conflicts away from the domestic sources of its strength, and not making commitments which it would have to defend at its peril.

Cleveland withdrew his predecessor's treaty for a canal through Nicaragua as well as the ones for reciprocity with Spain's remaining colonies in the Americas. But he approved renewal of the reciprocity treaty that bound Hawaii commercially with the United States, including a provision for a naval base at Pearl Harbor. When Britain and France protested the base, Cleveland told them that this was America's business. And when news arrived that German agents in Samoa were plotting to establish a protectorate over islands where a U.S. coaling station existed, Cleveland sent warships to substantiate a forceful protest to Berlin. Bismarck backed down. Most importantly, as the Cuban people continued their simmering revolt against Spain and as the American people clamored for intervention, Cleveland cited the long line of precedents for neutrality in foreign conflicts. He continued doing that throughout his second term as well.

The 1888 election of Republican Benjamin Harrison brought a different perspective on putting America First. James G. Blaine came back as secretary of state. His successor, John B. Foster (grandfather of President Eisenhower's John Foster Dulles), was similarly forceful. Rather than protest Germany's attempt to establish a protectorate over Samoa, Harrison negotiated a joint protectorate. The Harrison administration engaged in any number of ventures—for example, the threat of war with Chile over the treatment of drunken sailors that piqued American pride but came to nothing. Its most memorable one was acquiescence to the request for annexation of Hawaii made by the American community there which, in the administration's waning days, had deposed Queen Liliuokalani with the help of a U.S. Navy ship's crew. But the Senate postponed action on the treaty until Cleveland's second inauguration in March 1893.

Cleveland, refusing annexation brought about by such methods, urged Americans in Hawaii to restore the queen. When she made that impossible by demanding the plotters' beheading, Cleveland washed his hands of the matter. Hawaii would remain an independent republic awaiting circumstances that would permit annexation—as had Texas. So determined was Cleveland against annexing territory that, after open war broke out between the Cuban people and Spanish authorities in 1895, he spent much of his energy fighting off mounting pressure for the annexation of Cuba from Americans as well as from Cubans.

But Cleveland also showed what the Monroe Doctrine should mean to a powerful United States. In 1895, his secretary of state, Richard Olney, responding to friendly Britain's refusal to countenance U.S. mediation of its quarrel with Venezuela, told the British that America was now "practically sovereign" about matters it chose in the Western Hemisphere. Cleveland, who had been so scrupulous as to reject Hawaii's application for annexation, nevertheless so approved of Olney's course of action as to prepare for war against Britain should it persist in refusing American mediation. Note, however, the Cleveland administration's point: they had no intention of interfering in Latin American countries' internal affairs but every intention of preventing Europeans from doing so. At the turn of the twentieth century, Cleveland and Olney warned most clearly against the folly of American interference to right foreigners' wrongs.

The Cleveland administration's policy toward Latin America—energetic commitment against European interference in the hemisphere combined with its own refusal to interfere—illustrates perfectly what U.S. foreign policy had been about since John Quincy Adams: to seek peace by practicing peace while being ready to make war to keep powerful foreigners away.

William McKinley did not intend to shift the focus of U.S. foreign policy from America itself to the world scene. But he ended up doing just that. Historians point to the virus of Progressive imperialism then sweeping Europe and to the interaction between American elites' infection with it and the unfolding Cuban drama. Mistakenly, they conclude that America's adoption of imperialism was a foregone conclusion, or even that imperialism had been the essence of U.S. foreign policy all along. In fact, imperialism's sway in America *circa* 1898–1903 was due to the peculiarities of how McKinley handled the Cuban problem's climax.

As we have noted, American statesmen since Adams's time had tried to postpone potentially insoluble problems regarding Cuba—so close and important for good and ill that it could never be ignored. Every president since Monroe had believed that Cubans were incapable of ruling themselves. Yet racial and cultural differences made it ever imprudent to annex it. For this reason, Americans had continued to kick the Cuban can down Spain's road. In 1898, that had become impossible. Now what?

McKinley, who wanted to neither go to war nor take over Cuba, hoped the problem could be solved by legal finesse. But words do not change realities. He refused to think the matter through. He would fight, but without declaring war or recognizing the Cuban people's belligerency. Spain declared the war. The United States won it and saddled itself with an empire. He defined the temporary occupation of Cuba as establishing peace and preparing the natives for self-government—what we now call nation-building. Then as now, this was too clever by half, and ended up satisfying nobody. Interference in Cuba ended up transforming it into a cancer on the Americas.

On the other side of the world, possession of the Philippines, incompetently managed, eventually brought war with Japan.

American society's Progressive sector worshiped power. Because improvement of the human condition had been a subtext of the Civil War—on both sides—it is little wonder that passion for all forms of power swept the victorious North in its aftermath. With slavery eliminated, a consensus formed *circa* 1880 that America had become so good and powerful that no evils at home or abroad could stand before its energy and industrial miracles. That was the point of the era's most influential book, Josiah Strong's *Our Country* (1885). Powerfully, it argued that America's domination of the world had become inevitable, and that it would take place without a shot being fired—all because Americans were at the head of a progressive process that involved humans everywhere. In short, cultural progressivism predated the political version.

By 1917, when Woodrow Wilson told the YMCA that mere self-improvement is priggish and that virtue consists of improving others, upper-middle-class Americans had been imbibing such notions for two generations at summering places like Lakes Chautauqua and Mohonk. Progressive imperialism was to be gentle and, for all but such as Sen. Albert Beveridge (R–IN), who was not ashamed to speak the unspeakable (ruling others without their consent), it was not imperialism at all. But few were so clear or so bold as Beveridge. Pure intentions were the novelty of turn-of-twentieth-century U.S. imperialism.

Alfred Thayer Mahan's writings on the makings and logic of naval power, which influenced leaders such as Teddy Roosevelt and Henry Cabot Lodge to provide for at least naval defensive competence, if not supremacy, was a call for American power and grandeur—not a call to meddle in others' affairs. John Hay, TR's first secretary of state, who had been Lincoln's secretary and admired Seward (and hence Adams), wanted the opposite of interfering in China. His "open-door" policy intended to achieve equal access to and fair treatment of China by all nations, just as Anson Burlingame and William Seward had intended. Nor did

Elihu Root, who followed Hay at State, interfere or advocate interfering with Latin America. He intended the opposite.

Root also championed the acquisition of the Philippines, not just because he thought it would strengthen America's capacity to influence the Pacific, but also because he believed (as most other imperialists did) that by it, America could lead the world into a new kind of stewardship. Prior to the 1898 invasion of Cuba, Congress had passed legislation forever forbidding annexing the island. Nor is there any doubt about the heroic, self-sacrificing behavior of American administrators in Cuba, especially in Major Walter Reed's discovery of yellow fever's causes and its eradication in Havana. Rudyard Kipling's poetic celebration of turn-of-the-century imperialism, "The White Man's Burden," spoke of sending "sons to exile to serve your captives' needs."

Noble intentions, however, only masked the main fact: American elites were transcending their fiduciary obligations to the only constituency to which they owed allegiance, the American people. Note well: talk of higher obligations to mankind or to ideals veiled the fact that, from then on, the elites would follow their own wide-ranging fancies rather than the people's home-focused will. *In the name of mankind, or the greater good, or of the world's downtrodden, they disempowered American voters and empowered themselves. No longer would they feel they had to put America First. Now, they would put their own preferences first.* They had been the American public's servants. Now, they saw themselves as the rightful masters of U.S. power, and felt entitled to marshal the American people's forces for ends that the people scarcely understood, and when the American people objected, the Progressives felt entitled to malign them.

Nor could intentions affect the fact that, by not allowing Filipinos, Puerto Ricans, and others conquered in 1898 to enter the Union as States equal with others, the U.S. had abandoned its founding principle that political legitimacy derives wholly, entirely, exclusively, from the consent of the governed. The Supreme Court's decision in The Insular Cases cast aside the principles of the 1787 Northwest Ordinance and swallowed that poisonous pill. Moreover, by binding itself to "the white man's burden," the United

States was abandoning that principle's practical premise: its own absolute independence. Thus, Progressivism negated America's founding premises practically as well as theoretically.

These *practical* facts overshadowed the Progressive class's now merely *theoretical* premise that peoples everywhere want and are capable of the same freedoms as Americans enjoy. In fact, Progressives considered America, that is, *themselves,* uniquely qualified to lead mankind, even though morally and politically on a par with the rest of it. They squared that circle by assuming that mankind was yearning for that leadership, *their* leadership. In short, Progressivism covered an intellectual–moral power grab that reversed much that had made America, America.

For most Americans, however, America remained first. But imperialism had been merely one of Progressivism's manifestations. Progressive premises overturned the Adams Paradigm. By the turn of the twentieth century, the tone of American government—domestically and internationally—was being set by intellectual trends born in universities, spread through elite channels, and reflected by statesmen.

Theodore Roosevelt

Theodore Roosevelt had taken more than a few swallows out of imperialism's bottle. But experience in governing the Philippines soon convinced him that America should never do anything like that again. Having learned from his mistakes, he showed most fully how America could fulfill George Washington's and J. Q. Adams's view of foreign affairs by wielding world-class power for America's own maintenance. Also, though he had brokered the 1905 peace between Russia and Japan with the lightest of hands, Tokyo's anti-American riots had impressed upon him that the Japanese people's irrational ingratitude toward America outweighed whatever benefit America got from the peace between Russia and Japan. This confirmed his belief that statesmen must limit themselves to their own country's business. His corollary to the Monroe Doctrine was as anti-European as J. Q. Adams's original version had been.

TR embodied the principle of America First as much as anyone could. He most fully developed the Washington/Adams understanding of war's role in U.S. foreign policy. In his history of the naval/commercial side of the War of 1812—highly critical of Jefferson and Madison—and in his commentaries on Lincoln's conduct of the Civil War, he stressed the need to focus war on peace, and the need for congruence between ends and means. Lincoln and Washington had been the best of great men as well as the greatest of good men because they fought their wars aiming at peace.

In 1897, Roosevelt pointed to advocates of empire, who "protest against a navy and protest also against every movement to carry out the traditional policy of the country in foreign affairs," calling them "doctrinaires whose eyes are so firmly fixed on the golden vision of universal peace that they cannot see the grim facts of real life ... [who] prate about love for mankind, or for another country as being in some hidden way a substitute for love of their own country."

The Panama Canal and the Great White Fleet's voyage around the world were TR's proudest achievements. He gloried in these displays of America's power, yet he made sure to show foreigners that none of that power was necessarily directed at anyone. He was proudest that, during his presidencies, America had been at peace with all mankind. Historians' descriptions of him, at once as "imperialist," "isolationist," and "realist," would have led him to suggest the simple word *American*.

Priority and Seriousness

Americans of about 1910 might well have thought of themselves among nations as did sailors on Britain's newest battleship: "Fear God and dread nought." No nation wanted to hurt America, and none could have if it had wanted to. Geography helped. But much credit was due to generations of statesmen who had largely kept their priorities in proper order. Europe's and Asia's major powers had fought each other recently and were pursuing any number of quarrels from the Rhine to East Asia to

Africa through complex alliances and understandings. Competitive plans for mobilization were on hair triggers. But none of this was aimed at the United States, in no small part because American statesmen had not exposed their country to the vicissitudes of other nations' causes. U.S. statesmen's harsh experiences as international arbitrators had reinforced the traditional American bias for minding one's own business.

The U.S. Army was minuscule and would have weighed nothing on European or Asian battlefields. But no American had the slightest interest in sending it there. The experience in the Philippines had reconfirmed Americans' distaste for empire. The U.S. Navy had become a first-class shield for the Western Hemisphere. And that is where American statesmen intended using it. In the Civil War, Americans had shown that they could fight impressively on the largest of scales at enormous cost. But that had been for strictly American stakes.

In short, American statesmen had kept America itself first among their concerns, had pursued their country's interest guided mostly by justice, and had jealously balanced ends with means. Anchored to reality, they acted as serious men worthy of their responsibilities. Unserious successors would throw all that aside.

PART II—TWENTIETH-CENTURY POLICY IN PERSPECTIVE

The paramount purpose of John Quincy Adams's diplomacy had been to confirm—above all in Americans' minds—the Declaration of Independence's distinction between America's nature, and therefore purpose, and those of other nations. That distinction, that focus on America, had been the ship of state's compass, and the engine of popular support that drove it. Without that compass and that engine, U.S. foreign policy has drifted on the ruling class's currents and on the world's winds.

Chapters 4–10 examine U.S. foreign policy in the past century as it would look to John Quincy Adams. These chapters show what happens when policy is cut off from its natural primary focus on one's own country.

PROGRESSIVISM AND POLICY

By 1903, the issue of empire had lost importance to both sides. Everyone agreed that Hawaii should be annexed, that Cuba should never be, that sovereign possession of the Panama Canal Zone was good because it was "part of the American coastline," that Puerto Rico, Guam, and Samoa should be "territories"— outworks for America's defense—and that the Philippines should be independent as soon as possible. All agreed that there should be no more conquests. Ever.

But the division over empire had masked a deeper one, spread over both camps, which would truly shape America over the next century. Our focus here is on some of the ideas—the equality of the world's peoples, the importance of world opinion, a revised understanding of international law, the American establishment's own wisdom, etc.—the success of which made Progressive Internationalism the most influential current of thought about America's relationship with the world, and their consequences.

Under Theodore Roosevelt, Elihu Root served as secretary of war from 1899 to 1904 and as secretary of state from 1904 to 1909. As head of the Carnegie Endowment, he founded the Council on Foreign Relations. More than anyone, he was as much the father of Progressive American statecraft as J. Q. Adams had been the father of the previous century's statecraft.

The Patriarchs

Root mentored Henry L. Stimson, who was to be Herbert Hoover's secretary of state and Franklin Roosevelt's secretary of war. Stimson, in turn, mentored McGeorge Bundy, John F. Kennedy's National Security Council advisor. Bundy then mentored Anthony Lake, who served Henry Kissinger, Jimmy Carter, and Bill Clinton, and even advised Barack Obama. Root thus influenced generations of statesmen to hold that America must lead the world to a new and better kind of international relations, in which reason and persuasion would replace force. Under his guidance and legacy, the primacy of interest in America's leadership would replace the primacy of interest in America itself. Progressives wanted America to be better and believed *themselves* to be more and better than other Americans. They became *other* than Americans.

In 1907, with Roosevelt's permission, Root announced that the U.S. government would no longer put its solitary power behind the collection of private debts in Latin America, no matter how legitimate. What William Seward had done once as a gesture of good will, Root made into a principle. Root had been an imperialist because he thought it would strengthen America's hand among nations, but now America would also bend over backwards not to give injury or insult to any nation and to show the world a new kind of stewardship based on international cooperation.

For his work for the cause of international law, including the establishment of the International Criminal Court, Root received the Nobel Peace Prize for 1912. His acceptance speech distills his thought.

Building a better, peaceful world was about methodically "pulling up the roots" of war and selfishness, he claimed. Impartial international tribunals could settle the controversies that led to war. This better way of doing things was contagious and would build good habits. Since the first Hague conference of 1899, the participant governments had entered into 113 obligatory general treaties of arbitration. Thence, "the development of the peaceable settlement of international disputes ... waits upon the further development of international law by a more complete establishment of known and acceptable rules for the government of international conduct." In this context, Root saw the Hague conference of 1907 as really a lawmaking body that could transform international law from mutual bilateral commitments into commitments to abide by the decisions of multilateral institutions. Once nations made commitments to be bound by arbitration, and then by institutions, they would be bound. End of problem.

Root said that governments abide by international law because it is the most profitable thing to do. Modern economic well-being requires peace and order. Root assumed that everyone wanted economic well-being more than war. Root also argued that peoples, increasingly educated and possessing an "international mentality," would support only just demands:

> First, there has come to be a public opinion of the world; second, that opinion has set up a new standard of international conduct which condemns unjustified aggression; and third the public opinion of the world punishes the violation of its standard.... The spread of education, the enormous increase in the production and distribution of newspapers ... the telegraph ... the new mobility of mankind ... travel by steamship and railroad ... the vast extension of international commerce, [the nations'] dependence on each other for the supply of their needs will make sure that the peoples will push for peaceful, rational international relations.

Morality, as well as "economic science," demanded it. "When any people feels that its government has done a shameful thing and has brought them into disgrace in the opinion of the world, theirs will be the vengeance and they will inflict the punishment."

Root said self-interest and reason are not the biggest causes of bad international relations—feelings are. Root knew that more wars arise out of insult than out of injury. But he believed that "misunderstanding and prejudice are, as a rule, the fruits of isolation." As a result, the remedy is to get different people together to get them to learn about each other. "There is so much good in human nature that men get to like each other through mutual acquaintance." Each separate little kindness will seem meaningless, but together they will build solid habits of peace. The march of civilization is taking the world in this direction. "Civilized man is becoming less cruel." The world's moral level is rising. Let us not stand in the way of a better world.

Root persuaded President Taft to negotiate compulsory bilateral arbitration treaties. The Senate rejected the idea, prompting

Root and the partisans of the scheme to blame the American people for standing in the way of progress. It would not be the last time.

Nicholas Murray Butler, president of Columbia University (1902–1945) and of the Carnegie Endowment (1925–1954), believed that the world had become one big neighborhood, and that the familyhood of mankind, once theoretical, had become a practical fact because, said Butler, today we have dealings with folks in Bombay more easily than we used to have with a neighboring village. "Mankind has been climbing upward and neither standing on a level nor going downhill." He believed he could transform the world through international "mechanisms" for the resolution of international disputes. These laws and courts would be identical with those for resolving disputes within nations.

Stanford's founding president, David Starr Jordan (1891–1913), Herbert Hoover's mentor, believed "there is nothing in the world for us to fight for—at least not with sword and gun. Waste and greed and folly must be fought, but against these we need better weapons." He vowed: "We will leave all disputes to the decision of a tribunal of just men.... Above all, humanity ... this is the motto of the cosmopolitan clubs of our universities made up of men of all races." He could not imagine that the world was anything but these clubs, writ large.

The Great War's mindless slaughter of millions and the starvation of tens of millions, the utter negation of what these Progressives had lived for, sobered a few of them. Many, if not most, doubled down on their illusions.

Woodrow Wilson adopted Root and Butler's agenda. Even in October 1914, as the Great War was showing the futility of arbitration treaties as a solution to the world's problems, Wilson continued to advocate them: "The sum and substance of these [arbitration] treaties is that whenever trouble arises the light shall shine on it for a year before anything is done; and my prediction is that after the light has shone on it a year it will not be necessary to do anything; that after we know what happened, then we will know who was right and who was wrong." As the violence worsened under the lash of enraged public opinion in all belligerent countries, Wilson preached democracy as the solution to war—gasoline to quench the fire.

By the time Wilson became president, Progressive ideas had become mainstream. Unlike Adams, Wilson touted America as the champion of the rights of all peoples. He did his rhetorical best to erase the distinction between mankind's interest and America's. "Ever since we were born as a nation," said he, "we have undertaken to be champions of humanity." Even more so, Wilson asserted, America had "no reason for being" except to "stand for the rights of men." No purpose whatever. Adams and his successors had been rooted in reality. Wilson, at the head of his Progressive class, was leading America into the realm of imagination.

Prior to Progressivism, foreign policy could be measured by its effects on America's permanent interest. Progressivism substituted the Progressives' imagination—their private dreams. For America, these dreams all too often turned into nightmares.

Whereas statesmen from J. Q. Adams to W. H. Seward, Grover Cleveland, and TR had construed the Monroe Doctrine as a shield against extra-hemispheric meddling, Wilson began using it as a license to meddle in Latin America, sending the Marines first to Haiti, then to Nicaragua and to Mexico, "to teach them to elect good men." This left America sharing responsibility for local oppressors.

The Contrast

Prior to Progressivism, labeling any proposal or point of view as America First would have been meaningless. But, having cast aside fiduciary responsibilities, the Progressives' paramount premise is precisely that U.S. policy's proper primary concern must be with mankind as a whole, and with America only incidentally and derivatively. Therefore, Progressives have used the label "America First," implying a narrow-minded and selfish—an illegitimate—worldview. In 1939–41, FDR used it to smear calls for armed neutrality as pro-Nazi. In 2018, Robert Kagan, in a ten-thousand-word article for the *Washington Post*, was one of many who continued to equate it with "isolationism," "protectionism," and "resistance to immigration." Did he need to include "racism"? That followed in due course.

In 1915, three Republicans, former President William Howard Taft, future President Herbert Hoover, and near-president Charles Evans Hughes, formed a League to Enforce Peace—an organization of countries that would submit disputes to arbitration, and gang up militarily on any that resisted doing so. The League's members and sympathizers encompassed much of America's elite in business and law: Thomas Watson of IBM, Thomas Lamont of J. P. Morgan, Bernard Baruch, Henry Morgenthau, and others. A year later, Democrat President Woodrow Wilson effectively took the lead, declaring: "The interests of all nations are our own also. We are partners with the rest." America's establishment had well-nigh agreed that their country was merely at the head of mankind's common Progressive march.

For the Progressives, America belonged to history more than to the American people. Woodrow Wilson's entry into the Great War and his role in the Versailles Treaty for ends more fantastic than American—for example, "permanent peace" and "a world safe for democracy"—have set the tone for U.S. foreign relations and for schools of international affairs into our time.

None of Wilson's predecessors would have engaged Americans in a war for issues with zero direct relationship to their own security or prosperity, with marginal capacity to *affect* the issues' outcome, and with none to *control* them.

By contrast, TR said he would have warned Germany about America's interest in maintaining Britain's role in the Atlantic, hence that America could not afford a British defeat by a rising naval power. He would have cautioned Germany not to bring Britain into the war. Had such a president been in office, the Great War might not have started. But it having started, any of Wilson's predecessors would have maintained true neutrality and would have favored the peace initiatives that Wilson spurned. Had *they* entered the war, they would have done so solely to prevent the Atlantic, "the common possession of mankind," from becoming a hostile German lake. At the peace conference, they would have focused on that, and hence on discouraging a repeat of the

German invasion of Belgium and the Netherlands. They would not have staked America's reputation on drawing borders to be guaranteed by the League of Nations' ambiguities, or by their own.

The American people rejected the self-contradictory notion that Wilson's League of Nations could at once ensure that all would go to war for each, and that it would relieve each and all, especially Americans, of the need to go to war at all. Then the people rejected Wilson's party in the election of 1920. But because the Progressive orthodoxy had taken hold of America's best and brightest of both parties, logical reasoning proved weak against it.

Reacting to the exposure of his detachment from reality, and to the American people's resentment for the costs he had imposed on them, Wilson blamed his political opponents. To this day, Wilson's vindictive narrative is ruling class Progressive gospel: the American people's rejection of the League of Nations and refusal to "lead the world" caused World War II and risks causing the next world war also.

Wilson's 1920 electoral defeat notwithstanding, our Progressive establishment—disposing of America's wealth, heirs to the prestige that American troops had earned in the Great War, feeling entitled to world leadership, confident in their motives' purity, and believing that mankind shared their goals, plunged into world affairs, casting aside the American founders' America First focus. Following Wilson, they also dispensed with reconciling ends and means. They embraced a peace treaty pregnant with the bloody century of war that has followed. For this reason, as America's power has grown, Americans' security has declined.

Progressive internationalists wanted the League of Nations because they believed that it would eliminate the use of force. They vied with William Borah (R–ID) to prove their commitment to moral suasion alone, as well as with Gerald Nye (R–ND) to produce America's disarmament. In 1921, to universal elite applause, Secretary of State Charles Evans Hughes brokered the grand-daddy of modern arms control: the Washington Naval Treaties that "sank more battleship tonnage than all of history's wars," established naval ratios among the great powers, got nine powers to commit to the independence, territorial integrity, and equal access to China, and substituted the Anglo–Japanese alliance with an "alliance" between the U.S., Britain, France, and Japan, directed at no one. They also pledged not to fortify U.S. bases in the Western Pacific, thus disabling the U.S. Navy from contending with Japan there. But all that left Japan—with a new racial grudge—as the sole power in East Asia, while shedding the means by which America might have compelled respect for any ends at all in the Western Pacific.

Thus in 1931, when Japan first invaded China, Secretary of State Henry L. Stimson brought to President Herbert Hoover this "flagrant violation of the spirit and probably the letter of all the [1921] treaties." Hoover told him Americans must consider that Japan's primary violation was not of its specific commitment under the 1921 treaties but rather of its general commitment to the League of Nations. This had to be so, said Hoover, lest America be put in "a humiliating position in case Japan refused to do anything about what he called our scraps of paper or paper treaties." But Progressives' faith in treaties had put America precisely in the position of having to choose between humiliation and war. For the next decade, it chose humiliation. Then war.

No president from J. Q. Adams to TR would have placed America in such a position, for the same reason that none would have entered the Great War for abstract purposes or meddled with the Anglo–Japanese alliance, which meddling the Japanese regarded as an American racial insult. None would have made a treaty commitment to China's independence, or to anyone's, especially as they were depriving themselves of the means to keep the commitment. None would have practiced what TR called "peace with insult," combining "the unbridled tongue with the unready hand." That is because all of them would have fixated on America's own interest and on America's capacity to secure it. Steering by the America First compass, they likely would have avoided the Pacific War—and possibly even the European tragedy.

Wilson made America responsible for a Versailles settlement with many enemies and few friends. His Republican and Democratic Progressive successors then set out to support it with money and words—that is, impotently. They sponsored the Kellogg–

Briand Treaty's gauzy outlawry of war, imagining they were split-
ting the difference between concrete commitments, and none.
They were agnostic about the various regimes and movements
competing for influence in Europe—except for the Franklin Roosevelt administration's fraught romance with Stalin's Soviet Union.
They flooded Europe with money, which fueled all, and with sermons such as Cordell Hull's July 16, 1937, circular to the nations:

> [A]bstinence by all nations from the use of force in pursuit of
> policy and from interference in the internal affairs of other
> nations ... adjustment of problems in international relations
> by processes of peaceful negotiation and agreement ... faith-
> ful observance of international agreements ... modification of
> provisions of treaties ... by orderly processes ... in respect by
> all nations for the rights of others ... application of the prin-
> ciple of equality of treatment ... limitation and reduction of
> armaments.

Such sermons restrained no one, and only convinced the world of
American statecraft's imbecility.

Franklin Roosevelt and his Progressives were not faking imbecility. Whereas Winston Churchill had refused to treat Hitler as a
fellow statesman, FDR did not indicate that something was
wrong with Hitler until after the fall of France. At first, he had
resisted acknowledging reality because he sympathized with Hitler's statism. But after the 1939 Stalin–Hitler pact, the Democratic
Party's substantial pro-Soviet constituency demanded support
for Hitler because he had become Stalin's ally. As for Stalin himself, American Progressives—including FDR—never, ever, did
condemn him for anything. They were and remained in thrall to
communism as much as their European counterparts.

U.S. Progressives also supported Britain's virtue-signaling
opposition to Italy's 1935 invasion of Ethiopia, the sole lasting
result of which was to flip Italy to the German side, and hence to
make Hitler's uncontested takeover of Austria geographically
possible. They shared the British public's aversion to resisting
Germany and its blame of France for security-mania. Nor did U.S.

Progressives understand France's internal political demons and its military establishment's senile haughtiness. Yes ... FDR's brain trusters were not so brainy.

Power and Purpose

Until Pearl Harbor, the wars that began in China, 1931, and Europe, 1939, involved America's interests, but not necessarily America itself. World War II was not decreed by fate. Neither did fate decide that America must fight in that war, never mind on two fronts. Our statesmen's incompetence had a lot to do with events turning out as tragically as they did.

Japan wanted a major sphere of influence in Asia. American Progressives never discussed what a division of influences in Asia might look like. The U.S. had made possible Japan's uncontested invasion of China. Then, it demanded that Japan leave China, and backed that demand by a trade embargo without prospects of resuming normal trade relations in case of compromise. That left a starving Japan with only the choice of where to wage war. Its attack on America was meant to secure a sphere of influence that diplomacy had foreclosed. Can anyone imagine Adams or Theodore Roosevelt placing America and Japan in a bind as Franklin Roosevelt did?

Nazi Germany's primary interests were eastward, beyond German-speaking areas, where they collided with the Russian people and with the Soviet regime. That is why the 1939 Nazi–Soviet pact, which reconciled both sides' interests, at least temporarily, faced the rest of Europe with the harsh task of defining and defending their own interests with regard to Germany. Instead of doing that, France and Britain started a war over Poland without an idea of what these interests might be, without plans for doing any good for themselves or for Poland, and without the intention of doing anything but halfhearted defense.

What was *that* war to America's own interests? That was the question that the America First movement asked and that FDR refused to address. What should American statesmen have done diplomatically and militarily to guard those interests as well as

America's peace? Every president prior to Wilson would have focused on that. Between 1939 and June 1941, when Hitler invaded Russia, FDR was torn between the desire to help Britain and the Democratic Party's communist-friendly elements who supported Stalin (and, given the Stalin–Hitler pact, supported Hitler just as much). Moreover, FDR refused to address the America First movement's question: support Britain with precisely what, to achieve precisely what? Did he mean to declare war on Germany? If so, to what end? Under the circumstances, FDR's equivocations make some sense for himself and his party personally and politically, if not for America. Whatever else may be said of him during this period, he surely did not put America First.

By avoiding specifics, FDR protected those equivocations and managed U.S. politics preceding Pearl Harbor and Germany's declaration of war by accusing the America First movement of Nazi sympathies. Like Wilson, and so many others, when his incompetence caught up with him, FDR blamed his opponents. After December 7, his insistence on total war continued avoiding the practical questions while he accused his opponents of being soft on the enemy. As a result of Progressive political cleverness, U.S. policy pivoted from thoughtless war in 1917 to impotent self-righteousness in the '20s and '30s, to even more thoughtless war in 1941.

The first major U.S. act in that war was a supreme example of irresponsibility. In August 1941, FDR's and Churchill's Atlantic Charter *centrally* promised to restore Poland's freedom. But this was cynical, since both were placing no conditions on their aid to the Soviet Union, which had collaborated with Nazi Germany to dismember Poland and intended to keep its share—if not the whole thing. As the war wore on, FDR repeatedly refused Churchill's request to reconcile the two contradictory commitments.

J. Q. Adams would never have made contradictory commitments or pledges that the United States had no means of redeeming. Much less would he have entered into any unconditional alliance, especially with such as the Soviet Union, whose objectives were, by definition, hostile to America. One of J. Q.'s most valuable teachings is that even when an alien regime's short-term interests line up with America's, it is essential to separate that regime's purposes from ours in our own minds. But confusing them is precisely what our Progressives did, in World War I and in World War II. That confusion, especially with regard to Communist Russia, engendered precisely the "inordinate affection for another nation" among some Americans against which George Washington had warned in his farewell address. That "softness on communism," so powerful among some prominent Americans, fostered hostilities among us that endure in our time.

American Progressives would wage the Second World War in an even more millennialist manner than they had the First. The U.S. demand for "unconditional surrender" hid the absence of specific national objectives. What sane people fight for no concrete objectives? And since such objectives exist and are necessarily limited, what argument is there for letting enemy propaganda caricature them gratuitously?

For a century, America's founders and their successors had understood that any war must be fought in pursuit of a particular peace; for this reason, the means employed—military operations and the management of alliances—must make sense only in terms of the results sought. By nature, military success is only the gate to victory. Military success means victory only insofar as it brings about the particular peace desired. Washington, Adams, Lincoln, and TR understood that basic truth of statesmanship.

So did Winston Churchill and others anchored to reality. In 1944, Churchill's advice to FDR paralleled that of George Kennan from Moscow: by that point, Stalin needed America far more than America needed Stalin. As a result, wrote Kennan, this country should "play its cards to full advantage" to strike concrete bargains about spheres of influence while Stalin still needed America. But FDR refused to think specifically about such things, focused as he was on maintaining his international alliance with the Soviet Union and his Democratic Party's domestic alliance with its communist-admiring Progressive wing.

After World War II, Progressives dodged questions about what they were doing by erecting and worshiping the United Nations organizations, to whose allegedly omnipotent and omni-benevolent power they only *pretended* to abdicate their power. Beginning with the Korean War, the UN's existence allowed them to parry questions at home about whether they were acting wisely by asserting that they were acting legitimately. They did so in a pseudo-legal, pseudo-academic language, increasingly alien to the American people. Alas, not having to explain to fellow citizens what they intended, freed them from explaining it fully to themselves. Thus did they confirm their stewardship's stupidity.

U.S. officials from Chungking to Algiers, left without a compass by which to steer America's growing power, learned to play it by ear—developing the habit and taste for tinkering.

Anyone reading J. Q. Adams's instructions to U.S. ministers abroad cannot but be struck by the contrast. Even as, and perhaps because, the early nineteenth century's slow communications placed much responsibility on lower officials, Adams's letters explained in the greatest detail not just what the minister should do and not do, but why, and to achieve what ends.

By mid-twentieth century, American policy had left behind every vestige of J. Q. Adams.

STRUCTURAL FEATURES OF MODERN
U.S. FOREIGN POLICY

What U.S. officials did between World War II and 1989 had less to do with concepts (such as "containment"), with political promises (such as John F. Kennedy's to "help any friend … bear any burden"), with what was happening in the world, or even with the ballot box, than they had to do with the intramural clashes of ideology, identity, and interest within an ever-bigger, wealthier, and more independent U.S. establishment.

Prior to FDR, U.S. policy had flowed from the president of the United States and from the small number of persons associated with him. As this number expanded, and then exploded after World War II, no president or secretary of state exercised the same architectonic influence that J. Q. Adams, Lincoln, Cleveland, and TR had. Because this national security establishment—big enough to be self-referential—has put its identity and interests first, rather than America's, it has managed endless conflict as an end in itself and as a fount of profitable careers. In short, as part of the *administrative state*, it has institutionalized, embodied, and practiced all manner of corruption.

As Herman Kahn wryly noted in 1959, wherever two or more officials, academics, etc., are gathered, there is made what passes for U.S. policy. Hence what the U.S. government has done throughout the world ceased to fit into any reasonable definition of "policy" and became … simply a record of what officials did or said. Contrast this with de Gaulle's definition: "that ensemble of continued objectives, of matured decisions, of measures brought to term." Instead, the character, direction, and significance of U.S. statesmen's words and deeds have reflected principally the evolving identity of the establishment whose geometric resultant they are.

Presidents from Washington and J. Q. Adams to Herbert Hoover, and their secretaries of state, had mostly made their own decisions and explained them in the speeches they had written. Because their foreign policies were identifiable products of their own judgments, because Americans could hold them responsible, the American people could be confident that, regardless of the policy's actual quality, it would not stray far from their own concerns. But when foreign policy changed from an artisan product crafted by the president and his team into the opaque result of anonymous hands, conveyed by wordsmiths, it transcended its relationship with the American people. Foreign policy became the product of the modern administrative state, to which many contribute but for which no one may be held responsible.

Whether the bureaucracy's involvement improved or worsened the product is beside the point. J. Q. Adams would have opposed the process as much as the product.

Policy by an anonymous establishment is irresponsible by definition. Senators are just as happy for presidents to make war and to do business by executive agreements rather than by treaties because they prefer not to cast votes for which they can be held responsible. Even presidents try to evade responsibility. George W. Bush famously defended his 2003 decision to invade Iraq as the inescapable consequence of the intelligence agencies' judgment about Iraq's weapons programs. He hardly tried to explain the bureaucracy's basic decision to occupy the country indefinitely.

Nor was Bush unique: John Kennedy had defended his decisions regarding the 1962 Cuban missile crisis by referring to the latest close-ups of Russian missiles. In 2009, Barack Obama justified his decision to send another thirty thousand troops to Afghanistan by citing military advice to do so. The intelligence agencies, for their part, finagle for influence but accept no responsibility. Essentially, presidents have been saying "The experts convinced me, and that should be enough to convince you." But that is not how a republic is supposed to work.

Size over Policy

The U.S. foreign policy establishment's very size ensures irresponsibility and transcends the kind of relationship that America once had with the world. Some U.S. embassies resemble vice-royalties. The ones in Vietnam in 1962–75, Iraq in 2003–10, and Afghanistan in 2001–21 are the limit-case. The one in Iraq occupied over one hundred acres, had its own water and power, six hundred apartments, a shopping mall, an Olympic-sized pool, and once employed sixteen thousand people. Such embassies don't do Westphalian diplomacy. They exercise "guardianship" functions over other peoples. In sovereign Britain, the U.S. embassy does not superintend. But the U.S. staff in London numbers some eight hundred, only a few of whom are engaged in diplomacy. Most, as in all U.S. embassies, represent not just government departments—agriculture, defense, intelligence, commerce, and education. All manner of agencies also have their attachés, all of whom actually represent the interests of their diverse constituencies rather than any coherent U.S. policy.

The instruments and sentiments of influential domestic constituencies meld with and into what passes for policy. Today, for example, U.S. embassies hoist rainbow flags and celebrate "LGBTQ+ month," even in places where homosexual acts are against the law, such as Pakistan, and despite the fact that homosexuality is something that deeply divides Americans. Such gratuitous flaunting has nothing to do with relations between sovereign governments and everything to do with the changing character of domestic officialdom, responsible as it is to itself.

America First? No. For the foreign policy establishment's diverse members, their own careers and interests come first. Institutional interests come close behind. Then come partisan priorities. Finally, the substance of their diverse ideals comes in, far ahead of dead-last stuff like America's independence, its honor, its Constitution, its overall prosperity, and even its safety.

By contrast, there was nothing gratuitous, nor was there any expression of domestic partisanship about John Quincy Adams's insistence on making America's commitment to its own republican character crystal clear to Russia's government during the negotiations over the Monroe Doctrine. The tsar had expressed his own devotion to divine right monarchy in a document addressed to America. Adams's affirmation of republicanism—government by consent of the governed versus monarchy—is what then united all Americans and made sense of the policies that Adams was pursuing.

The Foreign Policy Business

In sum, today's foreign policy establishment is an array of constituencies whose people interchange with official-dom, whose interests in any given aspect of any given country range from and are mixtures of personal, pecuniary, and professional—for example, academics, think tanks, the media—to emotional. Whereas until the 1950s "schools of foreign service" taught primarily diplomatic history and languages, today's international relations curricula (573 U.S. colleges offer bachelor's degrees in international relations, and 196 offer master's degrees) are mainly preparation for careers in this array of constituencies. Success in these careers has nothing to do with advancing America's interests and everything to do with enhancing these constituencies' status, objectives, and careers therein.

Life within the upper reaches of these officials and entourages, in the universities, the foundations, the think tanks, and the media that cover them takes place in some of the world's finest venues: at Aspen, in Washington, at Stanford, and, at the top, at the Rockefeller Foundation's villa, first established by Pliny the Elder on the tip of Lake Como's gorgeous peninsula. The money comes from the government itself, as well as from foundations. Ford, Carnegie, Rockefeller, etc., have ever been the establishment's pantry, its voice, its hands and feet, as well as its employment agencies.

Some of the establishment's parts are funded by foreign governments that seek to influence American policy. Officials who serve in Saudi Arabia can see their predecessors who have pleased the Saudis enjoying retirement incomes that dwarf their government pensions. During Prince Bandar's tenure as Saudi ambassador

(1983–2005), few persons who wielded any kind of influence in Washington had not received some sort of present from him.

Tiny, rich Qatar's National Research Foundation partners with Texas A&M to designate grantees. Thus does it service the Bush '41 and '43's entourages and Texas establishment Republicans generally. To make sure that the influential people in the nation's primary energy state will not lack hometown voices that understand Qatar's points of view, it also runs chains of grants to the University of Texas, to Baylor, and to the University of North Texas. Qatar also hosts a branch of Virginia Commonwealth University, making it convenient for U.S. government personnel stationed at the air force base there to continue the degrees that bump up their credentials.

Researchers at the University of Arizona (longtime Senate Armed Services Committee Chairman John McCain's state) get Qatari money, as do ones at the Universities of Illinois, of Denver, Pittsburgh, Portland, Rutgers, Northeastern, and Northwestern— a total of fifty-one. Then there is the U.S. Qatar business council, headed by Patrick Theros, formerly the U.S. ambassador to Qatar, a living testament to the prosperity that comes from staying on the right side of a source of good deals. Dozens of Qatari-supported foundations, for example, the Washington Institute, Brookings, reach countless more grantees.

Ukraine has tried to make up for its lack of wealth and power by inviting influential Americans to share in the corruption of its domestic companies. The money that Ukraine funneled to the families of Democrats Joseph Biden and John Kerry and to Republican Paul Manafort is anything but unusual. Since many if not most U.S. officials and their families monetize their access to one another, foreign governments invest countless billions to open doors in Washington.

China, however, is in a class by itself among the lobbies. Because China's money reaches every part of the U.S. body politic, its power is beyond measure. Education? In 2019–20, some 370,000 Chinese students paid full tuition to U.S. universities. Few of our major universities do not enjoy research grants from China. The entertainment industry performs self-censorship to ensure its programs are distributed in the huge Chinese market. The National Basketball Association has more fans in and gets more money from China than from America.

Above all, corporate America has become so hooked on cheap Chinese labor and to a lesser extent on the China market as to transmit Chinese demands promptly and forcefully to both Congress and the Executive Branch's every part. After some employees of America's major accounting firms criticized China's suppression of freedom in Hong Kong, the Big Four firms issued a statement supporting China's crackdown. American Airlines, United, and Delta changed their websites to eliminate the word "Taiwan." The Disney company submitted its script for a movie to Chinese censorship. America's major media depend on Chinese officials' good will for access to the country. Through the media and through corporations, China contributes directly to U.S. politicians—the Clintons and Bidens being the prime examples.

Identity, Theoretical Differences, Practical Consensus

The biggest factor affecting this establishment, however, is less who pays for what than the Progressive establishment's evolving collective identity. In 1951, that identity took on the social and intellectual form that continues in our time, as it placed America's last prominent protagonists of the Adams Paradigm beyond its pale.

That year, Senator Robert A. Taft, the odds-on favorite for the presidency for 1952, had just published a book, *A Foreign Policy for Americans*, that argued for focusing policy on such of America's interests as could be secured by America's resources. The establishment feared those ideas' popularity and set about vilifying them and him. Opposition to Taft included seconding the corrupt deals that denied him the Republican nomination, including one that substituted one Texas delegation for another. That year also, Secretary of State Dean Acheson prevailed on President Harry Truman to fire the establishment's other *bête noire*, General Douglas MacArthur, from command of U.S. forces in Korea. MacArthur,

World War II's most successful soldier, had set about winning the war in Korea and expressed his professional judgment that victory is war's natural, proximate objective. As the fired general returned home to massive popular approval, the establishment consensus dismissed him as a dangerous dinosaur. The establishment hardly noted or cared that it was thus stigmatizing the public it purported to represent—and its sons who were fighting in Korea.

A decade later, President John F. Kennedy, who admired Mac-Arthur, was attentive to his warning against fighting a land war in Southeast Asia and considered instead his suggestion for a naval-economic strategy reminiscent of J. Q. Adams and TR. But by then, foreign policy had passed into the many hands of an establishment whose evolving consensus was reflected by professors such as Robert Osgood, Thomas Schelling, and Henry Kissinger, and conceived in such inherently meaningless terms as "international community," "leadership," and "world order." Kennedy gave in to it.

That consensus endures, despite the superficial differences between its Liberal Internationalist, Realist, and Neoconservative "schools." Equally, each of these schools believes that the world yearns for its peculiar leadership. Each sub-brand's leadership is different theoretically: the first pursues secular technocratic development; the second pursues peaceful, reasoned accommodation; the third pursues democracy. These theoretical divisions, however, merge in the practice of what has been called the Multilateral Liberal Empire. (See my essay "Some Call It Empire," *Claremont Review of Books*, Fall 2005.)

All three establishment factions believe themselves responsible for improving the world, for achieving some kind of "stable order." But at the most granular level, whether at State or the CIA, in think tanks or at conferences, all factions' White Papers, articles, and books say less about what America might gain from relations with any given country than about how to manage events there: who should govern, what parties' or movements' fortunes should be fostered or hindered, and how. All favor "arms control"— what Senator Richard Russell used to call "disarming while arming and arming while disarming." All want maximum discretion to manage foreign relations. All distrust the American people and try to minimize Congress's involvement in foreign affairs. All favor "special operations" and economic sanctions—the fantasy that they can engage in violence without the discipline of war. Thus do all effectively erase the distinction between war and peace.

The consensus's practical results, piled atop the other elements of corruption that have pushed statesmanship's natural focus into the background, have brought U.S. foreign policy to today's impasse.

POST–WORLD WAR II U.S. NATIONAL
SECURITY POLICY

The Cold War's main course followed substantially from our establishment's corrupt internal dynamic. On one side was the premise that communism and the Soviet Union were an implacable enemy to be eliminated by imposing all manner of constraints on it. On the other, the reverse: that the Soviet Union was as permanent a part of the world community as any other, and that integrating it into some kind of order to foster peace and progress was worth risking and paying for.

"Containment"—U.S. policy's nominal organizing principle from 1947 to 1989—was a compromise between these two sides among people with very different attitudes about communism and everything else. Moreover, the bright uplands of a post-colonial world beckoned the plurality of officials, who imagined a global order coordinated, if not run, by themselves in the United Nations' name. That vision had more to do with what the establishment actually did during the Cold War years than any opposition to communism, never mind putting America first.

The conflict between these tendencies first manifested itself dramatically in October 1956. That month, Hungarians overthrew their Soviet puppet government, chased occupying Soviet troops out of their country, and asked for America's help in holding on to freedom—exactly the sort of opportunity that the doctrine of containment anticipated. It just so happened, simultaneously, that France, Britain, and Israel attacked Egypt to reverse its national-ization and closure of the Suez Canal. The Soviet Union menaced Britain and France. The U.S. government, rather than keeping the Soviets off its NATO allies' backs and helping the Hungarians, chose to back the Soviet threats against Britain and France, forc-ing these to withdraw from the canal they had built and were managing. British Prime Minister Anthony Eden suffered a heart

attack, ending Churchill's dynasty. France's government began a
crisis that led to the end of the Fourth Republic. Meanwhile, as
the Soviets massacred the Hungarians, the U.S. government did
nothing.

Why the U.S. government acted as it did was not clear then
and has not become any clearer since. There was no single top-
down decision. Possibly, the U.S. government did not expect Britain and France to heed its public demand. When Secretary of
State John Foster Dulles visited Eden in the hospital, he reportedly
asked him "Why did you stop?"

Nevertheless, what the United States did turned out to be
epoch-making: beginning with the Hungary/Suez crisis of October 1956, the foreign policy establishment placed their interest in
avoiding confrontation with the Soviet Union—as well as their
preference for a Europe shorn of its colonies and for a world reshaped in their own image—ahead of anti-communism. Nothing
would ever be the same—not inside U.S. policy, nor between the
U.S. and its allies in Europe, nor throughout the rest of the world.

Containment versus Détente

Because the United States decided as it did in October 1956, conservative politicians throughout Europe who had
staked their reputations on identifying with America, lost credibility and found it more difficult to get public approval for deploying U.S. Jupiter and Thor missiles aimed at the Soviets. Leftist
ones found it easier to sell accommodation with the Soviets. Then,
in April 1961, the other shoe dropped. The Kennedy administration
informed the Europeans that defending Europe by threatening
massive nuclear response against the Soviets was no longer U.S.
policy; that henceforth NATO meant that the U.S. would help fight
a Soviet invasion on the ground, primarily by conventional means.

This would require substantial increases in European military
forces and, not incidentally, would ensure the widespread devas-
tation of Europe. During the Cuban Missile Crisis, the United States
dropped yet another shoe. To ask—rather than force—the Soviets to remove the missiles it had placed in Cuba, the U.S. withdrew

the Jupiters and Thors that had been placed in Britain, Italy, and Turkey at the cost of so much political capital. Thus did U.S. Progressives finish discrediting what had been the principal plank of postwar U.S. foreign policy, as well as the conservative politicians who had staked their reputations supporting it. As a result, since about 1963, *the NATO Alliance has been a bureaucratic reality masked by military pretense.*

During the ensuing fifteen years, U.S./European policy with regard to the Soviet Union and Eastern Europe consisted of competition to see whose package of concessions could most thoroughly satisfy Soviet demands. In the 1970s, this culminated in the Kissinger/Nixon policy of détente—of which the American people disapproved as much as they ever disapproved of anything.

So thoroughly did Americans reject Kissinger's détente that, in 1976, Jimmy Carter and Ronald Reagan—the next two presidents in a row—ran presidential campaigns against him, *simultaneously.* But that did not matter because no one was ever so lionized by the U.S. ruling class as was Kissinger. President Ronald Reagan, twice elected by landslides in part by rejecting détente, tried to restore containment as the core of U.S. foreign policy. But *Time* magazine's Strobe Talbot was correct: Reagan's view that the Soviet Union could and should die never became the U.S. government's policy. No sooner had Reagan left office than, as the Soviet Union was dying, the Bush 41 administration started doing its incompetent best to prop it up.

The Cold War ended when the Soviet Union died on Christmas Day 1991. But the foreign policy establishment's narrative is that it ended as its own expert negotiators integrated a reformed Soviet Union into the family of nations—just as anti-anti-communists had always advocated.

A World Reshaped

The Cold War notwithstanding, U.S. foreign policy since the 1950s has been principally about reshaping the world in the image of America's ruling class, as that class aggrandized itself at home. Keeping other countries from falling into communist hands—the public rationale for U.S. political, economic, and social interventions in other countries' internal affairs—was always contradicted by the fact that nearly always these interventions were on behalf of persons politically and socially like the Americans doing the intervening, regardless of their attitude toward the Soviets. That concurrence explains itself.

Specifically, the Americans doing the intervening and those on whose behalf they intervened were mostly Social Democrats, or Socialists—non-communists mostly, but emphatically not anti-communists. Such was Cord Meyer, the longest-serving chief of CIA's Covert Action section, whose 1980 book, *Facing Reality*, frankly explained that, like himself, the Americans who ran U.S. influence operations chose their counterparts only among the great international Progressive family, and differed from communists mainly with regard to means.

Through government, corporate, and philanthropic patronage (often intentionally difficult to distinguish), the U.S. promoted its own and its chosen favorites' cultures—art, music, literature—over conservative competition. The Ford Foundation, other major foundations, major international corporations, and banks took part. The Congress of Cultural Freedom (a covert arm of the CIA), which involved some of America's iconic cultural figures in its efforts, was the archetype. It prospered the careers of countless "good people." The results reshaped the world and America itself in ways that few foresaw.

We note in passing that the U.S. foreign policy establishment treated loyalty to the United Nations, and other international institutions, as yet another public rationale for pursuing its default policy of furthering its own objectives. That pretended loyalty served primarily to deflect criticism from within the U.S. body politic for what the establishment was doing. Prior to the late 1950s, the U.S. really did control all that the non-Soviet UN delegations did. What we might call the "UN made us do it" ploy worked well because of its novelty, especially as regards the Korean War. But the entry into international institutions of the so-called "Third World," which more often than not aligned with the communist world and invariably was embarrassingly corrupt, made the ploy less wieldy and more embarrassing with every passing year. Nevertheless, the establishment has never wholly abandoned it. More on this to follow.

It is important to note that, regardless of the verbal ardor of so many notable Americans for world government (for example, 1940 Republican presidential candidate Wendell Willkie, and the countless "Model UN" assemblies throughout polite America well into the 1970s), the U.S. foreign policy establishment never made the slightest move to diminish its own powers. Even in this century, as the establishment has invoked international institutions' rulings to influence U.S. policy, it has used such invocations to what it calls "international law," never to diminish its own powers, but to increase them against America's elected officials.

Self-Reproduction

In the 1950s, as France was fighting to hold on to its overseas *départements* against Algerian rebels backed by the Soviets, the U.S. backed these rebels diplomatically, as it backed and celebrated every other anti-colonialist movement. In fact, no Third World movement ever came to power without American help. CIA officers, especially, viewed themselves as the world's true revolutionaries. So much did the intellectual/moral patron of anti-Western Third Worldism Franz Fanon (author of *The Wretched of the Earth*) depend on the CIA that he ended his days in its care. Was Fanon "a CIA agent"? Did Nasser, Saddam Hussein, Castro, and others who also rose largely do so thanks to support from the CIA? Silly question. All sides used each other. More often than not, the CIA turned out to be the more naïve side.

In short, from the beginning, U.S. government meddling fostered people and produced movements and governments that were enemies of the United States or who had highly critical attitudes toward America or with agendas radically different from the American people's. That includes not just Egypt's Gamal Abdel Nasser, of whom Secretary of State John Foster Dulles spoke to his brother, CIA Director Allen Dulles, as "your colonel," but Fidel Castro as well—powerfully aided by CIA, though opposed by the

U.S. embassy in Havana. Once upon a time, Saddam Hussein was on the CIA payroll too. In Indonesia, we supported Sukarno, and then those who overthrew him; in Chile the leftist Radomiro Tomic, who brought Salvador Allende to power over Jorge Alessandri; and so forth. In Germany, the U.S. government supported Willy Brandt while opposing Franz Josef Strauss; in Italy, it was Lenin Peace Prize–winner Pietro Nenni over conservative Mario Scelba.

The U.S. government opposed Konrad Adenauer's and Charles de Gaulle's view of European unity consisting of self-governing nations, and strongly supported the current supranational bureaucratic European Union at every step of its evolution. The continual U.S. complaints about Europe's lack of military spending is no reason to forget that the U.S. government strongly discouraged Britain from having a truly independent nuclear force. The U.S. forced Britain to scrap its own Skybolt missile and tried to prevent France from having what U.S. officials called its nuclear "force de crappe"—no small insult to Charles de Gaulle's leadership.

One result of this activism has been the congruence, if not uniformity, of habits, minds, hearts, and tastes among America's, Europe's, and to a lesser extent the Third World's ruling classes. Its members mix in venues such as the annual World Economic Forum at Davos, Switzerland, and revel in their coolness. They want to perpetuate the world they have made and their role in it. Whatever differences exist within this international ruling class, there is universal agreement within it that the American people's preference for its own interests negates their own, and that American voters are the major threat to all that it deems good.

Nor did fostering the fortunes of one's own kind stop at the water's edge. Barack Obama is a case in point. It may not have been a coincidence that the grandmother who raised him was in charge of the Bank of Hawaii's department that financed the CIA's covert activities in Asia, and that young Barry Soetoro, his test results notwithstanding, got privileged access throughout his schooling, and to his first jobs, and to a host of left-liberal connections.

The CIA also built student organizations in America just as it did abroad, everywhere choosing the same Progressive human material. In America, these were the National Student Association

(NSA) and the Students for a Democratic Society (SDS). Just as happened abroad, however (e.g., Germany's Baader–Meinhof gang), the logic immanent in these human materials asserted itself. The groups turned anti-American, spawned the terrorist group Weather Underground, collaborated with the communist world against America in the Vietnam War, and became icons for millions.

In sum, having tried to reshape the world in its own image over more than two generations, the U.S. foreign policy/intelligence establishment became accustomed to believing that it has the wisdom, right, and duty to "nation-build" America as well as the rest of the world, regardless of what ordinary people in America or abroad may wish. Their own vision of themselves and of America remains their foremost concern.

Terrorism

What the U.S. national security establishment has done, is doing, and may do to substitute its judgment for that of America's voters, and/or to influence American elections, is beyond the scope of this book. Here we simply note that the Americans who brought terrorism to U.S. territory beginning in the 1960s were the children—always intellectually and often biologically as well—of the U.S. Progressive ruling class, and that today, this class pins the label "terrorists" on its domestic opponents. The U.S. ruling class's reaction to terrorism has reshaped America in ways once unimaginable.

Contemporary terrorism started when Egypt's Gamal Abdel Nasser, in the wake of Egypt's 1956 military defeat, hired a communist named Yasser Arafat to recruit fighters to wage war against Israel at a level of violence below what might prompt Israel to make war on him. The U.S. was not pleased: Nasser owed his power to CIA help, especially in brokering the alliance with the Muslim Brotherhood that had made possible his 1953 coup. Nasser, however, asserted his own priorities. Arafat's organization, Fatah, morphed into the PLO (Palestine Liberation Organization), and he went on to a murderous career. But because Arafat & Co. styled themselves "Progressives," U.S. policy never abandoned the forlorn hope of weaning them and similar groups to respectability. The United States has protected the PLO in its several phases of distress and continues to finance Fatah to this day.

In the 1960s, the U.S. ruling class's acquiescence to Castro's protection of American leftists who were hijacking airliners to Cuba, as well as its preference for losing rather than winning the Vietnam War, showed America's vulnerability. In those years, the Soviet Union increased substantially its investment in the terrorist training and organization center it had maintained in Karlovy Vary, outside Prague. There it published *World Marxist Review, Problems of Peace and Socialism* in several languages—a veritable workshop for terrorists. Europeans, Middle Easterners, Latin Americans, Asians, and Africans trained there and then infiltrated the West, often through Berlin. In 1965, this center organized the Tricontinental Organization, which held its conference in Havana that December. Its banner was a globe resting on crossed machine guns; its slogan: "One, two, many Vietnams."

By the 1970s, America had become the main focus of terrorists the world over. Their reasons mattered less. Later, Osama bin Laden's explanation was as good as any: America was showing itself not to be "the strong horse." As the Iranian revolution of 1979 unfolded, France's *Le Figaro* wrote: "It's open season on Americans." The season has not closed.

Terrorist violence itself, however, did not change America as much as did the U.S. establishment's choice to respond to it by increasing surveillance and policing of America's general population, rather than by following the example of Adams and Jackson and raiding the regimes that incite them, or by acting against the populations whence they come and the causes they serve. The Department of Homeland Security's charter attributes terrorism to impersonal causes—something to be endured indefinitely. Gratuitously, since 9/11, the U.S. government has given permanent U.S. residency or citizenship to some one million Muslims. We leave to the reader to imagine the intellectual reasoning and moral priorities by which the government decided to do this.

Even more recently, the Department of Homeland Security, the FBI, and something called the West Point Combating Terrorism

Center have published papers asserting that the primary source of terrorism in America is ... Americans "excessively concerned with their liberties." White Supremacists, you know! The Joseph Biden administration made that its official position and, perhaps unintentionally, its defining act. No more thorough reversal of George Washington's, John Quincy Adams's, Abraham Lincoln's, and Theodore Roosevelt's statecraft can be imagined, nor could there be a clearer illustration of the proposition that foreign wars have domestic consequences—especially mismanaged ones. See below.

Trade

Expansion of international trade was an article of faith among U.S. officials who planned for the post–World War II economy. Knowing that worldwide restriction of trade had helped cause and surely worsened the Great Depression, that the war had heightened dysfunctional habits of economic nationalism, and that the United States had the world's most productive and only undamaged economy, they used U.S. trade policy to stimulate economic activity in Europe and Japan. This consisted of lowering barriers to entry into the U.S. market while tolerating relatively high barriers to protect European and Japanese industries as they recovered from the war. At the same time, the U.S. Marshall Plan well-nigh required Europeans to lower trade barriers among themselves.

Acting as much in America's interest as in the rest of the world's, and since the two sides' interests happened to coincide, U.S. officials did not trouble themselves about whose interest they were putting first—thus neglecting one of J. Q. Adams's principal teachings: no matter the coincidence of interests between the United States and foreigners in any circumstance or time, one must never forget that, since times and circumstances change, American statesmen must take care above all to protect America's paramount interest in its own identity and independence.

Thomas Jefferson and Alexander Hamilton had differed about U.S. trade policy because Jefferson wanted America to be primarily agricultural and believed that farm exports would wield enough power to ensure independence, while Hamilton thought that America had to nurture its infant industrial economy to have the industrial capacity for military self-defense.

The Hamiltonian approach to international economics—reciprocity along with substantial protection for American industries—from which post–World War II policy departed, had long since turned American industries from infants into giants. For a century and a half, innovation and dynamism had helped produce a chronic shortage of labor in America. That meant that American workers enjoyed the world's highest wages by far. Because the cost of labor was high here, American products were often not competitive internationally. But as Henry Ford pointed out, American products were made and priced so that the Americans who made them could afford to buy them. By war's end they dominated the globe. In 1944–45, no one foresaw the U.S. being flooded with high-quality, low-priced goods from abroad. For this reason, as U.S. officials planned the postwar system, they did not intend to change this happy situation.

Nor did they imagine how it might change. For close to another generation, America's advantages were more than enough to overcome its high labor costs, while Europe's and Japan's regrowth, along with South Korea's and Taiwan's birth as suppliers and markets, boosted the American people's already extraordinary prosperity.

Major U.S. corporations set international economic policy early after World War II by establishing branches in as many countries as possible, especially in Europe. This allowed them more easily to sell abroad and to take advantage of lower labor costs outside America while the U.S. maintained one of the world's lowest tariff barriers. This worked well for America as long as the American economy's unique economic efficiency had outweighed American labor's high wages and salaries, making domestic products and services competitive at home and abroad as well as benefiting U.S. consumers.

By the mid-1970s, however, the combination of low barriers to imports into the United States with Japan's historically huge barriers and Europe's increasing ones were making for stiff competition. At the same time, U.S. corporations that had invested in Europe and Asia to produce for local markets began to use the lower labor costs in their overseas facilities to produce for U.S. markets as well. At this point, U.S. trade policy turned against the American people's historic prosperity and independence. Companies also moved more and more of their U.S. operations to lower-cost parts of the globe—first Europe, then Mexico and Taiwan, Japan, and Korea, and finally to China, the very mecca of high-quality, low-cost labor.

Thus U.S. corporations, by transforming themselves into foreign competitors, effectively de-industrialized America. This changed fundamentally what millions of Americans do with their lives and how we relate to one another. A society of people who make things is very different from one dominated by managers and financiers, served by a vast service sector. Changing to this latter model has meant high incomes for the financiers' managers, and those associated with government, and stagnating incomes for everyone else.

At this point, the U.S. body politic should have confronted the basic question with which Hamilton, Jefferson, Adams, and others of their ilk wrestled in the 1790s: what kind of country do we want to be? Who will decide what is produced here? What occupations may our people pursue, and how much will they be paid?

But the U.S. body politic did not confront these questions: first, because of the ingrained, unexamined sense that our exceptional prosperity is a fact of nature; second, because academics regarded as a panacea the economic truth of "comparative advantage," that all must benefit if each country confines itself to producing that which it does best at the lowest cost; third, because politicians looked at the American people strictly as consumers of products rather than as producers who live certain kinds of lives because of what they produce at a given price; and fourth, because officials forgot that maintenance of the capacity to produce certain essential things is the indispensable ingredient for international independence.

Nobody voted for changing the American people's occupational profile or for allowing the logic of "comparative advantage" to deprive the United States of sovereignty over key industries—from shipbuilding to pharmaceuticals to electronic components, including those for military purposes.

Nobody voted against it either, because the U.S. foreign policy establishment and educational establishment—and, of course, politicians—did not think of sovereignty over essential materials, products, processes, and skills as an issue. One might have expected the leaders of industrial corporations to make it their issue. But, U.S. industries having become appendages of the finance industry in recent decades, its leaders know and care less about their products than they do about stock prices. America First? For the economic as well as for the foreign policy establishment, America comes last.

UNSERIOUSNESS ABOUT WAR

Progressive thought looked away from the reality of war as the midwife of nations and the gravedigger of decadences, from the paramount importance of discerning what are and are not the necessary circumstances that call for briefly setting aside America's peace in pursuit of better peace. Rather, Progressive thought has complicated such discernment by blurring distinctions between war and peace themselves. As a result, under Progressivism, U.S. military forces at all levels have been planned and used in ways that have left them unable to secure victory, and therefore peace, on any level.

Because Progressive thought has clouded these most basic of realities, U.S. military operations have been planned and executed, not on the basis of standard military criteria, but rather on the basis of what will fulfill our foreign policy establishment's personal and institutional interests, as well as its evolving ideological criteria. The contact between U.S. military planning and reality, having produced results very different from those envisioned by those in charge of a military establishment costing some three quarters of a trillion dollars a year, have wrapped it in an atmosphere of unreality.

What follows traces the departures from reality made by modern U.S. war planning and conduct.

Nuclear Realities and "Declaratory Policy"

U.S. policy and weapons programs for war at the highest level have oscillated between two mutually exclusive paradigms, always including elements of both. The results at any given time have made sense only in bureaucratic and political terms.

The first paradigm, expressed in Bernard Brodie's *The Absolute Weapon* (1946) embodied the establishment's dominant reaction to the invention of nukes. Accordingly, because the establishment supposed that fear of nuclear weapons must be equally prohibitive for peoples everywhere forevermore, nuclear weapons have made major war virtually impossible. For this reason, because preparing to fight nuclear war would provoke it, America must not do so. Because strife among nations from here on can only take place via conventional skirmishes, America must engage in those skirmishes while maintaining only a quantum of invulnerable nuclear weapons to ensure perpetual peace at the highest level of warfare.

The U.S. military generation of World War II, however, believed that—since nuclear weapons have not changed the nature of man or war—we should plan to deter, and if necessary to fight, survive, and win nuclear war—the second paradigm. Possessing a nuclear monopoly and an expanding nuclear stock (but remaining largely ignorant about the location of things on which to disgorge it in the vast Soviet Empire), the military was confident that, by distributing it among an "optimum mix" of Soviet military and civilian targets, they could stop any Soviet aggression, protect America, and win the war.

By the late 1950s, improving reconnaissance as well as bombing and missile system accuracy made it possible to focus on military targets exclusively. Thus, as information and accuracy improved, America's military refined a "counterforce" strategy to destroy Soviet missiles and bombers. This, combined with America's multi-layered air defense and ongoing work on missile defense, made it doubtful whether any Soviet bomber or missile could have reached America in the 1960s. On a lower level, "tactical" nuclear weapons were integrated into the land, sea, and air forces' ordinary operations. President Eisenhower summed up the approach: "bigger bang for the buck." Nukes would economize American lives and allow the U.S. government to exert maximum power without militarizing society.

The Democratic Party's pull in the other direction came in 1957 when the Council on Foreign Relations published Henry Kissinger's *Nuclear Weapons and Foreign Policy*, a muted restatement of the Brodie thesis from *The Absolute Weapon*. The party's intellectual leaders believed that. But the Democrats ran their 1960 presidential campaign vowing to reverse the "missile gap" that they alleged Eisenhower had allowed the Soviets to open up, and they promised to improve America's capacity to fight at the highest level. Implementation of the Brodie thesis was the last thing the country expected from Democrats. But, after John F. Kennedy's victory, that is what Defense Secretary Robert McNamara delivered.

In 1963–64, building on Brodie's and Kissinger's thought, McNamara proposed that the Soviets and ourselves had reached an everlasting technological plateau, on which neither would ever be able to protect itself against nukes by any offensive or defensive means. For this reason, rather than for war-fighting, nuclear weapons should be built only for retaliation against civilian targets. This would produce mutual deterrence, which would ensure peace for all, forever. That meant that U.S. weaponry should aim not to protect America but to threaten to kill millions of Russian civilians. Never mind that killing civilians would do America no good and that the U.S. government had no intention of ever actually doing it. This was bluff advertised as bluff. They called this imaginary construct "declaratory policy."

Subsequent to this reasoning, the U.S. foreign policy establishment froze the number as well as the yield/accuracy combination of its strategic weapons. For example, the submarine-launched Poseidon C-3 low yield warheads were designed to be accurate only to a quarter mile, to spread destructive force far and wide but only sufficient to kill undefended civilian targets, and neither accurate enough nor potent enough to destroy the hardened Soviet missiles targeted on America. The United States dismantled its air defenses, decided not to defend against missiles, and spent some fifteen years trying to convince itself that the Soviet Union was doing the same things. *Invariably, the Soviets did the opposite.* Nevertheless, Henry Kissinger, as secretary of state under Presidents Nixon and Ford, codified all this and made it into the ruling class's default paradigm that endures in our time.

Placing "declaratory" or "pretend" policy at the peak of U.S. military planning has affected all the rest that the U.S. military does.

Dissent from this nonsense briefly prevailed during 1979–89. In 1980, President Jimmy Carter's secretary of defense, Harold Brown, acknowledged that the Soviets understood nuclear weapons differently from U.S. policymakers imagined and were making plans to fight, survive, and win nuclear war. "When we build, they build; when we stop, they build," he said. Carter's National Security Council, under Zbigniew Brzezinski and William Odom, issued Presidential Directive 59, which directed a return to a limited counterforce strategy. The Carter administration initiated programs to build equipment to carry it out. The Reagan administration completed those programs (the land-based MX missile and the submarine-based Trident D-5, designed to kill hardened military targets). The Reagan administration also talked of (but was talked out of) building missile defenses. Air defense of the United States, dismantled around 1965, remains nonexistent. Theoretically, the 1980s were a full repudiation of the McNamara/Kissinger paradigm. Practically, there was at most a partial return to the late Eisenhower one of fighting and defending at the highest level.

The next quarter century's administrations—Bush I, Clinton, Bush II, Obama—repudiated Reagan in practice rather than in theory. They reduced the quantity of U.S. strategic forces and essentially stopped their technical evolution. They removed nuclear weapons from ordinary ground, sea, and air operations because, as Clinton's defense secretary, William Perry, argued, their presence might make a president "feel less restrained ... in a crisis." They confined missile defense to a token "national" force, and prohibited missile defenses of troops and allies from being useful for national defense. Thus did these administrations ever more closely embrace the extreme Brodie paradigm. Rhetoric aside, the Trump administration changed nothing. Consequently, *it is difficult if not impossible today to explain how America might use its nuclear forces in battle to its own advantage.*

It is essential to keep in mind how total is the U.S. inability to conduct even the most elementary aspects of nuclear war. Counterforce targeting, even of the preemptive kind, no longer offers the protection it offered up to the mid-1980s, because Russia, China, North Korea, and even Iran have made or are making their land-based missiles invulnerable through motion or hardening in secret locations. By contrast, America's land-based offensive missiles are as vulnerable as they have been since the 1960s. Recently, the U.S. had possessed forty-one ballistic missile submarines. The 2020 number is down to fourteen, half of which are vulnerable, in port, at any given time. What could we do with the remaining seven? A lot of harm to others, for sure. But what good for ourselves?

A U.S. missile defense penetrable even by North Korea is the main reason why America's ultimate choice is to threaten to use its nukes in ways that do more harm than good, or to back down in the face of whomever might be serious about nukes. The lack of missile defense, although part and parcel of Progressive policy, is a technical–political subject unto itself (see *While Others Build*, McMillan, 1988) and is beyond the scope of this book.

In sum, without protection against enemy nukes through counterforce and/or missile and air defense, it is difficult if not impossible to imagine using U.S. nuclear weapons in ways that would do the American people any good. U.S. nuclear forces now serve primarily to deter America itself.

Fatal Skirmishes

Just as there is no such thing as a small pregnancy, there is no such thing as a small war—because any and all wars raise the most fundamental questions about any nation's existence.

In 1950–51, the decision to fight the Korean War at all, the manner in which it was fought, and its resolution, set a paradigm for all U.S. military actions into our time. Each of these ventures has been based on confusing the trivial with the essential, peace with war. Each pursued *arrangements* with foes instead of *victory*, sacrificed for tactical success, and ended in strategic defeat. Because all these skirmishes decreased foreigners' fear of America while increasing their contempt, each made subsequent ones likelier. All trained and equipped U.S. forces to operate unseriously. All have discouraged Americans, while accustoming our national security establishment to profiting from wasting America's human, material, and spiritual substance.

Secretary of State Dean Acheson's public exclusion of Korea from the list of vital U.S. interests in April 1950 was no slip of the tongue, having been coordinated with George F. Kennan's policy planning staff. It was based on the foreign policy establishment's mistaken assumptions about Communist China.

The previous year, when Acheson and his Progressive colleagues had facilitated Mao Tse-Tung's takeover of China by their failure to oppose him, they had bet that Mao would not challenge U.S. containment in Korea or anywhere else. As a result, when North Korea invaded the South as Mao's and Stalin's agent, Acheson and the establishment confronted an obvious challenge to themselves as well as to containment. For this reason, the invasion would have to be stopped, somehow. But Acheson and his cronies determined not to revisit their basic choices. Steadfast against confronting the Soviet Union and especially China, they ended up managing a self-contradictory policy with American blood.

The outcome might have been foreseen within days of the June 25 invasion, when Acheson persuaded President Truman to intervene but not to call this—and hence not to think of it as—fighting a war being waged by America for American purposes, but rather a police action on behalf of the United Nations for purposes that transcended America's. The pretense that American officials were not in charge in Korea helped these officials to deflect the American people's objections to what they were doing. When Truman/Acheson's firing of MacArthur made clear that U.S. officials were the ones commanding Americans to fight and die indefinitely without trying to win, these objections became bitter accusations.

The public said that if the Korean War was worth dying in, it was worth winning. Nor was there any material barrier to U.S. victory. Chinese troops in Korea were hopelessly outgunned. The U.S. military had a plethora of means at its disposal to cut them off and destroy them. Just as important, neither the Chinese nor the Soviets had gone into Korea to end up bringing America's wrath down on themselves. Nor, in 1950, had the Soviet Union, never mind China, any means of hurting America itself.

But the Democratic Party establishment's decision not to confront China and Russia resulted from: (1) reluctance to oppose communist governments upon which some of them and their constituents looked kindly; and (2) fear of any confrontation that might possibly involve nuclear weapons, even though the U.S. had essentially a monopoly of them.

This decision turned out to be the pattern for all subsequent U.S. war policy into our time—a generation after the Soviet Union's demise. Then, as later, the establishment justified it by arguing that American sacrifices serve purposes beyond the American people's understanding. Over the decades, they have given that purpose many names: "world order," "avoiding a bigger war," "strengthening the international community's solidarity," etc. This has served the essential political purpose of not confronting the fact that America's incompetent leaders are capable only of sacrificing American lives and losing wars. The rows of ribbons on their chests celebrate their contributions to defeats. Three generations of losers.

The American people demanded to know: if, as the establishment said, Korea was not the right war, why fight it? And if the establishment wanted to avoid any chance of war with Mao and Stalin, why were they fighting their North Korean pawn at all? If this so-called international community demands our defeat, what good is it to us? Maybe these experts were not so expert. In 1952, Americans voted the Democrats out of office. But the Korea paradigm had become part of the increasingly bipartisan establishment's identity. It has remained so.

"They are not serious."

How thoroughly our establishment had become accustomed to setting aside the realities of force and interest to avoid confrontation—and how ready it was to claim that deadly defeats are a kind of victory—became dramatically unmistakable in 1962, when the Soviets placed medium-range, nuclear-tipped missiles in Cuba in plain sight.

The Cuban Missile Crisis was a trial of spirit, not of force. The forces involved were not comparable. In those years, Soviet ships could not get out of port against U.S. opposition, much less reach Cuba, never mind fight the U.S. Navy. Their scarce dozen of primitive SS-6 intercontinental missiles, had they gotten off the ground, would have ended goodness knows where. Had the Soviets sent bombers against America, possibly not one would have gotten through what was then our thick, multilayered air defense. The Soviet leaders knew this. They also knew that the U.S. Strategic Air Command's 450 B-47s and B-52s, (then electronically invulnerable to Soviet air defense missiles) plus 170 Atlas and Titan missiles, 180 Polaris missiles, plus the Thors and Jupiters stationed in Europe would have left the Soviet Union far worse off than even the German invasion had. No, the Soviets were not stupidly risking war. Rather, they bet that the Americans would pay a price for the cessation of missile deployment in Cuba. The Soviets won their bet, bigger than they had reason to imagine.

The Kennedy administration neither destroyed the Soviet missiles, forced their removal, nor imposed any price on the outgunned Soviets. On the contrary, abstracting from the military balance, Kennedy offered, preemptively, to remove U.S. missiles from Europe and to guarantee the survival of the Castro regime in Cuba in exchange for the Soviet missiles' removal. To the American people, the Kennedy administration and its Progressive entourage denied that any bargain had taken place and presented the outcome as a great, shrewd victory. The U.S. media covered for Kennedy. Since that time, pretending victory has been part of the U.S. military's standard operating procedure.

But the fecklessness was clear to allies and enemies alike. When the crisis started, Charles de Gaulle had assured Kennedy of France's support "in war as in peace." Conscious of America's overwhelming military edge, de Gaulle had publicly bet on his country sharing America's triumph. He lost the bet. Disgusted with American leaders, this wise statesman uttered the most damning of his judgments: "They are not serious." The consequences of unseriousness have followed, in matters big and small.

Our establishment's unseriousness has theoretical roots. Robert Osgood, Thomas Schelling, and Henry Kissinger's theories provided intellectual support for the establishment's political and cultural turning away from the classic pursuit of victory.

Osgood (*Limited War*, 1957) and Schelling (*The Strategy of Conflict*, 1959) developed, and Kissinger translated into terms appealing to a wider audience (*Nuclear Weapons and Foreign Policy*, 1957; *The Necessity for Choice*, 1961), the core "realist" proposition. Namely: the logic of the choices available to any conflict's rational parties drives all to maximize their advantages and minimize their losses by moderating their objectives. According to this logic, illustrated by a simple matrix, the pursuit of victory produces only losers. Since war is politics by other means, wrote Kissinger, war's purpose must be the advantageous adjustment of interests. For this reason, and given the matrix, America's wars must be limited to the kind that "a great nation can afford to lose." Hence, Kissinger's "subtle task," as Jonathan Schell encapsulated it (*The Time of Illusion*, 1976), was to prepare our government "to negotiate and to settle for less than our traditional notion of complete victory." This brave "realism" reigned unchallenged in Washington during 1959–79.

The Soviet sponsorship of North Vietnam's campaign to seize the South reprised Stalin's successful strategy in Korea. Regardless of whether Soviet dictator Nikita Khrushchev had read Kissinger, he planned to lead the U.S. precisely into the sort of wars that Kissinger advocated and that the U.S. had shown in Korea that it was willing to lose. On the U.S. side, sending troops piecemeal to fight in Vietnam embodied the preference for confronting Soviet expansion by Kissinger's kind of war. That is why the Vietnam War turned out precisely to be a contest between one side that was determined to win and another that really did not mind losing. The Soviet and American strategies were in fateful synergy.

The establishment thought and acted in Vietnam in stark opposition to the conservative side of American life. The conservative candidate for president in 1964, Barry Goldwater, had protested, as statesmen from George Washington to Douglas MacArthur would have protested, that the war should be fought for victory or not at all. For that, Secretary of Defense Robert McNamara pronounced Goldwater more dangerous to peace than anyone on the communist side. As the establishment became ever more convinced of its kinship with the communist powers, and of its sociopolitical disdain for the conservative side of American life, it gradually decided to scuttle the U.S. war effort—to pull the political rug out from under those whom it had sent to fight the war.

But the communist side would not simply let the Americans walk away. In 1973, Hanoi returned 591 prisoners of war but held back some 302, demanding a ransom similar to what France had paid to get the last third of its POWs back in 1954. On February 2, 1973, the *New York Times* headlined: "Laos POW List Shows 9 from U.S.: Document Disappointing to Washington as 311 Were Believed Missing." Because paying ransom would have unmasked claims of "peace with honor," the subject was mostly scrubbed from the government and the press, except for Sidney Schanberg's reporting in the *New York Times*.

After America's defeat in Vietnam, Kissinger's wrote: "The dilemmas of Vietnam were very much the consequence of academic theories regarding graduated escalation that had sustained the cold war" (*Diplomacy*, 1994). He avowed that the U.S. ended up paying as much for defeat as it would have paid for victory. That understated the price of defeat. And he did not mention that these were his theories.

As the U.S. establishment worked to defeat its own armed forces in Vietnam, many among them adopted William Appleman Williams's thesis (*The Tragedy of American Diplomacy*, 1959) that America was on the wrong side of the Cold War. They blamed the military for militarism and—as President Jimmy Carter would say in the speech to Notre Dame that Anthony Lake had written for him—Americans in general for "inordinate fear of communism." This was not the first time, nor would it be the last, in which Progressive leaders blamed the American people for the country's troubles. This left the Americans who had borne the war's burden with distrust of their leaders, to which the Rambo myth's popularity and the continuing display of MIA flags in our time still attest. It engendered a distrust that keeps on getting deeper. In sum, Vietnam was a war, the loss of which imposed a heavy and continuing price on America.

What was the U.S. strategy in Vietnam? Who was the enemy? How was it to be defeated? *Ad nauseam*, President Lyndon Johnson repeated that the enemy was "poverty, ignorance, hunger, and disease." Accordingly, the military's role was to hold the line against the armed foe while the main strategic task was to have been accomplished by a legion of American political, social, economic, and educational nation-builders.

Thus, in Vietnam, the U.S. foreign policy establishment crossed the divide between war and its own default political modus operandi. In Africa and Latin America, as well as in Asia, they made and unmade governments, and directed their ministries' work. They aimed to conquer hearts and minds, to birth and build nations according to their imagination of what America should be. Nation-building would be mostly peaceful. The amount of violence required would depend on circumstances. They really believed that. Their successors still do. And whatever they do, they call it victory.

Confusing War and Peace

Vietnam had brought together the limited war doctrine with the longstanding Progressive practice of foreign policy for the theoretical purpose of improving the world and the practical purpose of advancing people they believed to be like themselves. The Cold War had provided this paradigm with a tenuous tie to vital American national interests. The Soviet Union's 1991 implosion removed that tie. It also freed the U.S. national security establishment from their last connection to war's natural discipline: that all wars put national existence at stake and that, nearly always, victory and defeat are the only options.

Having set aside this reality, the establishment has "worked with allies around the world militarily and socio-politically to thwart forces that would destabilize the U.S.-led international order." How many times and in how many ways have Americans been recited this mantra! In countless operations, with greater or lesser admixtures of military force and reformism, the U.S. government well-nigh erases the distinction between war and peace. Having done nothing else for generations, this mishmash is all they know.

They don't want to remember that foreign policy is about advancing America's peace, or to know that every involvement in other peoples' affairs is potentially a source of conflict; that giving aid to some can't help but make enemies of those who don't get it or don't get as much; or that when you support one side against another in their political struggles, you guarantee that your friends' successors will be your enemies. For this reason, Iran became America's enemy when the Ayatollah Khomeini replaced the Shah, on whom the Americans had doted. By the same token, the recipients of negative economic pressure cannot but regard such pressure as an unfriendly act—even an act of war. In short, managing foreign clients invariably involves some force. But inconclusive force is naturally endless because it does not aim so much to crush enemies as to police subjects. Some call that empire-keeping. But whatever else it does, it makes peace impossible.

The 1990–91 "Gulf War" is a case in point. The Saudi royal family had been U.S. clients since World War II. Iraq's Saddam Hussein had also been our client since 1979, when he replaced Iran's Shah in that role. U.S. politicians, never mind the U.S. State Department and intelligence agencies, courted him. In 1990, Saddam decided to play a bigger role in the region by annexing Kuwait. The Saudi royals, whose role he was reducing and whose people admired Saddam, asked the U.S. to make war on him. The U.S. government, instead of regarding the annexation as a local readjustment of power tangential to any vital interest of ours, chose to regard it as a threat to "world order." A magnificent exercise of U.S. military power followed that destroyed Iraq's army and "liberated" Kuwait." The U.S. military cried "Victory!" But no.

The Gulf War created problems where there had been none.

Machiavelli had warned: "Men are to be caressed or extinguished." That is, never do a *little* harm! Saddam had not been an enemy. Saddam, wounded by America but left in power, became an enemy. He rallied much of the Muslim world against an America arguably mean to Muslims and a paper tiger to boot. The Saudi royals were grateful, but now required a permanent U.S. presence to protect them against even some of their own people, including one Osama bin Laden. Previously friendly and powerless, this rich man's son became a deadly enemy—of America.

As a result, the "Gulf War" turned out to be the first of the many U.S. battles in the Muslim world that absorbed U.S. forces for a generation, reshaping them and America itself.

Since then, by whatever name, chronic use of force has been the reality of U.S. relations with the rest of the world. Eliot Cohen, iconic member of our establishment, expressed the sense of that relationship (*The Big Stick*, 2017): get used to it! But while the U.S. may regard what it is doing as merely managing world order, those against whom it uses force surely regard it as war.

The Americans who wage this no war/no peace for a living prosper by pleasing superiors, not by winning. Then, when they conclude personally successful careers, they get medals, the big pension, the house on the golf course, and the deal with the military contractors. They get those by putting themselves first and America last. But a succession of such successful careers leaves America ever worse off.

War on Terror

In the 1960s–80s, the U.S. government set a pattern for itself by pretending that the terrorists who were waging war on the West were something other than Soviet proxies (Claire Sterling, *The Terror Network*, 1981), and by preferring to endure small hurts rather than seeking to stop them. Instead, it began to impose internal security measures on America's general population.

Case in point: Fidel Castro's encouragement to hijack passenger planes to Havana (or Yasser Arafat's organization of airplane hijackings) were typical of early modern terrorism: acts obviously inspired and encouraged, if not organized outright, by some potentate or patron of some cause. Such indirect warfare succeeds insofar as the target does not respond directly. Moreover, governments that submit to indirect war ensure that its intensity will mount, and prove that they cannot defend their people. The U.S. government chose to endure the inconvenience of Castro-sponsored hijacking rather than to shut down Castro's regime in any of the myriad ways available, or to make an issue with Castro's Soviet sponsors. Instead, it chose to manage the problem by prohibiting the general public from carrying weapons on airplanes and requiring defenseless passengers not to resist hijackers.

That prohibition and that requirement are what made 9/11 possible. When Flight 93's passengers fought for their lives with bare hands, they acted in violation of U.S. regulations. Had they overpowered the terrorists, they would have been legally liable to prosecution.

The U.S. government's passivity in the face of low-level warfare had not escaped the Muslim world's notice. That passivity had become glaring when the U.S. endured Iran's revolutionary government's 1979 seizure of the U.S. embassy and its diplomats— a textbook act of war—behind the transparent screen that the perpetrators were private persons. This U.S. failure fit well with the Muslim world's default manner of warfare and politics in general— namely fighting more through unofficial groups, thus inviting their opponents not to hold them accountable.

By the 1980s, many of the Muslim world's governments and terrorist groups (all secular except Iran) were aligned with the Soviet Union. In 1983, Hafez Assad's Syria, the Soviets' principal proxy, and Iran's Revolutionary Guard Corps used Hezbollah to murder 241 U.S. Marines, thereby ending the U.S. effort to establish a pro-Western government in Lebanon. In 1986, as the U.S. and the Soviet Union were at odds over the deployment of medium-range missiles in Europe, Libyan terrorists infiltrated West Berlin from East Berlin and blew up a discotheque frequented by American soldiers. Only against weak Libya's Qaddafi did the U.S. deliver a warning strike. In short, the U.S. government was wedded to the fiction that terrorist groups and individuals are independent—"idiots" in the Greek sense of the word. But in the conventional sense of the word, the idiots were U.S. officials.

In the 1990s, the USSR having died, and given Iran's success, Muslim governments transitioned seamlessly to professing radical Islam and to using longstanding radical Islamic groups. By the same token, secular terrorists, for example, in the PLO, discovered their inner Islamic piety. Meanwhile, the U.S. government remained wedded to exculpating regimes—until the American people's furor following 9/11 caused a shift in focus—a shift so reluctant, partial, and confused that it resulted in our current, endless "war"—on nobody in particular because it's focused on "terror" in general. This is a war that, surely and not so slowly, is turning into a war among Americans.

No sooner had the hijacked planes struck the World Trade Center and the Pentagon than CIA Director George Tenet delivered the verdict: Osama bin Laden had done it, "game, set, and match." What, *precisely*, this individual had done remains unclear to this day. The CIA, having identified terrorism with bin Laden's al Qaeda, set out on a bitter bureaucratic crusade to squelch any notion that the terrorists were acting on any basis but personal religious preference. The idea was to prevent the American people's ire from falling on any of the governments or Progressive organizations dear to the U.S. establishment's hearts. Case in point, the CIA regarded the intelligence services of Ba'athist Iraq and Syria as allies because it had fostered their development and continued to receive information from them—which they took in with little skepticism.

This unwarranted exoneration of regimes and the subsequent ignorant military campaigns had undeniable consequences: In 2001, al Qaeda consisted of some four hundred men, mostly employed by the Taliban to fight their Afghan enemies. Nearly two decades later, the fighters who identify with something like al Qaeda number about thirty thousand the world over. Everything that the U.S. has done and not done in the name of anti-terrorism has managed radically to increase the main problem: disrespect for America.

Obviously the problem was that all Muslim governments, to some extent, so disrespect America that they incite and harbor anti-American terrorists. But which ones did and do so the most? And what to do about it? The facts of 9/11 pointed first to Saudi Arabia, home of the radical Wahhabi sect whose worldwide institutions are the foremost source of Sunni Muslim radicalism, whence all the 9/11 "muscle hijackers" had come, of whose identities we are still ignorant, whose authorities had facilitated the hijackers, as well as to Iraq. But Saudi Arabia was exceptionally well connected to our establishment. Iraq, on the other hand, was universally unpopular among Americans because, by 2002, Saddam was the Muslim world's most vocal and prominent anti-American.

Iraq's connections to al Qaeda itself were in plain sight. Al Qaeda had done nothing noteworthy until 1996, when bin Laden issued a "fatwa," the principal gravamen of which was America's ill treatment of Iraq. Such things seldom happen without money changing hands. At the same time, al Qaeda also incorporated a band of professional terrorists led by Khalid Sheik Mohammed whose acts from then on made al Qaeda a household word. These pros had been part of the secular Baluch community that had long served Saddam for money.

Throughout 2002, the CIA fought hard bureaucratically and hid much to discredit connections between any regime and 9/11, especially Iraq's. But nothing could counter the fact that, if an attitude adjustment were to be delivered to the Muslim world, overthrowing Saddam had to be the place to start.

The Bush administration settled on ridding Iraq of "weapons of mass destruction" as the invasion's official rationale because the establishment—principally the CIA—had refused to agree to an invasion premised on Iraq's responsibility for terrorism. Later, birthing "Iraqi Freedom," covered the government's own refusal to leave Iraq quickly. These rationales reflected agendas that had less to do with terrorism than with traditional Progressive foreign policy concerns: servicing allies, managing regions, and profiting from it all. Nevertheless, the Iraq War could only be sold to the American people as the War on Terror's centerpiece. But in fact this centerpiece had zero to do with fighting anti-American terror. Unintentionally, it did quite a bit to foster it.

The Iraq that the United States conquered in April 2003 was a British-created, mini-version of the Ottoman Empire. It forcibly held together Shia and Sunni Arabs, plus Kurds. The first two wanted to dominate each other, while the third wanted to get away from the other two. The moment that Saddam's regime disappeared, all set about their respective objectives—with knives, guns, and bombs—and never stopped. U.S. policy's practical objective, which endures today, "a united, democratic Iraq," is on another planet from the locals' concerns.

All sides tried to leverage U.S. power for their respective purposes, and all but the Kurds did so by killing Americans. The U.S. fought to stop Sunni and Shia from fighting each other, and to share power according to some formula acceptable to Saudi Arabia and Syria—governments that also were backing the Sunni at the time—and to Iran, that was backing the Shia. Absolutely none of that had anything to do with alleviating the terrorist threat to America. In practice, this U.S. government policy placed America itself at the tail end of a long list of concerns.

Sunni and Shia had made Iraq into a replenished minefield. U.S. troops died primarily driving around in that minefield. The establishment described the killers not as each other's principal enemies but as terrorists targeting our soldiers who, if not fought in Iraq, would come to feast on defenseless civilians in Middle America. Fox News still says stuff like that with a straight face. It claimed that by building "a united, democratic Iraq," America would convert them and their country from a nursery of terrorism to the prototype of a new, moderate Middle East.

In practice, however, the U.S. armed and paid both sides, supervised transfers of populations, erected physical barriers between them, called it victory, and left the country with more enemies than had been there before—minus five thousand dead, thirty thousand wounded, and maybe $2 trillion spent on military operations and nation-building.

Also, in notoriously xenophobic and war-loving Afghanistan, the U.S. government applied its default "nation-building" recipe:

strengthening the central government (though this meant disarming the very northern tribes that had won the 2001 victory
against the Taliban); spreading civilian advisers throughout the
land, bearing money and advice on how to live; and labeling and
fighting any who object as "terrorists." Whatever else happens in
Afghanistan, the United States will leave more ferocious persons
there with more grudges against America and fewer fears of it
than ever were before.

The experience of fighting today's Americans could not help
but make anti-Americans of many who had not been that. Countless Muslims in the rest of the Muslim world, in Europe, and in
America itself, learned that killing Americans could give meaning
to their lives. So alluring has this prospect become that, whereas
once upon a time anti-American terrorism tempted only exceptionally devout Muslims, now it tempts all manner of persons to
give meaning to murder by clothing their grievances with a thin
cloak of Islam.

Since Korea, the U.S. armed forces have accustomed themselves to operating with entirely secure rear areas, mastery of the
air, and underequipped opponents. These forces have developed
habits and indulge all manner of politically correct regulations
sure to doom them against militarily serious opposition.

The truest of truths about terrorists, always cited but seldom
taken seriously, is that they can hurt a country only by leading it
to hurt itself through misguided internal security. For the meaning of this, we may turn to Niccolò Machiavelli who, though the
opposite of a civil libertarian, argued that security measures
imposed on the general population weaken its allegiance—the
country's only true security. Arm the people! Machiavelli coun-
seled. And encourage them to cleanse the body politic. Our establishment did the opposite.

The major changes wrought by the War on Terror have been in
America. The establishment has applied internal security measures against the general population, on the politically correct
fantasy that any among ourselves are as likely as not to be terrorists. In sum, it demanded that Americans trust each other less
than ever, but that they trust the authorities more than ever. Thus

having diminished the natural distinctions between citizen and foreigner, familiar and alien, friend and enemy, our establishment accentuated the artificial distinction between rulers and ruled.

Moreover, Progressives have taken gratuitously to accusing whoever disagrees with them of "terrorism." After 9/11, our bipartisan ruling class came together on the proposition that, at home as well as abroad, America is at war against "terrorists" or "extremists" whose identity we cannot ever know and who are so evil that there must be no limit to fighting them. The Patriot Act of 2001 penalizes giving aid and comfort to their organizations, but it does not specify what qualifies any entity or person for such label. No law was ever voted to set any standard. Instead the Act empowers the president to make that designation without justifying it to anyone. By what standards is any American to be treated as a terrorist? In practice, those in power make up standards as they go along. President Obama defended non-judicial killing of Americans pursuant to their being classified as terrorists, saying: "It's not a bunch of folks in a room somewhere just making decisions. It's part and parcel of our overall authority … focused at people who are on a list of active terrorists." But the criteria for who is on such lists, and what is sufficient for each case, are indeed the exclusive purview of "a bunch of folks in a room."

Inevitably, those "folks in a room" deciding who the public's enemies are cannot abstract from their own private or corporate (or partisan) friendships and enmities. And so, the establishment's tendency to equate opposition to themselves with treason to the country has asserted itself.

Already by 2012 the Department of Homeland Security had published a study entitled "Hot Spots of Terrorism and Other Crimes in the United States, 1970–2008." It classified as "extreme right-wing terrorists" persons who are "suspicious of centralized federal authority" and/or "reverent of individual liberty." That year also, Col. Kevin Benson of the U.S. Army's University of Foreign Military and Cultural Studies at Fort Leavenworth, Kansas, and Jennifer Weber of the University of Kansas published an article in the *Small Wars Journal* titled "Full Spectrum Operations in the Homeland," arguing that the U.S. Army should prepare itself for contingencies such as "extremist militia motivated by the goals of the 'tea party' movement" seizing a small town.

In 2021, President Joseph Biden ordered the Department of Defense to purge the armed forces of persons whose way of thinking may be considered extremist or White Supremacist and to re-educate the ranks as prophylaxis against such attitudes. In the absence of objective standards for what these ideas might be, the purge can only be about partisan loyalty against the general population. In sum, the new American security state is committed to nothing other than the power of those in power. Like Orwell's Oceania, it is an endless end in itself.

Who benefits from all this? Not America's general population, who paid in blood, money, and decreased security, but all manner of officials—civil and military—who lived prestigious careers and enjoy opulent retirements. Contractors took trillions to the bank.

In sum, a half century of skirmishes has left Americans less respected abroad, more divided at home, and rightly wary of getting into more wars, but ill equipped morally and politically, as well as militarily, for any other kind of relations with the rest of the world.

You wouldn't know that from the torrent of self-congratulatory words that issue from the U.S. political–military establishment. Its members multiply America's problems by believing their own propaganda.

BELIEVING YOUR OWN PROPAGANDA IS DANGEROUS

The Pentagon's massive 2018 "National Defense Strategy" document, like previous ones, agonizes about whether the U.S. government should deal with two major contingencies at once, or should plan to stabilize one war, then pivot to win the second immediately after. Given that the U.S. government has not won any war in living memory, and that it has been constantly at war since 2001, it is all too clear that the document reflects the nearly impenetrable cocoon of self-deception, and corporate and individual self-interest, in which the U.S. national security establishment lives.

The countless presentations the Pentagon makes to Congress, the countless statements that presidents and lesser politicians have made about U.S. military power over the past half century, have been boasts of greatness combined with justifications for what the military has wanted—wanted primarily for its own service/corporate reasons rather than for winning wars.

The U.S. armed forces really are, incomparably, the biggest and best at most everything. We have more ships of higher quality than anyone else in the world; more air force squadrons, missiles, most manner of defenses—more of just about everything.

But the key question with regard to any weapon is: What is it good for? Where? In what circumstance? U.S. forces are as they are not to execute any strategy, that is, any plans for using what you've got to get what you want. They are as they are because of inter- and intra-service/corporate priorities, because of military–industrial collusion, and above all because of the national security establishment's self-regarding prejudices and tendencies. These people long ago discarded the actual winning of wars as the true gauge of military power. The DOD's dictionary of military terms does not contain the word "victory."

That is why the U.S. armed forces are classic parade ground

armies—superbly equipped, fabulously paid. They look good. But they are incapable of winning the wars that our national security establishment defines for them. In the crunch, U.S. forces would suffer from classic mismatches between ends and means. All foreseeable but disregarded.

The "National Defense Strategy" also lists and prioritizes a whole bunch of things that the U.S. government would like to see happen. But strategy—the connection between what you want and what you are doing, reasonably calculated to obtain any-thing—is just not there. A glance at the topmost priority tells the tale. That priority, naturally, is defending against attack on the United States. But in fact, *official policy remains not even to try defending against missiles from Russia or China.*

Defense, then, is merely a "declaratory" priority. The decision made during the Johnson/Nixon administrations, *circa* 1964–1972, to be unserious about nuclear war continues to relegate defense against missile attack to the "declaratory" category, and adversely affects everything else the military does. Mighty America's confrontation with crummy North Korea removes all doubt that defending America itself is not at the top of the U.S. govern-ment's priorities.

North Korean Exposure

North Korea is the quintessential "shithole country." With a GDP of $16.2 billion, about 0.03 percent of America's, its people are chronically malnourished. Its armed forces are more than a generation behind America's in sophistication. Yes, North Korea now has a production line of mobile land-based and sea-based ballistic missiles that could reach the United States. But its strategic forces are a tiny fraction of America's. Problem is, North Korea built its nuclear missile force in a way that perfectly exposes the U.S. government's unseriousness about war at the highest level—and consequently at all others as well.

When President Johnson reluctantly, and President Nixon wholeheartedly, agreed that America should never be defended against ballistic missiles, they knew that their decision would be unsustainably unpopular. For this reason, they hedged it with obscure rhetoric and expensive "research" programs that gave the impression that the country was as committed as ever to missile defense. Opposition to missile defense became part of the Democratic Party's identity; spending money labeled "missile defense" part of the Republican identity. The Democrats did not object as Republicans bragged about how much was being spent, and contractors of both parties took the money to the bank. Thus did each part of the establishment cover its priorities. But the American people remained uncovered. So effective has the establishment's hypocrisy been that at least half of America has never ceased to believe that we have a good missile defense.

The language of the policy's details furthered the confusion. Although the 1972 U.S./Soviet ABM treaty restricted defense of America itself to a single "site," whose land-based radar could not be "substituted for" by orbit-based fire control, it permitted America to defend against "non-strategic," "tactical" ballistic missiles. Because, by definition, these are missiles whose range cannot cross the oceans, the treaty did not permit any of the equipment for these "tactical" purposes to be useful for "strategic" purposes, i.e., for defending against the ones that can hit America itself. For geographic reasons, this distinction between tactical and strategic affects only America.

For this reason, unbeknownst to Americans, during the subsequent half century U.S. engineers have tried to provide for defending American troops abroad and U.S. allies while being careful lest the equipment they build be applicable to the defense of America as well. Especially have they shied away from using information from satellites for fire-control—that is, directly to program ground-based anti-missile interceptors so that they might be launched before the offensive missiles come over the horizon of radars located near the places to be defended. Early launch would so improve interceptors used for "tactical" purposes as to make most of them capable of defending as well against ones that can hit America. This restriction has made equipment in the "tactical" category extra expensive, unable to help protect America, *and* sub optimal against short- and medium- range missiles. Whoever would target America knows that, even if the American public does not.

In this century, U.S. policy has been to protect America itself *only* from a handful of missiles from anywhere, and to do so from a single site in Alaska. Politicians may have chosen this token measure to take away the argument, "We can't defend against even one missile." To accomplish the self-contradictory objective of building anti-missile weapons while making sure that they do not work *too* well, and that they can cover the whole country from one solitary base, the "national" interceptors themselves have had to be endowed with ultra-high speed. Gratuitously, they have also been required to hit incoming warheads directly, killing them by impact. These decisions' technical burdens have slowed progress and turned each interceptor into a near-billion dollar, not-so-sure shot.

U.S. policy's intent had been to defend America against the half dozen or so missiles that it presumed "shithole countries" such as North Korea and Iran might build. North Korea overthrew these ignorant expectations easily because the technology for making intercontinental nuclear missiles, and producing them in quantity, had long since ceased to be exotic. The U.S. government, for its part, has only begun to come to terms with the bankruptcy of this basic policy. Thus far, the government has concentrated on pretending that its cleverness has not been exposed. But pretense-as-policy has short legs. The question no longer is what shall America do with North Korea, but what will North Korea do with America?

President Trump, no less loudly than President Obama, demanded that North Korea "de-nuclearize." Fat chance! But these presidents' attitudes mirror the U.S. public's ignorant contempt for North Korea. The problem is that, not only do the U.S. armed forces have no way of de-nuclearizing North Korea, neither do they have the means safely to respond to even major provocations from North Korea. A YouGov survey reported by the *Wall Street Journal* shows a majority of Americans ready to demand a major conventional U.S. strike on North Korea were it to do something like seize a U.S. ship—which it has done in the past. The survey shows that the Americans who would so demand believe that the U.S. government has the capacity to intercept all or nearly all North Korea missiles. Not true. Under current policy, it is becoming ever less true. The U.S. public is merely reflecting what it has been told again, and again, decade after decade. Were North Korea to engage in such a provocation, the U.S. government—unable prudently to get into a war that it is in no position to sustain—would be placed in a highly embarrassing position.

There is reason to wonder how much any U.S. president understands the reality of U.S. vulnerability to missiles. At what point would they take the trouble to understand the difference between boast and reality?

President Trump was a vocal advocate of missile defense. He ordered the Pentagon to come up with a plan to provide it. On January 17, 2019, Trump released the Pentagon's Missile Defense Review (MDR) with words that might be summed up with Lucy's timeless promise: "This time, for sure!" Said Trump: "First, we will prioritize the defense of the American people above all else." And then: "The United States cannot simply build more of the same, or make only incremental improvements." Finally: "My upcoming budget will invest in a space-based missile defense layer…. Regardless of the missile type or the geographic origins of the attack, we will ensure that enemy missiles find no sanctuary on Earth or in the skies above."

But the MDR's eight thousand words contained no fundamental changes in current policy. None. Instead, the Trump MDR explicitly reaffirmed the basic no-defense policy: "While the United States relies on deterrence to protect against large and technically sophisticated Russian and Chinese intercontinental ballistic missile threats to the U.S. homeland, U.S. active missile defense can and must outpace existing and potential rogue state offensive missile capabilities."

Trump had said we would not "build more of the same or make only incremental improvements." But the MDR mentioned only one actual homeland defense addition: an additional twenty ground-based interceptors to be located exclusively next to the other forty at Fort Greeley, Alaska.

Nor is it as if those in charge of U.S. missile defense don't know what makes the biggest difference between horse-and-buggy interceptors and effective ones. All know and have always known that the biggest factor affecting the performance of surface-based anti-missile interceptors is whether you can launch them before the target comes into view of co-located surface-based radars. The MDR mentions in passing that "Russia maintains and modernizes its longstanding strategic missile defense system deployed around Moscow, including 68 nuclear-armed interceptors [meaning launchers that are loaded and reloaded from underground], and has fielded multiple types of shorter-range, mobile missile defense systems throughout Russia."

Why ever do the Russians (whose students outrank ours in math and science) think that these masses of interceptors—not nearly as sophisticated and expensive as ours in Alaska—can protect against intercontinental missiles? They know so because they know that their less-than-ideal interceptors are *targeted* by far-away radar systems, the very ones that *also provide early warning*, while the interceptors are located close to the places to be defended. They know that *unifying remote warning and targeting is the key to interceptor performance*. They have acted accordingly since the 1960s.

That truth is well known in America too. But because the establishment puts its proclivities first rather than America's interests, that practice, known here as Engage On Remote (EOR), came into tentative use only in 2019, only in the Navy, and only for the defense of overseas troops and allies. The Russians also put nukes on the interceptors to relieve the exquisite, failure-prone, and prohibitively expensive hit-to-kill technical requirements that U.S. officials have imposed on ourselves.

President Trump also made a big deal of sponsoring the establishment of a fifth branch of the military, the U.S. Space Force, dedicated to supremacy in orbital space—satellites being vitally important to all military operations. But when Russia tested improved devices for destroying U.S. satellites, the head of the

U.S. Space Command responded with an empty reference to "deterrence." It is empty because the United States does not have and is not about to acquire any capacity to protect its own satellites and to destroy those of others any more than it is about to acquire any serious anti-missile capacity. Why? Because the very same (chiefly air force) officials and contractors actually in charge of such functions put existing careers and money tied to current programs ahead of America's interest. They corruptly pursue their own advancement instead of putting America First. They proved no better stewards of their own interests than of America's. No sooner had the Biden administration taken office than its spokesperson treated the Space Force as a joke.

Sooner or later, somebody with executive responsibility has to know what America can and cannot do for itself, because if North Korea can so easily take advantage of our vulnerabilities, so can anybody else.

The Reality of War

War itself is the limit to the U.S. national security establishment's self-referential habits.

In 2019, news that the war games that RAND corporation runs for the U.S. government show U.S. forces "getting their ass kicked" by Russia and China elicited disbelief: "How could this possibly be?" The short answer is that U.S. forces fail in the war games, and would fare worse in real war, because these forces would be sent to fight the Chinese for control of the Western Pacific, and the Russians for control of areas west of the Niemen River, as well as north of Crimea. As wonderful as the weapons in the U.S. arsenal are in and of themselves, they would be irrelevant to the outcome in areas where the Chinese and Russians, respectively, would enjoy overwhelming advantages.

The war games dealt only with operational/tactical factors on the conventional level within the theaters of operation. But China and Russia are nuclear powers whose missiles can deliver nuclear warheads on the United States. Neither has been shy about pointing out that they might force the U.S. to choose between its objective in someone else's back yard and the loss of one or more American cities. If, perchance, Chinese or Russian conventional forces should have difficulty disposing of U.S. challenges in-theater, raising the nuclear specter would surely force the U.S. side to reconsider why we engaged in war in others' back yards *without the capacity to protect ourselves at home.*

Since nuclear weapons are fully integrated into Russia's ground forces, this rude awakening would likely come in the course of ordinary operations. In the Pacific, we might well see China anni-hilating Guam. Are U.S. nuclear missile forces so superior to Chi-na's that the Chinese would never do such a thing? Perhaps. *But if they did, then what?* What good would America do for itself by kill-ing a couple of million Chinese?

The nub of military questions is what forces are good to do what, where, against whom, and *in ways that do their country good.* The Chinese and Russians, respectively, have good strategic, oper-ational, and tactical answers for what they do. The U.S. side does not.

The Chinese want to control the Western Pacific militarily, largely from the land. They began by building hundreds, perhaps thousands, of medium-range missiles able to cover the sea out to the eastern edge of Taiwan, making them largely invulnerable by placing them in caves or on mobile platforms. To this they added excellent aircraft with cruise missiles, and diesel-electric subma-rines that would be placed—still and quiet—to wait for the U.S. carriers. Then, they developed the DF-21, a ballistic missile that can adjust course on re-entry and kill a carrier with a nuclear war-head. And then, they pushed that defensive envelope outward by building a network of artificial islands in the South China Sea, each of which has a military value that exceeds that of several U.S. carriers. China's primitive carriers and the rest of its huge navy would enjoy the inestimable advantage of operating under the umbrella of its land-based forces.

Note well that China's control of the Western Pacific already exists. To try undoing it with current bases and equipment, the U.S. would have to send irreplaceable carrier battle groups across the Pacific to battle their way through Chinese defenses. The U.S.

having studiously avoided fortifying Taiwan, the only nearby major U.S. bases are Guam and Yokosuka—over a thousand miles away from the action.

In the event of a war, the Chinese are certain to attack and degrade the satellite network, the full health of which is a prerequisite for U.S. military operations in the area. Since the U.S. has precisely zero means of protecting against kinetic anti-satellite weapons, we must assume that vastly inferior U.S. forces, whose perfect functioning is essential to their operation in an enemy environment, would not be able to function perfectly. But even assuming perfect functioning, the U.S. offensive in the Western Pacific must consist of a contest of attrition, a contest in which location gives China the overwhelming advantage. There is no substitute for strategic vision. China has it; the U.S. establishment does not.

On the Russian side, the operational objective is equally clear: maintain superiority in an area well known to, and easy to reach by, the home team against what the Americans can bring from far away. That area, east of Poland between Lithuania and northern Ukraine, was the scene of the great Soviet January 1945 offensive that crushed the Wehrmacht. One or perhaps two combat brigades would be the maximum that the U.S. could deploy there, probably by air through Warsaw. Russian operations would consist of encirclement by land and denial of resupply by air through its formidable S-400 air defense system. Russian operations will make the most of their distance from U.S. power.

Fortunately for the United States' politically correct, gender-integrated forces, Russia's default plan involves more maneuver than combat. The operational objective would be to turn U.S. troops into prisoners, then hostages. The same would apply to the southern theater—except that U.S. operations there would be aided by a U.S. carrier battle group that would find it easier to enter the Black Sea than to leave it; another reservoir of hostages.

For a half century, the U.S. military–industrial National Security establishment has been getting America's collective ass kicked around the world. Very large forces that cost the better part of a trillion dollars per year, being neither equipped nor trained to win wars, are irresponsible bluffs, always in danger of being called.

But the officials responsible live in a bubble of fancy and privilege. They put their interests first; as they end their careers on corporate boards and in their villas, and pontificate as "experts" on Fox News and CNN—while ordinary Americans pay and die.

DIPLOMATIC MALPRACTICE

For a century, the Progressive approach to international affairs has been to pervert U.S. diplomacy from a way to communicate reality into an attempt to substitute the establishment's fancies for reality. By pretending to substitute words for reality, U.S. statesmen diminished the United States' credit with foreigners and the American people alike.

Early American diplomacy had sought maximum understanding of the compatibilities and differences that existed between the United States and other countries, and it pursued mutual agreement between nations by persuasion. It largely succeeded because the statesmen of that age started from the premise that the boundaries of the possible are set by all sides' sovereign right and capacity to be the final judge of their own best interests. J. Q. Adams was particularly effective because he communicated America's main interests in terms of realities, using precise language.

But Progressive statesmen have used diplomacy to try accomplishing things inherently impossible. They have sought to ignore and "rise above" the very real differences between cultures and among sovereign nations; pretended not so much to adjust different interests as to advance interests that they incorrectly presumed all nations had in common. For this reason, they have communicated less realities than ploys to obscure them. Since precise, accurate language exposes unrealistic enterprises for what they are, our statesmen speak in coded, hazy terms.

Only by imprecision, not to say baloney, is it possible to pretend, for example, that cultures based on opposite principles really prize the same things or, as Woodrow Wilson did, that there can be such a thing as a "community of power," or that nations that are arming to defeat one another might give up that purpose by depriving themselves of some of their armaments, or that peoples in the process of resolving their differences through war can resolve them through "peace processes." The biggest bundle of baloney, that all humans share the American people's ideals, is as tragically misleading as the proposition that everyone and anyone is likely to think and act according to Judeo-Christian principles. Few are.

The practical problem of U.S. diplomacy is the unexamined notion that treaties—and especially "multilateral institutions"— can substitute for a government's willingness or capacity to act in its own interest; that international connections can replace taking care of one's own business. A glance at history—for example, France and Britain's behavior during the 1920s and '30s—indicates that confidence in foreign partners diminishes incentives to think clearly about what one must do for one's own country. Following Woodrow Wilson, U.S. policy has made "multilateral" arrangements ends in themselves. But the notion that treaties and/or international bureaucrats will serve your national interests is not founded on reality.

Henry Kissinger provided the theoretical basis for diplomats to obscure the issues intentionally, and he made it standard U.S. procedure, calling it "creative ambiguity." Accordingly, regardless of what all sides of a negotiation may say, each participant must assume that the others agree with its own objectives. All sides then work together to find *common language that admits of varied interpretations*. All sides can then claim success. Thereafter, each side can put its own interpretation on the supposed agreement and do what it would have done without the negotiations in the first place. This pretense is a cheap, disgraceful caricature of diplomacy.

Kissinger made "creative ambiguity" his hallmark in negotiating the SALT/ABM treaty of 1972 and in the negotiations that ended the U.S. role in Vietnam. Of course, it is easier to convince oneself to afford losing a war or to retreat from a purpose than it is to persuade the other side not to seize a victory handed to it.

Progressive statesmen's standard behavior is to act as if the world can be shaped by pretend-arrangements. Pretense makes it possible to pursue abstract objectives. But aiming diplomacy to achieve ill-defined objectives, failing to distinguish America's own business from that of others, has made it difficult for American statesmen to understand others' business, as well as to pursue America's own. This has helped lead U.S. diplomacy into bureaucratic egocentrism.

Speaking in Vain

During the Cold War, as the Soviet Union deployed a massive apparatus of propaganda and political warfare to enlist the world's peoples in its struggle against America, the U.S. government felt it necessary to counter by speaking to foreign publics directly through proclamations, through semiofficial radios, as well as through clandestine influence on the world's media. This "public diplomacy" extended to communications with the Soviet Empire's own peoples, whom the U.S. government correctly judged to be communism's captives. Necessary as it was to counter worldwide slander of America, "public diplomacy" engendered the habit of developing an official U.S. position on just about everything that happens anywhere on earth, and proclaiming it loudly.

As a general rule, however, this is highly destructive, because it inserts America in others' business without cause ("Who do these Americans think they are, anyway?"), and because it does so in the name of the American people, who almost surely know and care nothing about the subject of any given U.S. proclamation. Schools of diplomacy used to teach that a government should "take note" only of such events as it plans to do something with or about, and officially ignore anything and everything else. Forgetting that lesson is another of Progressive diplomacy's dysfunctional features.

In America, the constitutional discipline of ratification by the Senate and of appropriations by the House had kept foreign affairs firmly within the bounds of "government by the people"—until Woodrow Wilson himself transcended them, ironically by practicing "secret diplomacy" in the name of "open diplomacy." Wilson, having taken control of transatlantic communications during the 1919 Versailles peace conference, pretended to Europeans that

Americans demanded their assent to his plans, and pretended to Americans that the Europeans demanded that Americans assent. But as he deceived others, he ended up deceiving himself. When he presented his plan for Senate ratification, his gauzy rhetoric did not match up with the plan's text, leading first the Senate, then the voters, to reject him.

Subsequent Progressive diplomatic dreams, based as they have been on intentionally obscuring reality, have also created disillusion.

Self-inflicted Harm

Progressive statesmen touted the United Nations as "the last, best hope of mankind" (as if somehow history were about to end). But that institution had always been a fraud on the American people, founded as it was on the Progressive lie that the Soviet Union's objectives were compatible with America's and on a charter that granted the Soviet Union three votes to every other country's one. Progressives continued to foist it on America even after it had become the ludicrous plaything of obscene Third-World despots masquerading as models of human rights.

The entire arms-control enterprise, from the Washington Treaties of 1921 to the SALT treaties of the 1970s to our time's marathon U.S.–North Korea nuclear negotiations, has been based on setting aside the obvious fact that, when the parties involved really intend to limit their armaments, such agreements are unnecessary, and they are futile when the sides have no intention of weakening themselves. Reality is that no government has any power to control any other government's armaments. As Walter Lippmann observed in 1943, the original disarmament treaties had disarmed only those who wished to disarm themselves. Exquisitely drafted arms control provisions are comical in their powerlessness. For example, the SALT II treaty's distinction between bombers capable of intercontinental nuclear missions from those that are not depend on features that show "Functionally Related Observable Differences" (FRODS).

Continuing U.S. financial support to countries and entities

that continue to incite and support terrorism is the most glaring example of how invincibly ignorant is the proposition that diplomatic engagement can induce governments to act against their own purposes. Between 1995 and 2018 some $5 billion flowed from the U.S. government to the Palestinian Authority. U.S. law, of course, prohibits funding for "acts of terrorism." But the State Department has argued that, since the governments and agencies that receive U.S. money pay for things other than "acts of terrorism," money going to these entities does not fund terrorism but rather shifts the Palestinian Authority's internal weight against terrorism. Yet money is fungible, and Palestinian Authority textbooks continue to instill the cult of terrorist martyrdom against the Jews and their friends—mainly the Americans. And the PA continues to pay salaries to the families of imprisoned terrorists that increase with their crimes' severity.

In 2018, however, the Trump administration cut some $700 million that was to have gone to the PA and to the UN refugee agency—a small departure from Progressive practice.

Nevertheless, the habit of claiming underlying agreement in the face of the opposite is deeply rooted in U.S. diplomacy because it makes possible for diplomats to succeed even when their success comes at the cost of America's failure.

NEITHER NATION NOR EMPIRE

Though Progressive thought confuses America's interests with causes that transcend or oppose them, as well as with the notion that America is somehow first, it also shuns outright imperialism—not least because the American people reject instinctively the notion of ruling others. But, by harnessing America's power to this confusion, American Progressives have sought to manage the world and to weaken the unique characteristics that make America a nation. For this reason, U.S. foreign policy since the twentieth century has been neither that of a nation that minds its own business nor of an empire that controls its foreign subjects by force—neither fish nor fowl. Ours has been the foreign policy of a nation that imitates empires, or of a mostly make-believe empire that is forgetting what it meant to be a nation. It is a policy that puts its executors first.

On Whose Behalf?

The peoples who came to America intended to rule themselves, not others. They intended no conquest, said J. Q. Adams, except of the wilderness. Adams shared the intentions of the early settlers who had purchased land from the Indians. "Agreement of soul with soul," he called it. But not even President George Washington, never mind J. Q., could justify excluding settlement from the bulk of the country to preserve a hunter-gatherer way of life. U.S. foreign policy was to be about enhancing and preserving America itself.

John Quincy Adams, like the rest of his generation, foresaw the inevitability of the American people's expansion over the North American continent, and the attraction that they would exercise over the rest of the hemisphere. He wrote to his father: "The whole continent of North America appears to be destined by Divine providence to be peopled by one nation, speaking one language, professing one general system of religious and political principles, and accustomed to one general tenor of social usages and customs." In his presidential inaugural address, Adams spoke of other peoples' admiration of the American people's rights and blessings: "The forest has fallen by the ax of our woodsmen ... liberty and law have marched hand in hand." Yet Americans would mind no business but their own.

Like the rest of the founding generation, Adams was acutely aware of the American people's defining characteristics, and of these characteristics' fragility. Let us reiterate what Adams thought of this American nation:

> [These Americans were]: associated bodies of civilized men and Christians, in a state of nature, but not of anarchy. They were bound by the laws of God, which they all, and by the laws of the gospel, which they nearly all, acknowledged as the rules of their conduct. They were bound by the principles which they themselves had proclaimed in the declaration ... by all the beneficent laws and institutions, which their forefathers had brought with them from their mother country, by habits of hardy industry, by frugal and hospitable manners, by the general sentiments of social equality, by pure and virtuous morals.... [By living together, they had already developed] all the moral ligatures of friendship and of neighbourhood ... combined with that instinctive and mysterious connection between man and physical nature, which binds the first perceptions of childhood in a chain of sympathy with the last gasp of expiring age, to the spot of our nativity, and the natural objects by which it is surrounded ... the feelings under which the children of Israel "sat down by the rivers of Babylon, and wept when they remembered Zion."

America was a lot more than a set of ideas. It was a peculiar people in a peculiar place, with distinct habits.

The shortness of our common history, the diversity of our origins, and the lack of a peculiarly American literary corpus have never prevented the American people from being obviously unique. Since before de Tocqueville and into our time, visitors from abroad have remarked upon the differences that strike them when they land among us: the religiosity, the patriotism, the ease, confidence, and openness with which people deal with one another; the ubiquity and honor of work; the generosity; the sense of equality and of possibility, such as are found nowhere else. Abroad, Americans are easy to spot by a certain confidence and nonchalance by the way they walk and bear themselves.

French colonists used to delight in black and brown school children reciting "our ancestors the Gauls" in perfect French. But, as Lincoln said, the "electric cord" that makes Americans American is believing as the founders believed that no man may rightly rule another without his consent. Thus do Americans, descended from all nations, often speaking foreign-accented English, refer to "our Founding Fathers." Today as in 1776 and in Lincoln's time, rejection of entitlement to unearned deference is still the source of the "free and willing spirit" (Psalm 51) that makes the great American nation.

That nation today is a long way from the New England colonies' Puritanism. Especially in the past half century, our ruling class has done much to remove the Bible, which had been America's national book, from American life. Nevertheless, the American people can be understood only in biblical terms. In America as nowhere else, for good and for ill, discourse about public—and private—affairs is about justice, righteousness, and equality.

The American Empire

More often than not, America's upper classes have preferred to set aside our American national concerns and peculiarities and to take up what they believe is our duty to help uplift mankind. They have done so, not for the sake of the American nation that exists, but rather to make amends for its real and imagined sins against their own ideas of what America should be but is not. But they have done it for what they believe is righteousness' sake.

Because the core of America's nationhood—the Declaration of Independence's statement that all men in all nations have the inalienable right to govern themselves as they see fit—Progressivism's ruling belief that the "more progressed" should have power over the "less progressed" is seldom expressed openly. The wave of explicit imperialist sentiment that washed over America at the turn of the twentieth century was a partial exception and vanished as fast as it had risen.

Not since Albert Beveridge in 1898–1901 has any prominent American openly advocated that we rule others without their consent. "Self-government and internal development have been the dominant notes of our first century," he said; "administration and the development of other lands will be the dominant notes of our second century … the Declaration of Independence does not forbid us to do our part in the regeneration of the world. If it did, the Declaration would be wrong."

Nevertheless, since then, prominent Americans have acted as if the U.S. government had the right and duty to set the course and standards of other peoples. President George W. Bush's statement in his 2005 second inaugural address that "the survival of liberty in our land increasingly depends on the success of liberty in other lands" was the perfect example of the Progressive "one-world" sentiment that dominated American statecraft for a century. Like nearly all Progressives, Bush did not talk about ruling foreign inferiors. That sentiment has manifested itself in many ways, however, including gratuitous imputations of virtues, purity, and entitlement to non-Western peoples. Still, whenever prominent Americans have confused America's interests with those of mankind at large, they have done so in a way that rationalizes their own assumption of the right to lead, to teach, to help, to act as sheriff, and to provide world order.

Note well: U.S. elites do not intend to "lead" foreign peoples to think or behave by the standards of ordinary Americans whom they consider unrefined, uncouth, and racist. (Not incidentally, regarding Americans as excessively conscious of the differences between Whites and Blacks requires Herculean efforts to overlook

that, everywhere else on the planet, even the most minor racial
differences mean far more than major ones do in America). No,
the standards to which our establishment intends to lead the
world, which they often call "world standards," are their own very
peculiar ones.

This is doubly ironic because Progressive thought has always
assumed that all men everywhere share the same fundamental
objectives. On the basis of that self-evident falsehood, thinly
veiled by imprecise language and euphemisms, they have little difficulty in their own minds removing the distance between identifying America with themselves and using America's muscle to
nudge, or to push (or maybe to force), foreigners in desired directions—especially those who stand in the way of "progress"—as
they define it; that is, of their own preferences, of themselves as
teachers, guides, maybe masters of less-progressed foreigners. For
this reason, a ruling class empowered and established to superintend foreigners developed the means and the mentality to superintend fellow citizens, whom they are supposed to serve. Nor is it
any obstacle to officials accustoming themselves to confuse their
personal and corporate interests with America's—and to place
them ahead of other Americans' rights and interests.

Imperialism Turns in on Itself

Once upon a time, in the 1950s and '60s, as the U.S.
government was ramping up its influence abroad to fight the
worldwide Soviet challenge "by any means necessary," its leaders
agonized about how to ensure that the tools for influence abroad
would never "blow back" to contaminate our domestic relations.
But the sense of entitlement that comes from the exercise of
ever-growing, ever-less-accountable power overwhelmed that forlorn hope.

The civilian and military bureaucracies that constitute the foreign policy establishment make the decisions about what the two
hundred thousand troops today deployed in eight hundred-plus
bases in 177 countries do, as well as about what the bureaucrats

themselves do in Washington. And that very much involves these bureaucracies' corporate interests, as well as the personal interests of their leaders. These interests very much include their political preferences—above all the natural preference for themselves as rulers.

For practical purposes, these are the people who know most about the things they do about foreign and domestic matters. In their own view, they are the ones who "know best." This imperial apparatus is so fragmented and self-regarding as to make it impossible for it to put America as a whole ahead of its many self-regarding concerns.

Does that mean that the imperial/bureaucratic tail wags the national dog? *In the establishment's view, its members are that very dog.* This, as we have seen, has meant helping to steer the nation into a variety of inherently endless commitments that have subsumed if not submerged the American people's concerns and interests with other countries' and blurred the distinction between war and peace. No differently from Louis XIV, the establishment's members have come to see themselves as the state itself, and to look upon those who disagree with them as enemies of the state.

Most recently, we have seen intelligence and military officials using the powers given to them by the American nation to interfere with the American people's own self-governance. The U.S. ruling class's campaign against Donald Trump's candidacy and presidency began with intelligence officials crafting out of whole cloth the maliciously false story of his collaboration with the Russian government. And indeed, fifty former senior officials deflected attention away from documents that showed the influence-peddling scheme of Trump's 2020 election challenger, Joseph Biden, by attributing them to "the Russians." Wholly lacking evidence, they weaponized the prestige of their government positions. But our empire-keepers who see themselves as the nation's guardians—like countless other Praetorians since the original Roman edition—are mere usurpers.

Returning national security policy to its proper focus on

America First rather than on other nations or on the establishment is essential to the Republic's maintenance.

Whether and to what extent that focus is possible, however, depends on the extent to which the United States of America may remain a republic in any meaningful sense of the word. As we mentioned at the outset, a country's foreign policy can only reflect its character. Unfortunately, today ours is very much in question.

PART III—RETURN TO REALITY

The world and America itself never were what Progressive ideology imagined. Since Woodrow Wilson, our foreign policy establishment has been dealing with caricatures of reality, aiming to reshape them into their own image. America, said Secretary of State Dean Acheson in 1948, would have to be "the locomotive at the head of mankind." And in fact, under Progressive leadership, what he called "the continued moral, military and economic power of the United States" did make big changes around the globe. American Progressives tried to foster a world in which national identities would mean much less, and in which differences in civilization would be quaint reminders of innocuous folklore—at most like Disneyland's ride "It's a Small World After All" among differently costumed dolls singing the same song. In this wished-for world the UN, led by the United States, would enforce peace to the extent that peace did not result from economic interdependence's replacement of contrasting ideas and truly diverse civilizations.

This conception never even gestated. Until the mid-twentieth century, Western colonial rule had masked mankind's enduring civilizational differences. As colonialism ended, these resurfaced. The Cold War, by pressing the world's peoples to take sides for or against communism, also had obscured peoples' underlying concern with matters peculiarly their own. That too had masked civilizational differences. And though the American people were willing enough to support interference in other nations' affairs, so long as it could be justified as necessary to counter a mortal enemy to themselves, no sooner did President Bush 41 talk of fighting for "a new world order" than they too reverted to natural concern for America's own affairs.

After the Cold War's end, it became ever more obvious that the Russians were more Russian than ever, the Muslims more Muslim, the Indians more Indian, the Chinese more Chinese, etc. While Europeans and U.S. Progressives have done their utmost to cut their own ties to their civilization as well as to subordinate their national identities and interests, it seems that every other people group has done the opposite.

In the emerging environment, which we now examine, the levers by which U.S. policy sought to move the world either no longer exist or are no longer connected to life.

In this environment, the J. Q. Adams Paradigm calls us back to reality. The primary feature of international reality is each and every government's near-exclusive focus on its own interests. For this reason, as the U.S. government looks to the future, it must do so by putting America itself at the forefront of its concerns. But what does putting America First mean in our time?

Adams's principles provide no recipes. Neither does this book. The first part of what follows, chapters 11–18, is about how Adams might regard the differences between today's world and the past's— beginning with America itself—and what that suggests for specific problems. Chapters 19–20 discuss the meaning of Adams's principles.

EVOLVING AMERICA

What is the twenty-first-century America that U.S. foreign policy should serve, and how can the country as it is today be served? It is very different from the country that became great in the nineteenth century, that out-produced all others combined in the wars of the twentieth century's first half, and that put men on the moon. Changes in America itself raise the question of the extent to which it may be possible for what America has become to have any foreign policy at all.

Today, leaders in government, the media, education, and corporate life deny the legitimacy of voters who oppose them, considering them and their way of life "deplorable," "ugly," and even "terrorists." They refused to accept the 2016 election's results and led substantial constituencies endeavoring never again to accept any electoral outcome with which they disagreed. They fear the rest of Americans, whom they call systemically racist. After the 2020 election, they designated the public's tendency to White Supremacy to be the armed forces' and intelligence agencies' principal focus.

These Deplorables, etc., feeling maligned from above, have come to believe that most, if not all, that they hear from their leaders is false. They have come to disrespect and fear their own government, and to regard it as a source of harm all or most of the time.

What foreign policy is possible for a people who hate each other? Our only guide is Lincoln's foreign policy in the Civil War. Knowing that his domestic adversaries counted on help from Europe, Lincoln doubled down on America's traditional policy. He abstained from unnecessary foreign involvement and took what little friendship where he could find it. (Russia, in those years.)

Because we Americans have become a people with characteristics different from those we had as recently as in the mid-twentieth century, U.S. foreign policy cannot deal with as many topics as then. Domestic political divisions may take out of rational consideration any issue whatever. It follows that any and all government policy in this new America henceforth will have to be far more focused on what Americans, diminished and divided, are willing—or even able—to do together. But hyper-partisanship is not the cause of profound changes in the American people's habits of heart, mind, and practice. It's only a result.

To these changes we now turn our attention.

The Way We've Become

Figures give some sense of how today's Americans are losing intellectual, moral, and political resemblance to earlier generations. In 1830, Horace Mann, the father of American public schools, estimated that nine out of ten of his fellow citizens could read the King James Bible. During World War II, only 4 percent of some 18 million draftees were illiterate. But despite (or because of?) massive expenditures on education over the subsequent two decades, 27 percent of the Vietnam War's draftees were judged functionally illiterate. In our time, the Literacy Project estimates that 45 million Americans are that way. A third of California's fourth graders cannot read a simple sentence, and half of its high school graduates read only at that minimal level. Reading the King James is beyond many if not most of today's college graduates. Today, U.S. fifteen-year-olds rank twenty-fourth out of seventy-one countries in science and thirty-eighth in math.

These trends started at the top of America's educational system. While 2,817 high school students scored 750 or better on each half of the SAT in 1972, by 1994 only 1,438 made this score though the test had been made easier. In 2019, American college students spent less than a third of the time studying as did their grandparents. Students at Harvard and Stanford study less than those at Podunk State. No matter who you are, the less you study, the less you learn. As a result, today, educational pedigree is inversely related to performance. Prestige institutions sell prestige.

And as the bell-curve of intellectual achievement shifts leftward, the bell-curve of school grades shifts rightward. Increasingly, "A" is the default grade in America. Is it even possible to argue that we are as well-educated as those who came before us? Among all classes and races, some 70 percent of U.S. students report having cheated on exams or papers. This means that U.S. schools have habituated successive generations to lie for self-advancement, as well as to lie to themselves about themselves. In sum, America's schools have crippled America's minds and corrupted its souls.

That corruption affects especially America's elite institutions—including law enforcement and the military. In 2015 the U.S. Military Academy, to avoid having to expel growing numbers of cheaters, loosened the unforgiving honor code by which it had lived. Cheating having burgeoned as a result, in 2012 West Point considered but rejected reinstating it. Tolerated, lying from on high is to be expected. Truth and honor are relics of despised former ages.

No one should be surprised at our elites' increasing ignorance, incompetence, and corruption as well as at the general population's increasing inability to follow directions—never mind arguments. Reason is becoming ever less relevant to interactions among Americans than is identity politics.

Declining Moral Quality and Potency

In 1965, Daniel Patrick Moynihan published a set of statistics about America's Black population that all regarded as measures of personal, social, and national disaster. The chapter headings sounded the alarm: "Nearly a quarter of urban negro marriages are dissolved, nearly a quarter of negro births are illegitimate, almost a quarter of negro families are headed by females, the breakdown of the negro family has led to increased welfare dependency [and crime]."

But, in 2021, the disastrous numbers for 1965's Blacks looked good in comparison with those of our time's *White* population. A glance at the data compiled by Charles Murray about the twenty-first-century White population in this century shows it having taken on many of the sociological characteristics of the Black family, including low rates of marriage, high rates of unwed motherhood, and declining work ethic. Our time's White divorce rate is about 40 percent; the White illegitimacy rate is 25 percent. White men who don't marry or stay married, who don't go to church, now exhibit the same tendencies as did Blacks with regard to work: they tend to work less or just to drop out of the labor force and live off women, public assistance, and crime. On balance, twenty-first-century Whites are more dysfunctional than 1960s Blacks.

In the nation as a whole, women alone or with children are almost 40 percent of households, and just under a third of all households are on public assistance. Crime rates and other indices of social morbidity for America, as a whole, dwarf those of Blacks a half century ago.

Americans of all races and classes are also shunning religious institutions—rapidly. Just in the half decade between 2012 and 2017, some 5 percent more reported "seldom or never" going to church or synagogue. Almost half of Americans are now in that category. This is an essential index of collapsing responsibility because churches teach that though you may escape your responsibility to man in this life, you can never escape your responsibility to God for eternity. Since churches are also perhaps the major avenue of involvement with the community, increasing secularization is yet another way in which individuals are losing habits of honesty and cooperation—otherwise known as a key part of "social capital."

Religion itself—the sense and the reverence for God, the awareness of objective standards of good and evil, the factor that America's founders—irreligious ones included—considered essential to republican life, is also waning. That is in part because government has increasingly banished religion from public life, including the Ten Commandments and nativity scenes. Fifty years ago, as Apollo 8 orbited the moon on Christmas Eve and the astronauts were streaming live TV of the lunar surface, they also were reading Genesis Chapter 1 to the world: "In the beginning, God created the heavens and the earth...." Today's U.S. government would not allow that.

But the decline in churchgoing is also due to many religious leaders' joining the Progressive critique of American civilization. People resent being deplored from the pulpit quite as much as they resent it from the secular high, mighty, and media. That is why the more Progressive churches—including parts of the Catholic Church—have lost parishioners, while the more conservative ones have gained them.

These unmarried and unchurched, these not-so-hard-workers and cheaters, these porn-watchers, are not happy. Between 1999 and 2016 the suicide rate increased by nearly 30 percent. During the 2020 Covid-19 shutdowns, the suicide rate increased to the point that the U.S. Centers for Disease Control and Prevention restricted reporting on it. Suicide is now the second biggest cause of death among teenagers. Increasing use of opioid drugs, fentanyl, etc., is less a cause than a consequence.

Yes, part of the change in *overall* U.S. personal morbidity is due to the now near-total disappearance of family life among Blacks. Only 28 percent of Black children are born in wedlock. Fewer than half of this lucky minority reach adulthood with both parents still together. The near-disappearance of family life among this 12.8 percent of the population (it persists primarily in TV commercials) has proportional effects on overall figures. A fourth of all Black men spend time in prison and—conventional wisdom notwithstanding—being sentenced to prison in America takes a lot more than casual misbehavior. But if we look at Moynihan's figures *for 1940*—2 percent illegitimacy for Whites and 16.8 percent for Blacks—we get a hint of how different with regard to commitment, responsibility, and hence social potency *all of us* are from the Americans who bestrode the globe in the mid-twentieth century.

Ever since then, as the American people's personal and social potency have declined, schools have increasingly taught that America is evil, and a succession of no-win wars have further drained the reservoir of patriotic dedication; today's young people bear little resemblance to those who offered their lives in World War II. Were they to fight to the death, they would likelier do it against the other side of domestic divides.

Divisions

Today's great divide among Americans is not between the races, between those with more or less money, or between blue- and white-collar occupations. It has nothing to do with race or even with money, per se. Increasingly, the American people are a collection of subcultures that have become classes, and risk becoming castes. These, along with social health and ills, functions and dysfunctions, differences in orientations and concerns, are spread—unevenly—across the traditional social categories.

Sorting ourselves out into congenial groups is one of the American people's congenital features. In 1636, Roger Williams led his congregation out of Massachusetts to found the Providence Plantations colony. In the 1840s, Brigham Young led his Mormons out from among the people who rejected them and founded Salt Lake City. Today as well, Americans continue to sort themselves out. As a result, American society is increasingly made up of relatively homogeneous, coherent, subgroups *very different from each other, according to what is important to them, to what they love and hate.* The sharing of loves and hates through modern communications is the major means by which physically separate persons constitute subcultures. These different identities of sentiment have become America's real constituents.

For practical, political purposes, the several subcultures are arranged into two main alignments: either with or against the people, habits, and ideas that have been governing America and setting its tone for the last half century. As in the rest of the Western world, the great divide is to be with or against a remarkably uniform ruling class. These divisions largely between the rulers and the ruled have nothing to do with foreign policy, and little with any other policies. So deep is the several subcultures' disdain for one another that the American people at large either believe only the perspectives coming from their own group, or believe none at all.

The two main alignments are in a cold but warming civil war. Within these alignments, two of these subcultures are prototypical.

Every January 22 since 1973, anywhere from four hundred

thousand to three-quarters of a million people, mostly young and of modest means, have trekked to Washington, DC, from throughout the country in the worst of winter to protest the Supreme Court's imposition of legal abortion. The numbers continue to grow because the pro-life movement is a major component of a growing cultural area, related to but not coterminous with millions of conservative Catholics, evangelical Christians, Orthodox Jews, and Mormons. It is also related to the burgeoning practice of homeschooling. This subculture reproduces above the national average and has established a tacit but effective barrier to marriages between persons who hold opposing views on whether there is a right to life or a right to abortion.

An example of this trend's demographic significance may be seen in the fact that, if continued for another generation or so, it would, among other things, make the Modern Orthodox into the majority among U.S. Jews. Though there is no logical connection between commitment to the sanctity of life, distrust of government education, service in the military, or ownership of guns, in fact the subcultures that focus on these matters are compatible, do blend into one another, and are in opposition to the other main subcultural alignment.

Near-worship of abortion and disdain for religion (theophobia) are the principal totems of the vast and wealthy subculture associated with government—most office-holders of both parties and the bureaucracies—the leadership of major corporations, the education establishment, the media, etc. These define themselves largely by looking down on the rest of America. Asserting very specific preferences with regard to just about everything—codes of behavior, of language required or banned—they make it a point to impress a sense of inferiority on those they consider to be of lower classes.

Since the mid-1960s, this subculture's wealth has grown disproportionately to the rest of society. But wealth defines this subculture less than the way it is acquired—mostly through government-connected corporations and privileged access to finance. It is wealth connected to power, and it adds to the subculture's pretense of entitlement to rule. This ruling class's capacity to extend favor as well as to punish, its capacity to wield quasi-public power with private discretion, is something new in America. Never before has it been so important for Americans to be on the right side of the right people, and so costly to cross them.

In 2020, this ruling subculture, including its members in government, radically increased its efforts to expel dissenters from positions of influence in society, and to suppress potential dissenters into silence. They labeled disagreement as "hate speech" and penalized it. They used Google and social media to cut conservatives' capacity for mass communication.

Then in May 2020, magnates of virtually all the nation's major corporations poured billions of dollars into violent organizations, Antifa and Black Lives matter, that physically sacked and burned America's urban centers, supported by the Democratic Party's state and local politicians and egged on by the major media. They meant to show average Americans that submission is the only path to safety. But government-led or -approved physical attacks on dissenters raise the prospect of civil war less like nineteenth-century America's and more like the twentieth-century Spanish horror.

Because today's American government is aligned with one side of the population against the other, it is less trusted, less legitimate, and in the last analysis, is less powerful than ever.

Today in America, as throughout the West, government has become arguably the major source of society's decay. Here and now, as it has ever been, social and political life flourishes and rots from the top.

Legitimacy Squandered

Over two generations, the United States' ruling class transformed America's regime through high-profile campaigns that have had less to do with their ostensible goals than with increasing the power of one sector of society over another. As a result, broad publics are withdrawing legitimate consent from their rulers.

The manifold increase of spending on education, for example, diminished the American people's literacy, numeracy, and scientific knowledge. But it did swell, enrich, and empower a class of educational personnel and contractors from kindergarten to graduate schools. The Civil Rights movement promised fulfillment of the Constitution's promise of equality before the law, but it morphed into a byzantine system of preferences and discretionary powers over schooling and employment that empowered its managers and increased racial resentments.

The environmentalist movement ended up as an industry of regulations that enrich the wealthy. Feminism and the movement for sexual equality promoted irresponsibility toward women through divorce and abortion, poisoned intersexual relations by presuming men guilty of sexual assault, let men into girls' bathrooms, and enriched lawyers. The War on Poverty swelled America's underclass but made fortunes for the "helping professions." The trillions spent on post-1945 wars produced defeat after defeat. They killed some 115,000 Americans, crippled twice that many, and filled corporate boards with rich, retired generals. In 2020, the U.S. government spent some $5 trillion, placing the country essentially under house arrest by treating what was essentially a flu epidemic as if it were a plague. Thus it erased millions of small businesses and swelled the big ones. It made the rich richer and the poor poorer, weakened the weak while swelling the strong.

All these campaigns have been based on propositions touted by the most highly credentialed persons in America—experts certified by the U.S. government, enshrined by academia as science's spokesmen, and fawned upon by the media working in concert to forbid disagreement. All have increased the ruling class's discretionary power—as well as wealth.

Coming Apart

As persons in power have made/observed/enforced laws and regulations to benefit the subculture of which they are part, the United States' effective constitution has become "stop me if you can." This diminution in the sense of obligation to the rule of law spreads from society's commanding heights to the general population.

The Supreme Court long ago began to use its discretionary power to try shaping American society according to its members' sociopolitical preferences, constitutional text notwithstanding. *Dred Scott*, *Lochner*, *Plessy*, *Roe*, *Kelo*, and *Obergefell* are just a few of the decisions in which its naked partisan will has contradicted constitutional text or has shined through perfunctory constitutional verbiage. President George W. Bush accompanied his signature of laws passed by Congress with "signing statements" by which he declared intent to enforce/administer those laws in ways either not specified in their text or, as some charged, in opposition to text. President Barack Obama went far beyond that by announcing that his administration would simply refuse to enforce laws with which it had come to disagree—for example, the Defense of Marriage Act and the Religious Freedom Restoration Act. Will trumped law, period.

Today, the practice of selective enforcement of laws, and of selective prosecutions, has become standard for office holders of the Democratic Party. Individuals and subcultures that continue to follow laws with which they disagree are behind the times, late in joining self-dispensation from the law. It would have been strange indeed had not the assertion of personal/partisan prerogative over law migrated into the general population. Increasingly, Americans sense that they had better look out for themselves.

Ever since deepest antiquity, Thucydides tells us, going about armed has been the ultimate measure of lack of civilization. Today, some twenty-two million Americans hold permits to carry concealed firearms. To these must be added the perhaps fifteen million who carry guns legally in the nineteen states (plus four, with conditions) that do not require permits to carry guns in public. Between March and October of 2020 some seven million Americans bought guns for the first time. Five million more did so during January 2021. That means that perhaps a fourth of able-bodied American adults feels so threatened by their fellow citizens (understandably, women now make up the majority of persons requesting permits), so abandoned or threatened by their government, as to go through the trouble and expense of walking around armed.

What Can America Do?

In sum, the U.S. establishment is an overfed, cancerous, and inward-looking organism, using ever-inferior human material and doubling down on failures. It loses wars and spends trillions that produce the opposite of whatever it advertises. It lies, predictably, as a matter of course, and it exudes contempt for the governed. Its members pull rank and put themselves first. Always. The establishment has accustomed the American people to notice that virtually all that comes from it relates to personal and partisan advantage.

The administration that came into office in 2021 officially accuses its opponents of deep-rooted racism, and states that rooting out widespread White Supremacy is its foremost preoccupation. The paramountcy of their war on domestic dissent diverts and disables America among nations. China's media abound in commentary as insightful as it is derisive of America's "*baizuo*," white liberals. Surely, these rulers are adrift among a people and in a world beyond their understanding.

Americans now view their rulers as corrupt, even when they are not, and as enemies, even when they are not. The population's sullen stares preface more energetic resistance.

Whatever thoughts today's foreign policy establishmentarians may have of wielding influence such as that of George C. Marshall, abstract from the fact that it had flowed from an exceptional people, that it was managed by men of a different caliber. But that American people and that American polity are gone. Three generations of defeats erased the early twentieth century's triumphs.

On July 5, 2020, as Russian President Vladimir Putin was driven past Moscow's U.S. Embassy and noted that it was flying the rainbow flag in celebration of the LGBTQ+ movement, he reportedly mocked America. That hard-bitten realist might well have expressed his judgment in the words by which Charles de

Gaulle had characterized U.S. Progressives six decades before: "They are not serious." Seriousness—what parents look for in a son-in-law—is statesmanship's minimal requirement. Contemporary American statesmen don't rise to the minimum.

Whether a people so governed, diminished morally and intellectually, and at war with itself can support any foreign policy at all is by no means clear. Surely, however, the only policies that might gather popular support are few, simple, and obviously grounded in compelling reality.

JOHN QUINCY ADAMS'S PRIORITIES

Foreign policy is hardly the principal means by which to establish the virtues on which republican life depends. But John Quincy Adams's principal business today would be to minimize the ways in which foreign policy diminishes them.

George Washington had defined America's objective with regard to foreign countries: "Observe good faith and justice towards all nations; cultivate peace and harmony with all." Washington valued international peace and harmony so that Americans would not have to concern themselves with foreigners. Why? Because what concerns America itself is incomparably more important than anything concerning the rest of the world.

For Adams as for Washington, the United States' achievement of independence was the most important event in mankind's secular history, because self-rule allowed Americans to live lives of unprecedented freedom and virtue while respecting all who respect America. Today, as two centuries ago, maintaining what remains of that unique way of life is the objective to which Adams would subordinate all others. That is why, today as ever, he would judge that the American people's untrammeled exercise of collective liberty—of sovereign self-government—is indispensable to achieving that objective.

Closely related would be his concern for squaring policy with America's real military forces as well as diplomatic realities. For him, political responsibility is also the touchstone for calculating the proper relationship between ends and means.

Adams would find that fulfilling his primary geopolitical concern—excluding the influences of America's enemies from the hemisphere through friendship with our hemispheric neighbors—is also more challenging than before and requires methods different from the ones he had used. Adams would back off our extensive political involvement in a Europe increasingly unable to fulfill commitments. He would regard Russia much as he had in 1823 and act accordingly. But because China's expansion into the Pacific impinges inherently and directly onto America's core interests, he would find today's China to be a historically peculiar problem. On the other hand, he would find that the principle of commercial reciprocity by which he had lived and the diplomatic principles by which he acted are as applicable today as ever. By the same token, he would regard the problems posed by today's Middle East as that of the Barbary Pirates writ large.

Independence and Unilateralism

John Quincy Adams described the Declaration of Independence as "a beacon on the summit of the mountain, to which all the inhabitants of the earth may turn their eyes ... a light of admonition to the rulers of men; a light of salvation and redemption to the oppressed [holding out] to the sovereign and to the subject the extent and the boundaries of their respective rights and duties; founded in the laws of nature and of nature's God." By this, Adams told us that *independence means the exercise of collective moral responsibility through self-rule.* Collective liberty.

Collective liberty does not necessarily comport with individual liberty, much less the complex of virtues that all since Montesquieu (who followed Cicero, who followed Aristotle) have recognized as essential to the republican way of life. But none is as likely a guardian of its own individual liberties and virtues as is the people itself. The Declaration of Independence is such a beacon—in and from America—because the American people were in fact guardians of a rare set of virtues. For this reason, America's exercise of unilateral responsibility for its own actions versus the rest of the world is the necessary (though not the sufficient) condition for individual liberty.

It should not be necessary to reiterate that Adams would not prescribe today anything resembling what some call "isolationism," any more than he practiced it two hundred years ago. The United States of America was founded foremost to preserve and promote a unique way of life in North America. "Go ye and do likewise," said J. Q. Adams to the rest of the world. Putting America First means putting forth an example that others may follow.

To guard the independence that made possible our way of life requires practicing unencumbered freedom of action. Since any and all commitments to foreign powers impose restrictions on one's collective liberty, concern for that liberty requires minimizing commitments. For commitments to foreign powers to be consistent with self-government, they must be made by the American people itself. The Constitution's requirement for at least two thirds of the Senate to approve treaties is especially relevant in our time of sociopolitical division because it makes sure that America makes only those few commitments on which nearly all can agree. That is the only way in which involvement in foreign affairs can help unify a nation rather than divide it.

Today's ubiquity and speed of international interaction makes it easier than ever for Americans to find allies abroad for their quarrels at home. Our ruling class's commitment to internationalism often serves precisely to enlist foreign allies in its struggles to diminish the American people's freedom of action and republican responsibility. Adams would not imagine that reducing international commitments and the re-adoption of unilateralism could repair this facet of the American people's modern dysfunctions and divisions. Reducing commitments can, however, place practitioners and people squarely before their responsibilities for their own future. Hence J. Q. Adams's primary task would be to exit from internationalism's structures and to debunk the rationalizations for them.

Around the turn of the twentieth century, U.S. administrations of both parties had begun by expanding arbitration treaties into something like an international court. Then they promoted the League of Nations and put faith in treaties ostensibly curbing arms, guaranteeing borders, and outlawing war. They devalued treaties and conducted international relations by executive agreements and mere bureaucratic harmony. They entered into countless alliances and commitments that they had little if any intention of honoring. They created the United Nations, and they are now flirting with the European Union as a model of international relations. That slippery slope, Adams would argue, has involved imagining that it is possible to surrender responsibility for our own business. It also involves suppressing international law based on agreements between sovereign peoples, substituting customary transnational legal processes for law among nations. That illusion involves delegating to international institutions of what had been the right to self-rule. Adams would explain the qualitative chasm between solemn treaties and voluntary, ad-hoc international arbitration among sovereign peoples on one hand, and permanent alliances as well as international "structures" on the other.

He would debunk the pretend-history by which our foreign policy establishment has ruled: that the American people's refusal to be sufficiently international was a cause of World War II, and that the relative peace since then is due to America's having learned to subordinate itself to the world's needs. Or, as Barack Obama encapsulated the matter for the UN in 2009, "Giving up freedom of action ... binding ourselves to international rules over the long term—enhances our security," or as former Secretary of Defense James Mattis put it, "Our strength as a nation is inextricably linked to the strength of our unique and comprehensive system of alliances and partnerships." Truth, Adams would argue, is exactly the reverse.

Adams would revisit the debate over the League of Nations, reiterating the point he had made during his time in office that nations pursue their interests regardless of the presence or absence of treaties. He would confront the unfounded claim that U.S. membership in that body might have made it possible for it to fulfill Woodrow Wilson's utopian expectations. He would point out that the American people in the 1920s and '30s were as averse to international commitments and war as those of other democracies, and hence that there existed an unbridgeable gap between the pretenses of that era's treaties and anybody's willingness to back them up.

Then Adams would explain that the United Nations is based on the self-evident lie of an "international community" that shares basic standards and objectives and whose judgments we must respect. But the sentiments and judgments that come and go among the world's governments are sometimes monstrous, often bad, and always not our own. His point would be that, in the context of what the Declaration of Independence defines as the only legitimate government, no argument exists why we should obey norms created by persons not responsible to ourselves.

With regard to alliances—of which NATO is a prime example—Adams would argue for withdrawal, not because of any calculus of relative contributions and benefits, but rather because specific commitments are justified only by the alignment of specific interests in specific circumstances. Today's U.S. alliances are general commitments of indeterminate length, not for specific goals but rather for the sake of broad relationships. In short, they celebrate themselves, are ends in themselves that usurp judgment, and foreclose consideration of our interests regardless of time or circumstance.

Twentieth-century U.S. statesmen made the mistake that President Monroe was about to make in 1823, in consultation with former President Jefferson, when he proposed an alliance with Britain containing something like NATO's Article 5—until Adams convinced him otherwise.

Adams would use the history of NATO's post-Soviet expansion as a means of confronting Americans with the reality of commitments. As Poland and the Baltic states were about to accede to the treaty, and given that its Article 5 famously states that members must treat attack on one as an attack on all, some asked whether the United States would wage nuclear war to counter any Russian attack on these new members. Honest answers to this question were embarrassing—for example, Boston University Professor David Fromkin's suggestion that these states be offered the treaty, minus Article 5. But, Adams would have asked, what sense does it make to invite someone into a house without the roof? Adams would press home reality: What would you do were your bluffs to be called? Don't bluff, he would say.

By the same token, Adams would ask Americans to revisit the diplomatic transactions that resulted in Ukraine's delivery of the world's third largest nuclear arsenal to Russia *circa* 1994, in exchange for a less-than titanium-clad U.S. guarantee of independence and territorial integrity. The U.S. government extended that guarantee because it never contemplated redeeming it. Everyone knew that this commitment was pure pretense. As a result, in 2014, when Russia violated Ukraine's territorial integrity by taking the Crimea and threatened the rest's independence, the U.S. government betrayed its commitment and became mired in a diffuse effort to manage the mess it had helped create. Adams would not have made the commitment. Instead, Adams would have offered "honest friendship" to both Russia and Ukraine as they worked out their relationship, sobered by each other's nukes. All would have benefited from U.S. officials' thoughtful abstention more than from their irresponsible "engagement."

In sum, Adams's recommended withdrawal from institutions and treaties would result not in de-valuing American commitments, but in taking them seriously, making only the ones that we must and intend to keep. The man who famously said, "America does not go abroad in search of monsters to destroy," was neither bashful, weak, nor apologetic. Neither was he "soft" on monsters, nor an "isolationist," but the very idea of a statesman.

Of Arms and Oceans

J. Q. Adams's diplomatic involvement in the Napoleonic wars and America's part therein (War of 1812) reinforced his appreciation of George Washington's and of Adams's father's armed neutrality—especially the "armed" part, because neutrality alone had not saved from invasion the Russia where he was stationed, nor America from suffering outrages by both Britain and France. Jeffersonian America's lack of physical and intellectual armament had led to military disasters, including the burning of Washington, D.C. Moreover, Adams was acutely aware that while the oceans are America's commercial lifeline and buffer from the world's major powers, undefended oceans provide enemies with easy access. For this reason, two hundred years ago, Adams advocated maximum U.S. military—and especially naval—power. He would do the same today.

Adams would be appalled by the U.S. military budget's enormity and by the discrepancy between size and capacities. Official policy calls for the military's ability to win two wars at the same time. What wars are you talking about winning? Adams would ask. Against whom? Where? With what? How? Current forces, he would argue, serve a national security policy on autopilot. He would press for tailoring forces to fulfill basic functions.

Homeland defense, Adams would say, means firm control of the North Atlantic, of the eastern and central Pacific, as well as assured access to the rest of the oceans. It means control of orbital space over America. And that in turn means defense of our territory against all missiles from anywhere. No stranger to technology, he would quickly learn that doing this requires orbital-based fire control for surface-based interceptors, as well as for surveillance and tracking. Above all, it means placing weapons in orbit that are capable of protecting our satellites as well as striking missiles from anywhere to anywhere as soon as they clear the clouds. What does the U.S. military do, he would ask, if it does not do these things?

The U.S. Navy is, incomparably, the world's biggest and best, but best for what? Adams would say that the primary purpose of any navy, especially of navies whose country is as dependent on the sea as is America, is to dominate the sea approaches to themselves, operating under the cover of land-based air power. But today's U.S. Navy is all about projecting power to the world's far corners—imperfectly and at great danger to itself—while short-changing its primary mission of sea control.

Nor do we do sea control through bases. The U.S. has acquired naval/air bases in Bahrain and Qatar, best fit for intervention in the Middle East while giving up bases in the Azores and Iceland, fit for controlling the Atlantic. Adams would reverse this choice of bases and missions, judging that securing the oceans makes far more sense militarily and in every other way than trying to meddle in the Persian Gulf. He would return the base at Subic Bay, Philippines, to its former dimensions, refurbish Clark AFB, retain the U.S. presence in the Horn of Africa (Djibouti), and would do whatever necessary to keep in friendly hands the land keys to ocean control in Panama, Singapore, Gibraltar, Suez, and the capes of Good Hope and Horn.

Inverted priorities—neglect of functions essential to ourselves combined with consuming attention to peripheral concerns of ours as well as to others' business—is the essence of irresponsibility. Adams would right foreign policy priorities by regrouping American forces now scattered and vulnerable all over the globe, mostly back onto U.S. soil.

Today, these spread-out forces are dedicated to tasks that they are insufficiently manned and equipped to carry out. Whenever force is to be used, the U.S. government depletes units located hither and yon to concentrate them in the place and on the task at hand. This is an awkward and inefficient way to put task forces together. It also depletes the forces left behind and invites aggression against them. Adams would note that, were U.S. military forces based chiefly at home, they might spring in force, properly constituted, to meet needs quickly and then return home. Under Adams, all would know that, when a U.S. task force leaves home, it is neither a "show of force" (i.e., a show of weakness) nor a half-hearted measure.

Adams, like Churchill after him, had learned from history that island nations, natural sea-powers, must limit their overseas land operations in scale and in time, taking advantage of mobility, speed, and capacity to concentrate. Britain, the late eighteenth-century's superpower, had lost its American war in part because it stopped thinking in terms of counterforce raids to focus on occupation. Adams would remind today's Americans of that.

Adams would withdraw U.S. troops from Europe, Korea, and Japan—which have abundant resources to take care of themselves—as well as from many other places. Long gone are the days when U.S. troops abroad were in sufficient number and with sufficient armament to fight major battles against major opponents with a chance to win. Today, they are essentially strategic tripwires and political placebos. Adams would disdain both functions as fraught attempts not to face reality. Reality is that, compared to Chinese and Russian forces, locally deployed forces on our side are insufficient and outgunned; that only the locals—Europeans, Koreans,

Japanese—can right regional balances; but that the locals are not inclined to do so in part because of the U.S. presence.

He would consider Taiwan a special case. The island nation of 23 million people is the geographic and political bull's eye of China's drive to control the Western Pacific. Insofar as the U.S. government is serious about countering that drive, and understands what it takes to do so peacefully, it has no alternative but to fortify Taiwan militarily and politically.

By weaning allies from dependence, Adams would make it possible to see just what they are worth, what they really want, and what they may be willing to do for themselves. Any number of East Asian governments want U.S. support against China. Adams would urge giving it, insofar as these governments were willing and able to contribute to U.S. objectives regarding China.

Adams would withdraw troops from Afghanistan, Iraq, Saudi Arabia, Syria, Bahrain, Qatar, and Turkey because most of the strife within and among them does not involve us. He would manage relations with them reciprocally, with statecraft's ordinary tools, selling arms to some and not others, admitting students from some and not others, giving and withholding favors according to the ebb and flow of interest. He would leave no doubts among any that America's primary interest in their regard concerns suppressing any incitement or toleration of anti-Americanism, and that the U.S. government will impose dire economic as well as military consequences on them for any harm that might come to us from their jurisdictions.

But for such warnings to carry weight, Adams would want to take care of our unfinished business with regard to Iran. There is no need for America to build an anti-Iran coalition in the Middle East, because Sunni Arab Saudi Arabia's, Egypt's, and others' opposition to the spread of Persian Shia Iran's influence is part of the natural order of things. And it is true that much of Iran's bluster against America, including its statements about its weaponry being aimed at America (and even at Israel), thinly masks Iran's real focus on its regional rivals. Nevertheless, Iran has continued to commit acts of war against America. Suffering that war and Iran's continued growth in power is imprudent. As a result, Adams would impose total secondary sanctions on Iran, possibly including blockade—not to democratize its regime, but to kill this enemy for its enmity to America and to do it in exemplary fashion.

As we discuss below, Adams would disagree strongly with using economic sanctions in the ordinary course of international relations because he considered such sanctions to be acts of war to be used as such, with deadly seriousness. But the Islamic Republic of Iran started a war with America, and Adams would want to finish it, as well as to show the consequences of harming Americans.

Adams would renuclearize U.S. forces, reversing the trend since the George H. W. Bush administration to banish them from ordinary military operations, even as the rest of the world is integrating them. He would return to military orthodoxy, according to which enemies are designated wholesale by statesmen rather than sorted out retail on the battlefield, the killing is done by the big guns, and cities are to be bypassed.

Of Arms and the Republic

John Quincy Adams never imagined that his successor, General Andrew Jackson, who defeated him in a bitter election and ran the government far differently than he, might focus America's armed forces on his voters as likely terrorists. Were Adams asked about President Joseph Biden's 2021 order to purge the armed forces of persons and thoughts opposed to his party and to seek out terrorists among them, he could only fall back on fundamentals. Namely: war on domestic socio-political opponents disables any country among nations at the very least. The Republic's survival depends on stopping it, cold.

He would note that this self-defeating war is possible only because the armed forces—and the Intelligence agencies—became so large and self-regarding that they lost their republican character and became part of a partisan oligarchy. Hence restoring that character—insofar as that may be possible—requires shrinking them. And stripping them of the prestige that they are weaponizing.

The secrecy that surrounds intelligence agencies, and their America-unique separation from the government's foreign/military operations, shielded the decline of their work's quality and usefulness. The media inflated their mystique. Meanwhile, their upper levels merged into America's decadent ruling class. Using the unwarranted assumption that they know what ordinary mortals cannot, and professional secrecy to shield their pronouncements from substantive scrutiny, Intelligence officials have supported the ruling class against domestic challengers by covering up evidence against them, as they did for the Biden family, by smearing opponents as foreign assets, as they did to Donald Trump, as well as by purveying as fact their opinion that opponents are part of shadowy, subversive, violent organizations.

Adams would note that the U.S. government's current theory of Intelligence—that secret information is essential to understanding foreign regimes and their intentions—is historically groundless. He would note that U.S. attempts to operate by that theory have produced only high-level decisions muddled by non-responsible and often dis-informed partisanship masquerading as secret Intelligence. Statesmanship, he would argue, requires intelligence of the ordinary kind, informed by the statesmen's own knowledge, experience, and good diplomatic reporting. Because espionage is useful—often essential—in military and sometimes diplomatic operations, Adams would transfer those functions from the CIA and (part of) the FBI to the armed forces and Foreign Service.

Adams would find it difficult to believe that the Biden administration really meant to purge from the armed forces significant numbers of persons out of tune with its ideology—if only because it is impractical and unsustainably disruptive—or actually to use the military to pursue domestic political opponents. Nobody can be so crazy as to want civil war. He would bet that Biden & Co. intended an inexpensive but effective campaign to rally supporters by intimidating opponents. Nevertheless he would note that making bellicose moves with deadly weapons, even unseriously, risks the most serious consequences—like playing with fire.

Trade

Violent conflict over the 1794 Jay Treaty that granted trade privileges to Britain was the principal event of John Quincy Adams's young adulthood. Free trade with and reciprocity to all had been pillars of the foreign policy that his father had helped erect. The Jay Treaty's supporters, including J. Q., were not happy that circumstances were forcing departure from those pillars. Later, they eliminated privileges as fast as circumstances permitted. But they did impose tariffs, to provide government revenue as well as to protect the development of domestic industries.

For the Jay Treaty's intellectual godfather Alexander Hamilton, for George Washington, and most definitely for J. Q. Adams, tariffs were not any abandonment of principle. Nor were they primarily about economics. They were about supporting America's independence.

The Revolutionary War had established absolute juridical independence and tenuous military independence. But because Americans produced almost nothing beyond a bountiful agricultural surplus, the United States of America was the most economically dependent of nations. Achieving practical independence required cutting Americans' near absolute dependence on customers, and above all on suppliers. And that required acquiring sovereignty over essential industrial goods. Alexander Hamilton had "written the book" on that in his 1791 *Report on Manufactures.* That, in turn, meant imposing tariffs: protectionism. The American people would have to pay higher prices for imported manufactured goods and/or buy inferior American-made goods. To some extent, economic rationality would have to be sacrificed to the *ratio* of statesmanship.

Hamilton's report had stressed what everyone knew: Americans had secured military independence only thanks to foreign guns, powder, textiles, and shoes. Far from arguing for autarchy, Hamilton had stated the obvious: no nation can expect to maintain political independence while dependent on foreigners for the essential physical means of securing it.

Like Hamilton, Adams preferred to regard trade strictly from the perspective of classical liberal economics: willing seller and willing buyer. Following Montesquieu, he believed that mutually beneficial commerce can happen only among equals, absent coercion. Unlike the British of the day and so many others, the Americans did not look at international affairs as a means of exploitation. Adam Smith's 1776 *The Wealth of Nations*, which celebrated classical liberal economics, including the principle of comparative advantage, had found widespread acceptance in America. Americans also looked at classical liberal economics as an avenue to peace.

George Washington had said that Americans would make trade an instrument of peace as well as of prosperity by neither giving nor seeking special privileges, by "forcing nothing" in commercial relations. Americans could not prevent other nations from pursuing mercantilism. But American trade negotiators could minimize its effects by pursuing reciprocity.

Yet Hamilton had convinced Washington and his followers to make exceptions to the axioms of liberal economics in favor of statesmanship's principal good: independence, on which all else depends. For this reason, Adams was quintessentially American in tempering a principled preference for free trade with the economic requirements of political and military independence. He supported protective tariffs to establish these essentials, as did Henry Clay and as did their admirer, Abraham Lincoln. For them, money was a means of fostering independence—not an end in itself.

They knew that, as Adam Smith had argued in the 1795 prosecution of the East India Company's Warren Hastings, trade privileges are corrupt and benefit politically privileged sectors of all sides' economies at the expense of less-well-connected ones. That sort of micromanagement fosters the opposite of domestic and international harmony. They also knew that the most successful of mercantilist countries, Spain, awash in gold as it was at the seventeenth century's outset, had reduced itself to impotence because its people were losing the desire and capacity to produce things. Money had sapped the life out of them. Spain's decline showed pure mercantilism's folly: power is not something that money can buy. Money can even destroy it.

Some Americans of the founding generation, notably Thomas

Jefferson, James Madison, and Thomas Paine, believed that America's status as the world's superpower of agricultural commerce would allow it to buy the physical requirements of independence. But the War of 1812's catastrophes reaffirmed the common sense that America must possess the industrial capacity to fend for itself. For this reason, though all favored free, reciprocal trade and nobody thought in terms of complete economic self-sufficiency, debate about trade among Americans focused on the practical question of what American activities so contribute to America's identity and independence that they ought to be protected.

Because Europe and Japan's recovery from World War II was essential to maintaining America against the Soviet challenge, Adams might have agreed with America's sacrifice of reciprocity in the war's aftermath: low barriers to the American market, coupled with toleration of high barriers for entry into foreign ones. But because the several rounds of international trade negotiations that have occurred since the 1970s have been concerned with securing advantages for favored constituencies rather than with America's principal interest in its own security, Adams would have looked askance at them.

In our day, mercantilism being even more prominent than it was two hundred years ago, Adams would say that focusing on America's own interest in our own identity and independence is more important than ever. Today's mercantilism aims at far more than piling up "hard currencies." It is about power, not money. Political leaders seek to draw into their own sovereign sphere the skills and capacities that place their country at the top of the value-added food chain, embodied in what any given country's people do, in what they produce, in the occupations in which they engage. Today, technology being more important than ever to economic performance and military power, the acquisition of technology, legally and illegally, is high on the list of modern mercantilists' goals. But the intelligent ones know that technology, like money itself, is only a component and that power itself requires making and using all of power's tools.

Recognizing that we were in a war with the Soviets, albeit a cold one, Adams would have approved of the Pentagon's and Commerce Department's scrutiny and limitation of exports to the Soviet Union. But the Soviets' use of trade against us was limited to the acquisition of pieces of military technology—famously, computers and guidance systems—as well as to the development of small lobbies of companies that benefited from the trade, for example, PepsiCo and Occidental Petroleum. The Soviets never combined military, commercial, and political threats to America.

China combines them, far more effectively and on a far bigger scale, and it does so with an economy intertwined with America's in countless ways. Through economic power, China has made itself a significant factor in U.S. domestic politics. China's comprehensive cold war against America, Adams would say, makes it necessary for us to shape our trade policy according to the practical principles in Alexander Hamilton's 1791 *Report*, rather than by blind adherence to the theory of comparative advantage. During this young century, precisely such blind adherence has allowed China to manipulate the U.S. economy into a position of dependence for the essential physical components of power that recalls our young Republic's dependence on foreigners for its own independence.

The Chinese government's main asset was and remains its dictatorial control over the world's biggest reservoir of intelligent, disciplined labor. It offered American companies the prospect of manufacturing in China with negligible labor costs and a permissive regulatory and tax environment. The many companies that accepted this offer abandoned their American factories and workers, taking their technology to China. They enabled the Chinese to make things even as Americans lost the ability to make them. China is now the primary source for U.S. basic pharmaceuticals, electronics, and the rare earths for modern batteries. In short, the Chinese and their U.S. corporate partners deindustrialized America.

Adams would wave Hamilton's *Report* under our noses and ask whether we really want to be an independent nation.

In terms of trade policy, the main difference between America's dependence today and two hundred years ago is that today's state of dependence resulted from our choices. It could easily be remedied were Americans to choose to do so.

Because Adams so sharply distinguished between peace and war, he regarded trade, and the negotiations necessary for it, as part of the workings of peace. Therefore, he would argue that the latter day U.S. practice of using trade privileges and sanctions to try forcing other countries to do what they don't want to do is foolish. Governments, he would say, neither will nor can sell out interests on which their members have staked their positions and likely their lives. He would also say that sanctions are inherently acts of enmity, indeed of war. As such, unless they are part of overall war plans reasonably oriented to victory, they are almost certain to yield little except increased enmity. Adams had read Machiavelli's warning against doing one's enemies a *little* harm.

But although Adams thought it counterproductive to use tariffs as political sanctions, and although he much preferred trade arrangements based on reciprocity or the "most favored nation" principle, as president, he did not hesitate to impose tariffs on British textiles to pressure Britain to relax its prohibition against American ships engaging in the carrying trade within the British Empire. In short, fire is often the best firefighting tool.

NEIGHBORS AND RELATIVES

In 1825, Secretary of State Henry Clay, writing on President J. Q. Adams's behalf, instructed Joel Poinsett, newly appointed U.S. minister to Mexico, that Mexico was to be considered "most important" to the United States. In the intervening two centuries, Mexico has only become more so. How important it is and how wise is the Monroe Doctrine, we almost learned the hard way when the administration of Mexican president Jose Lopez Portillo (1977–82) negotiated permission for the Soviet Union to operate consulates in the ten Mexican cities closest to the U.S. border. The Soviets' embassy in Mexico City, their largest, had long been the headquarters for their massive subversive operations against the United States. By the late '70s, with Soviet power in full flow and America beset by malaise, opening these consulates would have turned our southern border hostile. Only the election of Ronald Reagan in 1980 and of Miguel de la Madrid to Mexico's presidency in 1982 prevented this catastrophe.

John Quincy Adams knew that friendly borders are like oxygen: when you've got them, you don't think about them. When you lose them, you can't think of anything else. Having read Thucydides, Adams knew that great as Athens's losses in the Sicilian expedition had been, nothing so sapped its life as did a small fortress the Spartans established at Decelea, on the edge of Athenian territory. That is why Adams devoted the greater part of his time as secretary of state to relations with the Spanish possessions in or near U.S. borders, especially Florida, Cuba, and Mexico. As Spain's hold on them was loosening, his first priority was to keep them out of the hands of any power that might use them against America—Britain first, but really anybody, including pirates. Because Spanish America's peoples were innocuous at worst, the danger was limited to that.

Notwithstanding Mexico's iconic complaint, "so far from

heaven, so close to the United States," the United States' relationship with Latin America had been mostly symbiotic. In living memory, our southern border was largely unguarded, with persons flowing in both directions, without formalities, to mutual benefit. That happy state is gone, never to return.

Today, Adams would judge Latin America more consequential than ever. Its people, connected to us by land and blood, our relatives as well as our neighbors, are younger, poorer than ourselves, mal-governed, restless, and over twice our number. As the latest caravan of would-be migrants heads from Central America to the U.S. southern border, Americans recognize the existential threat that such mass migration poses. Those who come are no longer primarily itinerant workers, but persons who seem to be moving from Central America's welfare rolls to ours. Since such migrants tend to vote more for Democrats than for Republicans, the Democrats try to increase their number among us and to marshal them for their own advantage by convincing them that Republicans are their enemies. As a result, today's mass migration from Latin America heightens the danger of political war among us, over and above the danger of deculturation and increased criminality.

Adams and his successors had favored immigration. But today he would recognize that removing immigration as a partisan and societal bone of contention is a prerequisite for peace at home even more than for foreign policy. He would also recognize that this is impossible so long as so much immigration is either through penetration of a porous border or by exploitation of laws (asylum, birthright citizenship) that were never intended to be avenues of migration. For this reason, reluctantly, he would cast aside those laws, abandon the informalities that had served the hemisphere so well for two centuries, and favor the management of a southern border impenetrable without official permission. Good fences, he would judge, are now essential to good neighborliness.

America's founding generation had few illusions about Latin America. The Monroe Doctrine envisaged no sort of attempt to uplift it. Nevertheless, there was unanimity of hope that all would be better off if, over time, standards there approached standards here. William Seward—Adams's admirer—looked forward to the time when sections of Mexico and Canada would have so approached the U.S. socially, economically, and morally as to apply for admission to the Union as states. Meanwhile, even this most hopeful of Adams's disciples thought of immigration strictly in terms of what may be in it for us.

There is growing acceptance among us of the notion that letting people into the country, whether for labor or as prospective citizens, should be on the basis of merit. But what do we judge meritorious? Answering the question, whether openly or tacitly, is unavoidable. Abraham Lincoln, also Adams's admirer, said that our lands were made for free farmers who "when they look through that old Declaration of Independence ... 'We hold these truths to be self-evident, that all men are created equal,' ... feel that that moral sentiment taught in that day evidences their relation to those men ... they have a right to claim it as though they were blood of the blood, and flesh of the flesh of the men who wrote that Declaration, and so they are."

Adams would suggest that, once the establishment of an impenetrable border had restored our capacity to choose, the choice of who is to be admitted be made by criteria openly specified by law. Not unlikely, Lincoln's criteria for citizenship would be met most likely by intact families with trades or professions, and a record of contributions to their communities.

It is no exaggeration that the violence and corruption that reigns from the northern Andes through Central America, throughout Mexico, and spills over our border, is rooted in part in our own American people's growing taste for mind-bending drugs. U.S. consumers pay Latin American drug-trafficking networks some $70 billion per year—some of which comes from U.S. taxpayer subsidies to drug users through Supplemental Security Income (SSI)—and all of which has empowered some of mankind's most destructive people.

Networks of traffickers have broken down societies throughout this region by corrupting authorities as well as by enlisting hungry young men, and partially replaced them with their own sociopolitical power structures. Kidnappings and all manner of extortion supplement their income from the drug trade. The U.S.

legal and penal system's permissiveness allowed the gangs to grow in U.S. territory. In short, one of the United States' sociopolitical illnesses infected Latin America, where it became an epidemic that now spreads among us in virulent form, including via the migration of people from the region.

Adams would regard as perverse, unjust, and destructive the increasing domestic decriminalization of possession and use of narcotics alongside stepped-up efforts to curb the trafficking: perverse because decriminalizing use of drugs increases the casual demand for them, and hence increases the cartels' incentive to increase production and import; unjust and ineffective because it tries to shift the battle against the drug epidemic from the Americans who cause it by using the drugs, onto the mostly foreign people who merely service Americans' increasing demand; destructive of our neighbors because no part of their societies is immune to the drug dollars' corruptive effects. Adams would advise either total legalization of such drugs, or the imposition of draconian, summary punishments for any and all involvement with them.

What Is Nearest Is Dearest

America's reduced capacity to exercise power makes friendly Latin America all the more essential. As previously noted, the Soviet Union's placing of nuclear-tipped missiles in Cuba in 1962 was foredoomed because the U.S. could be sure of stopping any and all Soviet traffic with little if any risk. The Castro regime itself survived only by America's leave. But today, were Russia to send missiles to Cuba—never mind were it to home-port ballistic missile submarines there—any effort to stop it would have to contend with a Russian submarine force roughly on a technical par with ours and with Russian strategic forces in many ways superior to ours. Also, given military asymmetries, China could place missiles in Venezuela more safely than we could place them in Taiwan. What would we do were China to do that openly? Even Iran could place missiles in Venezuela. Then what?

In the strongest terms, Adams would chastise the American statesmen who facilitated Fidel Castro's and Hugo Chavez's rise to power in Cuba and Venezuela, who failed to overthrow them when they aligned themselves with America's enemies, and who are yet complicit in their regimes' survival. He would note that Castro pioneered a system of dictatorship based on the secret police, the military, and on radical privation of the population that others have learned to imitate. He would deploy the maximum of incentives and disincentives to discourage or to penalize foreign governments from acting in any way favorably to these regimes. He would regard visits by Chinese or Russian military units—especially the Russian security forces in Venezuela and Russia's support of its anti-American regime, as major international provocations, direct challenges to the Monroe Doctrine and challenges to America's very nationhood to be dealt with accordingly.

Adams would cut Cuba, Venezuela, and Nicaragua off from any intercourse with the U.S. and impose secondary sanctions on European or Asian governments and companies that sustained them. Certainly he would look for ways of imposing costs on China and Russia to more than counterbalance whatever strategic benefits they thought to gain from their involvement against us in our neighborhood. That was the Monroe Doctrine through TR, and it should be the Monroe Doctrine now.

FOURTEEN

MUSLIM CONTAGION

For the very reasons that John Quincy Adams judged Latin America to be most important to the United States, he would judge the Muslim world to be of the least importance. Muslims are not our neighbors. Their lands are on the other side of the globe. Nor are they our relatives. Until the twenty-first century, their numbers among us were inconsiderable. Typically, they do not marry outside their communities. Barack Obama's statements to the effect that "Islam has been woven into the fabric of our country since its founding. Generations of Muslim immigrants came here and went to work as farmers and merchants and factory workers, helped to lay railroads and to build up America" are counterfactual, dishonest, and meant to deceive.

By any objective standard, the Muslim world is sick—a sickness congenital to its civilization that can only run its course. It is beyond the reach of foreigners to cure. In the roughly half century prior to our immediate time, the U.S. ruling class, beguiled by misjudgments and consequent to reliance on easily accessible oil and gas, became unduly engaged with that world's affairs. Initially because of competition with the Soviet Union, U.S. officials tried to channel Muslim countries' politics, got involved in wars among them, and imported some of their hatred along with its carriers. Interference in their affairs has always been counterproductive.

The Soviet Union's death a generation ago removed much of the Muslim world's geopolitical significance, and American technology for hydrocarbon extraction removed the economic one. The consequent drop in world energy prices also removed the basis for the clientelistic way that the Muslim world's leaders rule and made it impossible for them to continue attributing their civilization's inadequacies to the West. As a result, now, as the Muslim world's components focus on exacerbated quarrels within and among themselves, and as the U.S. ruling class's illusions fade, this anomalous period of seeming importance is ending. More than ever, limiting America's involvement with peoples who have little to give but trouble seems the essence of prudence.

Obama mentioned that Thomas Jefferson and John Adams had copies of the Koran—but did not mention that they got those copies to try to understand what the Barbary pirates' envoy had told them—that Muslims are bound by their faith to capture and enslave Christians. In fact, when America first encountered Muslims, those Muslims were not acting as contributors to the American nation, but as pirates against it. John Quincy Adams himself was forcefully unequivocal about what to do with the pirates: exterminate them physically as mankind's common enemy. Then as now, all manner of piracy is a practical matter, not a religious, never mind a racial, one.

The reasons why Americans and Muslims who take Islam seriously are like oil and water go beyond religion's specifics. The role of Sharia, Islam's law of secular and spiritual life (Islam does not distinguish the two) is the chief external. Just as important are the customs and values of Islamic societies, which Muslims typically do not distinguish from their religion. Their denigration of work—considering it proper only for slaves and losers—sets them at odds with Westerners. The religion itself deems non-Muslims enemies who, if not converted, are rightly to be enslaved or killed.

Only in the early nineteenth century, when Napoleon invaded Egypt, and France and Britain conquered North Africa, did the Muslim world begin to feel the relative effects of its Sunni majority's eleventh-century disengagement from the realities of reason (Robert Reilly, *The Closing of the Muslim Mind*, 2014). Since that time, that civilization, now of some one billion people, has refused to revise its own intellectual/civilizational choices, and has remained faithful to a faith that defines itself as at war with the rest of the world. Islam, Samuel Huntington noted, "has bloody borders"—and has been increasingly at odds with itself about how to deal with the rest of the world's painfully superior power and prosperity.

Between roughly 1830 and 1960, Westerners built the Muslim world's material infrastructure and educated its human infrastructure. Western sanitation systems and health care radically increased life spans, and hence levels of population. After Western companies turned over oil's bounty to Muslim governments, its glitzy cities have been designed by Western engineers and built by Asian laborers—the same combination that extracts and transports the oil. In fact, Muslim countries' dependence on the West for the food and technology that supports populations five times those of Adams's time is greater than ever. But, since the 1950s, Muslim peoples have been ruled by their own in various corrupt imitations of Western practices—disastrously.

The essence of the problem is the impossibility of enjoying Western standards of material comfort and civil freedom while adhering to the Koran's moral and social prescriptions. Muslim societies' traditions, which reflect those prescriptions as well as local habits, add to a problem that is internal, endemic, and without evident solution.

For two hundred years, Western-educated Muslims have lived as Westerners and tried to imitate various Western systems of government—all of which is contrary to basic Koranic injunctions. They have adopted Western language and dress, set up monarchies, republics, and military dictatorships. They have tried socialism and dallied with Nazism, aligned themselves with Americans and with Russians. But corruption and despotism are the main things they have delivered to their peoples.

Since the Muslim Brotherhood's founding nearly a century ago, and increasingly since the Iranian revolution of 1978, any number of Islamist movements have challenged the Westernizers, arguing that whoring after the West, departure from Islamic theology and law, are the sources of the people's misery. Today, most if not all of the Muslim world's regimes give lip service to some version of that proposition. But more Islam has not helped. Wherever Islamist parties have taken power—beginning in Algeria in 1970, to Iran in 1979, to Turkey in 2001—religious practice has declined, corruption has increased, and the standard of living has fallen.

Today's Muslim masses are not happy. They know they are very poor in comparison to the West. They are young but live under governments that kill hope. Their culture tells them to blame the infidels for their troubles, and their religion tells them that fighting infidels is their duty. This has proven to be an explosive combination. Most of the region's governmental groups are anything but sound. Revolution is active or brewing among them, without exception. *The borders and regimes that have existed since World War II's aftermath should not be expected to last.* Anything is possible, except stability.

Egypt, the most populous Arab country, is malnourished, growing demographically, perpetually on the verge of famine, and on a knife's edge between military and Islamist kleptocracies. The future of Saudi Arabia, the largest and richest country, is disputed by the descendants of King Saud's several wives. During the last dynastic struggle, in 2005, the half-brothers had marshaled opposing military forces. The Gulf states too, flush with cash and even more bereft of protection, struggle as oil prices show no sign of ever again generating enough to subsidize a growing, youthful population, most of whom have never experienced the need to work. All look anxiously at the downtrodden Shia tribes that live in the vital oil-producing regions. These, in turn, look for opportunities to revolt, and to Iran to provide them. So do the Shia minorities in all the Gulf states. In Bahrain, they are the majority.

Shia Iran has ably exploited its fifth columns throughout the region. Its Persian identity helped its pan-Muslim credentials as it became a main sponsor of the Muslim Brotherhood. Iran strikes fear with its missiles, its nuclear program, as well as with its proxies. Turkey, under Islamist party rule since 2001, is also subverting the region through the Muslim Brotherhood as well as by supporting its favorite groups as it tries to re-establish something like the caliphate that died officially after World War I. It also has invaded parts of Iraq, Syria, and even Libya.

Geopolitical order, to the extent it existed in the twentieth century, had been Britain's gift to the region, delivered from its great base in Aden, and via its anti-Russian alliance with Iran. After that ended in 1956, the U.S. tried fostering an order acceptable to the Sunni Saudis and the Shia Iranians. That fell apart in 1979 when Iran's pro-American Shah was overturned. U.S. attempts to broker peace between Shia and Sunni resulted in the occupation of Iraq for a disastrous decade. The mere possibility of fruitful U.S. involvement ended in about 2011 when Turkey, a nominal U.S. ally, turned against any and all supported by the United States, and aligned itself with Russia.

Vladimir Putin is now the region's arbiter. Russia's interest, however, is the security of its naval and air bases on Syria's coast. For this reason, Russia does not support Turkish or Iranian aggression, but is friendly to local efforts to resist it. Yet this unstable arrangement looks more like order than anything that has existed in the region since Britain left it after 1956.

America's Role

As noted earlier, the Third World is substantially a creation of U.S. foreign policy. But ending Europe's colonial empires and influence did not turn out with its peoples becoming America's eager pupils as Progressive ideology imagined. Nowhere is this clearer than in the Muslim world. We cannot know what post–World War II sentiments for independence in France's and Britain's colonies and protectorates would have produced without U.S. involvement. But the U.S. government did support those movements, heavily, and the results speak for themselves.

In 1953, the U.S. government birthed new nationalist regimes in Iran (the Shah) and in Egypt (Gamal Abdel Nasser). The previous year, it had brokered the formation of the Arab Socialist Ba'ath, the party that took power in Syria, and in Iraq in 1968 with the help of a CIA agent named Saddam Hussein, supplanting yet another U.S. supported dictator. The United States was key to delivering Algeria—legally an integral part of France—into the hands of the Marxist FLN (National Liberation Front).

By then, it should have been clear to Americans that none of these movements was going to follow Washington. Each had its own agenda. U.S. policy ended up following them. It was friendly to their regimes' demands for ever-increasing shares of oil revenues. Iran's U.S.-supported Shah led the charge for recognition of sovereignty over the oil and fostered the founding of OPEC (Oil Producing Economic Community). U.S. policy, founded as it

was on opposition to those movements' former colonial or
neo-colonial status, was also tolerant of their relations with the
Soviet Union, their hostility to Israel, and their increasing use of
terrorism.

U.S. relations with the Muslim world may be the most vivid
illustration of the fact that U.S. foreign policy has had less to do
with America's interests than with the personal proclivities of the
persons in charge of it. In each of the world's regions, policymakers identify with the local self-identified Progressives and their
agendas. In what the State Department used to call "the hot sand
and curry circuit," this was no different from elsewhere. The State
Department's and CIA's Arabists were much like their predecessors, the "desert-loving Englishmen" of the T. E. Lawrence era—
only less competent. They were also more susceptible to corruption,
especially after 1970, when local potentates became sovereign
over floods of oil money. Early U.S. Arabists also shared a bit of
genteel anti-Semitism, which blended seamlessly with their constant comparisons between the Muslim population's great wealth
and numbers, and Israel's poverty and puny size.

After the 1956 Arab–Israeli war, when Egypt, and later, Syria,
started using Soviet-aligned persons as terrorists against Israel,
and these started targeting Americans, the Muslim world became
a problem for America. During the 1973 war, when OPEC insti-
tuted a general oil embargo and terrorism ramped up, it became a
big problem. After the 1979 Iranian revolution mobilized a substantial part of the Islamic population against us, it became a
nearly all-consuming problem. Nearly half a century's experience
proves that U.S. efforts to deal with it made it worse.

Equally problematic is U.S. Progressives' increasing identifica-
tion with an anti-Semitism that is now wholly stripped of gentil-
ity. This poisonous mixture of incompetence and malevolence
made for waging the War on Terror in a way that made it a domestic political disaster more serious than any foreign failure.

Anti-Western terrorism had arisen from Islamic resentment
of the West, sharpened by domestic unhappiness for which the
West was held responsible, as well as by growing contempt for the
West's weakness—especially among governments. Governments

fed it, in part to channel resentment away from themselves. Worthless U.S. military action spread contempt for "infidels" to the general population.

As pointed out above, growing Islamist unrest also contributed to ordinary Muslims' contempt for their governments, and spurred these governments' resentment for their neighbors. Opposition increased between Sunni and Shia, monarchies, and other regimes. Today, Turks, Arabs, Persians, Berbers, Egyptians, Palestinians, Mesopotamians, Kurds, and the countless groups they sponsor are at each other's throats. Concentration of the Muslim world's attention on itself has relieved its pressures on the rest of the world. A blessing for the rest of mankind.

As these realities developed, the U.S. foreign policy establishment preferred to ignore them. Our foreign policy establishment continued trying to impose their visions of order. Foremost among these was the objective of peace between the Muslim world and Israel, premised on the domestication of the PLO and other Palestinian terrorist movements, coupled with Israel's fuzzing of its status as the Jewish State.

But U.S. officials failed to see that intra-Muslim strife had made the Palestinians into a tool for some Muslim governments against others, and that Israel itself had become a weighty potential ally for some of these governments. As Iran and Turkey became ever more threatening to Sunni Arab regimes, these regimes made peace with an Israel that did not threaten them. This left Arabs and Israelis free to concentrate on confronting Iran. It also made irrelevant two generations of U.S. policy according to which official accords between Israel and the Palestinians was the key to peace in the Middle East.

The Bottom Line

Safety from terrorism really is America's principal, if not exclusive, concern with regard to the Muslim world. John Quincy Adams would remind us that foreign countries' internal nature, needs, and vicissitudes will always trump whatever roles we might want them to play. He would judge that the essence of

prudence regarding the Muslim world is to avoid as much conta-
gion as possible from ills that are not of our making and that we
cannot control. He knew that destroying what he called pirates
(and we know as terrorists) is a prerequisite of all civilization, and
he would shake his head at the moral weakness by which the West
has allowed pirates to hold Western Civilization hostage under
the banners of Islam itself, or for Islamic causes.

Adams would counsel zero patience with that. In 1816, he had
told Britain's Lord Castlereagh that if America had a navy a third
the size of Britain's no one would hear of the Barbary Pirates ever
again. Today, the balance of forces between America and the Muslim world being even more one-sided than he could have imagined, he would advise acting accordingly.

The essence of U.S. Mideast policy's incompetence, Adams
would say, is *the lack of focus on what we want for ourselves from the
region—which is not much.* Adams would urge us to minimize
conflict with Muslim states by not involving ourselves in their
quarrels with one another, and by being ready and willing to use
our overwhelming military and economic power utterly to devas-
tate them if they make war on us or gang up on Israel. He would
minimize contact with that world, including by students and
tourists, and especially all manner of immigration. Restrictions
on contact with any given country might be loosened after considerable periods during which that country had suppressed
incitement.

Today, no less than in 1818, Adams would remind our government that it has the duty, right, and power to hold any and all foreign leaders responsible with their lives for anything that happens
under their influence that endangers Americans. Prior to Progressivism, U.S. foreign policy toward the Muslim world had had no
trouble distinguishing between their problems and our business.
Today as ever, dealing successfully with foreign cultures requires
recovering the capacity to understand that world's peoples, as well
as the problems they pose in their particularity and intractability.

He would not have waited for 9/11 to hold responsible any
regime or potentate that defied America's warning to cease and
prevent incitement of terrorism, and he would not hesitate to

punish individuals who murder Americans. He would have considered Saudi Arabia, Wahhabism's mother-house; Qatar, home of terrorism's chief propaganda organ, al Jazeera; and the Palestinian Authority, as having placed themselves in a state of war with America as much as Afghanistan's, Iran's, and Iraq's regimes, and would have responded with ultimata—and, if need be, war—to end their unacceptable behavior. The danger for America in our time is that no one in the region fears us. Instilling a healthy dose of fear, Adams would advise, is an essential part of peace.

After 9/11, Adams would have used secondary economic sanctions and sea/air blockade (very much including food) on their potentates and peoples. Because none of these societies can feed themselves or even maintain their own essential public services, they quickly would find themselves hungry, out of refined fuels, with the wherewithal of modern living breaking down because of lack of spare parts. Their populations would be driven back to pre-modern life that they no longer know how to manage, and in numbers far too great for survival. Neither the most entrenched of dictators nor the fieriest ideologues could escape blame for bringing on catastrophes that can be easily avoided or ended by crushing any and all advocacy of terrorism far more brutally than Americans would.

Knowing that the Muslim world had lived peaceably alongside the West when the West had left it no alternative to doing so, Adams would be confident that it would resume peaceful ways as soon as the West ceased to tolerate anything else. But occupying them and mixing U.S. troops with their populations would never cross J. Q. Adams's mind.

FIFTEEN

THE INDUS AND THE GANGES

The sub-continent between the great rivers that fascinated early Americans is home to a billion and a half people who preserved much of Britain's high quality educational system, who birthed two indigenous nuclear powers, and who produce a bountiful harvest of medical doctors and engineers, some hundred thousand of whom enrich America. India imposes itself on our consideration because it wages simmering wars against China and the Muslim world, both of which it borders, and is a perennial target of Russia's imperial ambitions. These challenges, which also impact its identity as a nation, are very peculiar to India. Americans cannot help but be interested spectators of how Indians handle them. How much and how little they mean to America is a textbook illustration of the nature of international relations.

Americans can be happy that, in the twenty-first century, India is neither an enemy nor inclined to act with enemies of the United States, and that constructive relations with it have become possible.

It was not always so. Though Mahatma Gandhi, the father of India's 1947 independence from Britain, represented a peculiarly Hindu mentality, Jawaharlal Nehru, the country's first prime minister and head of the dynasty that ruled for the next half century, was a British socialist—intellectually, morally, and politically. He was ill disposed toward America. His dynasty imposed a socialist economic system that further impoverished historically hungry India. By 1960, India's per capita GDP was only about $100 per year. Nor until after that dynasty's demise did it start climbing to the current $2,100. Nehru, lionized by the U.S. foreign policy establishment, was also the principal advocate among newly independent nations for aligning themselves largely with the Soviet Union against the United States, though under the label of "Third World."

Internally, the Nehru dynasty—conformant to its Western socialist understanding of things—tried to transcend the Indian subcontinent's fundamental division between Hindus (about 73 percent of the population) and Muslims (about 23 percent) by joining both under socialist secularism. It failed. British rule had kept that division from producing massive bloodshed. But in 1947, as the British left, Muslims retreated to their majority areas west of the Indus and east of the Ganges, while Hindus in these places went in the opposite direction. These areas became Pakistan and Bangladesh, respectively. In the process, Hindus and Muslims killed between one and two million of one another. These mega-massacres dwarfed the killing of 374 Hindus by British-led Sikh, Gurkha, and Baloch troops in 1919, which had turned Nehru into a leader in the drive for India's independence.

Contemporary India, ruled by a Hindu nationalist party, has given up pretense of equal citizenship for Muslims, and of anything but hostility to Muslim Pakistan which, in turn, sees its alliance with China as the surest guarantee of its survival. China provides Pakistan all manner of economic and logistical assistance, and it helped Pakistan acquire nuclear weapons. Pakistan gives China land access westward, passing southward of Russian-controlled territories. Together, Pakistan and China keep India militarily preoccupied on its northern borders.

Throughout the Cold War, the United States was as effectively allied with Pakistan as India was with the Soviet Union. Pakistan's traditional military rulers, British trained, were friendly to the United States and were key to defeating the Soviet Union's drive to possess Afghanistan. The United States did not have to ask. Pakistani Muslims' objection to Russian conquest in the subcontinent was in the nature of things. Even socialist India was grateful for America forcing the Soviets to retreat. The rise of Islamism worsened U.S. relations with Pakistan, even as the passing of the Nehru dynasty and India's focus on China as the greater threat improved India's relations with America. The number and success of Indian immigrants to America also played a role in that improvement.

Good as good relations may be, as aligned as some U.S. and Indian interests are, and as much as some Americans dream of some sort of alliance with India, John Quincy Adams would have Americans repeat to themselves: "Time and circumstance, time and circumstance." The American people have no possible interest in being party to oppressing Indian Muslims in any way, or in further alienating Pakistan, much less in who controls the Himalayan high passes between China and the sub-continent. Nor do U.S. diplomats have to make the case in Delhi that the Indian Navy should be unfriendly to Chinese penetration of the Indian Ocean or should share intelligence on it with the United States. Such actions are in the nature of things. But nothing could persuade India to send its navy through the straits of Malacca into the South China Sea to back up the U.S. Navy in a confrontation with China.

In short, with regard to India as well as other nations, basic principles apply. Reciprocal economic relations with the peoples who live on either side of the Indus and the Ganges make as much sense in the twenty-first century as they did in the eighteenth. But who the peoples who live there, and what they believe may be necessary for them to remain themselves, are exclusively their own business. It would make no more sense for Americans to try intruding on the Indian government celebrating the Hindu god Ram atop the ruins of a Muslim mosque than do U.S. efforts to encourage "moderate Islam" in Pakistan or anywhere else. We may be happy that India abandoned socialism. But it had adopted it without our say-so and abandoned it in the same way.

Quarrels such as those over Kashmir and the Himalayan passes that excite Indians, Pakistanis, and Chinese should leave Americans cold. Where interests align, little if any effort to coordinate them is necessary. Where they do not, attempting to make them so is largely futile. Elementary.

POST-EUROPEAN EUROPE

Europe, the ethnic origin of most of us, the cradle of our civilization, home of the peoples most like ourselves, with which our economy is most intertwined, is the part of the world we believe we know best. But it is ceasing to be like anything we have ever known or imagined. As a result, what had been the most reliable anchor of our foreign policy is becoming a problem we really don't yet understand. The reason for this may well be how easily Europe fits into the ideological categories by which our establishment misunderstands America and itself.

Today, Britain, France, Germany, Italy, Spain, etc., are disappearing in the most fundamental, biological aspect: in Germany, for example, 42 percent of all births in 2017 were to migrants from the Middle East or Africa. That percentage will rise. Natives' birth rates are far below replacement levels (Italy's is 1.34 births per woman). Together with the migration of young Middle Eastern/African people, these rates are changing Europe's biological character fast. Mohammed was the most common name given to boys born in Berlin in 2018. At this rate, by the present century's end, Germany's population of Germanic young people will be the size of a minor country's youth, and Germany's Muslim youth will have sealed Germany's future as a Muslim country.

Europe's cultural character is changing even faster. This is due in no small measure to what the class of people that has ruled Europe for the past half century—including religious authorities— has done to devalue their people's Christian and patriotic affections, and to look down on their own way of life. France's IFOP polling institute found that, in 1999, 70 percent of young adults had been baptized, along with 48.8 out of 100 children aged 0 to 7. Six years later, in 2005, the baptized proportion of the 0–7 cohort had fallen to 40 percent. By 2010, it was down to 34 percent, and by 2015, to just 30 percent. In short, France's population is increasingly cutting itself off from its roots. It is awash in alien migrants, despised by its leaders, and despising them. Thinking of and treating such countries as they were in previous decades makes no sense.

The infection caused by the injection of unassimilable Muslims into a continent suffering from critical demographic deficiency will ensure that European civilization may prolong its existence only within self-contained enclaves of particular, regional cultures. Particularity is the essential element: no part of Europe can possibly remain European unless it walls itself off from the Muslim flood that is washing over the rest, and, most crucially, unless it reproduces itself well above replacement level. Only a few parts— Hungary, northern Italy, parts of France have even acknowledged the need for the latter. As well, Europeans serious about reviving a dying civilization would also have to restore their relationship with Christianity while breaking relations with current religious leaders. While that is very difficult, Latin Americans have proved in recent decades that it is not impossible.

Visitors to Europe, never mind residents, barely recognize the human content of their surroundings from what they had been a generation ago. The migrants' offenses against public safety and the restrictions that the establishment has imposed on native populations on the migrants' behalf are just some of the efficient causes of a political revolt for which no end is in sight. It should not have surprised anyone that ordinary Europeans are rejecting the entire class of public figures, including religious ones, that have led to daily life being lived less confidently, less freely, less joyously.

Charles de Gaulle had sought strictly to limit non-Europeans' entry into France because, he said, the French are "racially white, of Greek and Latin culture, and Christian religion." They can integrate those who are not these only "in homeopathic doses." To suppose otherwise, he thought, is to deny one's own existence. But that is precisely what Western Europe's leadership has done with regard to immigration, and hence with regard to culture and religion as well. De Gaulle, who regretted that many Frenchmen were abandoning Christianity, had also tried to bolster French identity by promoting devotion to its secular bases. Like him, many in France had placed hopes on the secular sacredness of patriotism. But that sense has waned even faster.

In the rest of Europe's states, traditionally less patriotic than France, internal political cohesion has simply collapsed. The traditional parties are discredited, and the ruling classes are under siege by disaffected populations, especially by the young. Without constituencies outside the establishment, they fear elections and think of nothing but safeguarding their status.

Their very capacity to marshal people for any common purpose whatever has well-nigh disappeared. Increasingly, the levers and buttons in the Atlantic Alliance's control rooms are connected to nothing.

Proposals from traditional elites to remedy Europe's impotence are obviously unserious—for example, French President Macron's proposal for a European Army to serve "a kind of empire, as China is and how the U.S. is." It is surreal to imagine that today's Europeans, who are disinclined to hazard discomfort, never mind lives, for their national governments—only about one in five might be inclined to fight for his own country in the direst circumstances—would hazard them for Europe's supranational elites, whom they increasingly despise. They are in revolt against environmentalist policies that have raised prices for electricity, heating, and gasoline as well as against migration and deculturation.

The only certainty is that the Europe of states with structured, responsive societies and high-quality educational systems—the Britain, France, Germany, Italy, etc., we used to know—is past history and can never return.

That is why the political, diplomatic, and bureaucratic issues of Euro-American relations, such as levels of military expenditures, are largely meaningless. What essential elements of national existence and preservation would spending more on national defense buy? Not only does today's Europe neither contain nor produce the kinds of statesmen who lifted it out of World War II's rubble (Germany's Adenauer, France's de Gaulle, and Italy's De Gasperi), it no longer produces even the inept ones who ruled in the last generation (Germany's Gerhard Schröder or

France's Valéry Giscard d'Estaing) and is sidelining the likes of them who remain on the scene. Our establishment would like for such to return. But they won't.

The movements that are now rising in Europe have similar demands: loosen the EU's grip or leave the EU entirely; cut the ties between government and privileged corporations; stop migration; provide public safety. They define themselves by opposition to current rulers, by local allegiances—small-scale, tepid nationalisms—and by the desire to reestablish the way of life that is vanishing. That secular desire for cultural identity is strong enough to have fostered an increase in religiosity among those who share it— along with increased distance from current religious leaders. Above all, from Warsaw to London, Paris, and Milan, the people don't want to be ruled by the international personages that meet at Davos each winter. But no one should mistake their sentiments for the sort of nationalism that had existed in Europe in the previous three centuries.

The U.S. ruling class—virtually identical with Europe's—insists on seeing these populist movements as a passing phase rather than as Europe's medium-term future, because it does not want to understand them, or itself. Until America's ruling class stops imagining that the likes of Angela Merkel and Emmanuel Macron represent anything but a crumbling order, it will not be able to inquire what the movements now rising in Europe portend for the old continent and its relations with the rest of the world. To what extent are these movements capable of geopolitical engagement? What is their image of the United States, and what are the areas in which they might wish to or be able to cooperate with us?

Increasingly, the question will be to what extent any of Europe's traditional nations may retain meaning or even remain whole. It remains to be seen which of Europe's several constituent parts will cohere enough to deal with the demographic and cultural breakdown that afflicts the whole continent. How they do so will vary according to the character that each of these parts developed over past centuries.

Poland's consistent past, for example, is a guide for understanding its future and perhaps for understanding others. Simply, the Poles maintained nationhood based on Catholic identity (*Polonia, semper fidelis*) through centuries of subjection to the Russian, Austrian, and Prussian empires. That and their history of often-heroic behavior suggest that Poland will remain a coherent entity. Its enduring connection with Polish Americans suggests that U.S. policy can confidently expect to find Polish interlocutors. How much America may be able to do for Poland is a different matter. The other peoples of the former Soviet Empire, especially the Hungarians, share a concern for national identity that is likely to last, and that will almost certainly make it possible to deal with them as whole units. That will not be the case in Western Europe.

To what extent and for what purposes Germany will hold together is by no means certain. History suggests that the three Germanies traditionally associated with their characteristic drinks—wine (West), beer (South), and schnapps (East)—will be as different socially and politically in the future as they were in the past. The Bavarian South and the Rhenish West may be expected to continue exhibiting more conservative ways, be less attracted to any sort of radicalism, and be more open to relations with the United States than the former East Germany. Only Bavaria seems to have any sense of nationhood. Yet none of that may prove relevant.

As Great Britain devolves into its parts, the same may be said of England. In 2016, the British people voted by referendum to leave the European Union. England voted overwhelmingly to leave, to reaffirm its national identity and special relationship with the United States. Scotland voted to remain, and Wales was close. Britain's establishment, well-nigh unanimous for remaining, spent the subsequent three years trying to undo the people's decision. This devastated the public's faith in the country's political institutions and ensured a political revolution the likes of which Britain has not experienced since 1832, if not 1688. No one can know where it will lead.

France, as de Gaulle wrote, "was made by strokes of the sword." But, the sword of kings or emperors long sheathed, France is in the throes of a long-term rebellion against its elites, tempered chiefly by the people's habitual, sullen, grudging obedience to "the State." Modern France is, and is likely to remain, one and indivisible in its fecklessness and discontent. Its deep divisions—urban gentry versus the French "deplorables," religious versus modernist—are nationwide. France, the most united and patriotic of Western European nations, hungers like no other for leadership in which it can believe. But this leadership is nowhere to be found.

Italians don't believe in leaders. Economically, socially, politically, northern and southern Italy live by different standards and belong to different worlds. As the decades pass, its regions' evergreater legal autonomy strives to match the human reality. Affection for America, however, is one of the few things Italians of all regions have in common. Disdain for their country's and Europe's ruling class is another. Italian voters from all regions have been rejecting the country's establishment, represented by the Democratic Party (PD). But such has been the establishment's centripetal attraction to other parties' politicians who, one after another, campaigned against it but ended up enabling it to govern by contracting parliamentary support for it. Italian voters' anger, however, ensures systemic eruptions.

Throughout Western Europe, the establishment deplores the voters in the name of democracy. But who wins or loses the next rounds of elections will hardly affect Europe's fundamental problems or its direction.

The only sure thing that all this uncertainty means for America is that U.S. policy will not find support in the usual places, among the usual people. Countries, parties, and movements within Europe may be willing to help with this or that American concern, each for their own reasons.

John Quincy Adams would note that we have little to hope from today's Europe. He would also note that because there is even less we can or should do about what is happening there, America should not modify its policies to please European governments or elite opinion. To follow Europe's lead is to share its foolishness. Europe's NATO members have essentially tried to pay diplomatic and economic ransom to the Muslim world. And they have urged America to follow their lead. In so doing, they have facilitated the rise of anti-Semitism among themselves and complicated American efforts to safeguard Israel. Europe is increasing its economic dependence on China as well as on Russia. Adams would tell these friends that America does not share their choices and warn them of the consequences.

Since Europe's cultural, social, and political pillars are crumbling, Adams would view his main task as getting America clear of the falling rubble—disengaging America from institutions and people from which European people themselves are disengaging. The question of what good we can do for ourselves and what harm we can avoid would be his lodestar.

Adams would deal with the EU only when absolutely necessary, and then only second-hand, by reducing U.S. representation to it before withdrawing entirely. Instead, he would negotiate directly with interested nations as much as possible. As member countries considered leaving or loosening ties with the EU, Adams would offer them bilateral trade treaties with the United States. In addition, he would cease to treat EU decisions as binding, other than ones contracted with America.

Adams would reject the idea that Europe needs the United States to protect it from Putin's Russia, because conquering and occupying even Ukraine, never mind Germany, France, Italy, etc., is beyond Russia's physical as well as political capacity. Adams would note that Europeans have even less interest in defending themselves than Russia does in attacking them. Indeed, in 2019, the Council of Europe reversed its 2014 decision to expel Russia, made in the wake of Russia's annexations of Crimea.

Regarding whatever genuine fears of Russian domination they might have, Adams would suggest that shifting from reliance on Russian gas to reliance on American gas would be the most concrete measure available to them to assert their independence, and that theirs and America's conclusion of a long-term agreement on relations with Russia is a more effective guarantee of peace than the maintenance of a NATO bureaucracy whose command levers are connected to armies that have neither the capacity nor the intention to fight.

More insistently, he would ask them to reconsider their con-

tinued support of anti-U.S. regimes in Latin America, since this
endangers the American people's friendship.

At the top levels of European life, Americans will find pomposity, lassitude, emptiness, and renunciations. But below that, Europe will continue to hold millions of people yearning for Western Civilization's ways of life, with whom Americans can find common ground. Perhaps the greatest contribution that Europe may make to America over the next half century will be the individuals who may choose to take their talent and energy across the Atlantic and become Americans.

WHAT IS RUSSIA TO US?

From the founding of our Republic until the 1917 Bolshevik coup, Russia loomed small in U.S. foreign policy, and vice versa because the interactions between the two countries' geopolitical and economic interests were few and compatible. Given that these fundamentals have not changed, we should expect that the two countries' policies may gradually return to that long normal. But, for both countries, transcending the intervening century's habits will not be easy.

The Russian bear is licking the Soviet era's deep wounds as it growls behind fearsome defenses. Few other than Dostoyevsky imagined a tragedy as momentous as what the Communists inflicted on the long-suffering Russian people. No one knows whether or how it may be possible to undo its profound effects. Russia's population is less than half of America's (a tenth of China's) and declining. Despite efforts to boost the birth rate, its demography is likely to recover only slowly as the dysfunctional effects of the Soviet era on the behavior of men toward women may gradually give way to traditional Russian culture.

The despair that manifests itself in alcoholism will also take a long time to dissipate. Russia's economy is perhaps one eighth of America's. Nor is its culture friendly to the sort of entrepreneurship, trust, and cooperation that produces widespread wealth. Authoritarian rule will continue to provide essential structure to social life, especially by appealing to nationalist sentiments. The only sure thing is that, since Russia stretches from the Atlantic to the Bering Strait, since it borders both Europe and China, and since its military forces are fearsomely, intelligently built, it cannot but affect us.

U.S. liberals believed the Soviet Union's dissolution was impossible, and conservatives flatter themselves that they caused it. But virtually no one among us believed it was happening. Then, our establishment was well-nigh unanimous that Russia would evolve in a liberal direction. A decade of deep but ignorant involvement in Russia's internal affairs followed.

Americans had preached democracy to Russians and others within the Soviet Empire as part of the struggle against the Soviets' worldwide challenge. Russians did not have to be told that they were captives of a tyranny, but they appreciated America's attention to their plight. After the Soviet Empire fell, pro-democracy activists in and around the U.S. government redoubled their efforts to "democratize" Russia and the other former communist countries according to their own lights, not realizing how deeply this would be resented. They also got too close to former Party officials, as these used their Western connections to buy and to loot Russia's assets.

The Clinton administration combined ignorance and self-contradiction by trying to load onto Russia the hopes that the U.S. establishment had long entertained about global co-dominion with the Soviets, while on the other hand they pushed NATO to Russia's borders in the Baltic states and interfered massively in Ukraine. Russians came to see America as an enemy. Few Americans understood Vladimir Putin's 1998–99 rise as the reassertion of a bankrupt, humiliated, resentful Great Russian people.

The George W. Bush administrations fumbled at the new reality. Cleverishly, they courted American public opinion by publicly disavowing the treaty obligation to limit U.S. missile defenses, while simultaneously trying to appease Russia by continuing to limit them in fact. And as the Bush team struck a tough pose by formally objecting to Russia's dismemberment of Georgia, they effectively condoned it. The administration's dishonest incompetence earned contempt from all sides.

The incoming Obama administration tried to go further along the same self-contradictory line by withdrawing anti-missile support from Eastern Europe and quietly promising even more restraint. But when, in 2014, Putin took Crimea, Obama imposed economic sanctions, meddled even more in Ukraine, and agreed to station token NATO and American troops in Poland and the Baltic States. Then, for what seems to have been the most tactical of domestic political calculations, the Obama administration and therefore the U.S. establishment decided to try explaining the course and results of the 2016 U.S. election campaign as "Russia's attack on our democracy."

All this produced a mess of appeasement, provocation, insult, and enmity without much of an international point on either side—another lesson in the consequences of incompetence mixed with self-indulgence at the highest levels.

Although today's Russia poses none of the ideological threats that the communist Soviet Union did (and though we have no directly clashing interests with it), Russia is clearly a major adversary in Europe and the Middle East. Its technical contributions to China's military, and its general geopolitical alignment with China, are most worrisome for the United States.

But what is the point of enmity between Russia and America? What other than Soviet inertia and wounded pride motivates the Russians? The U.S. maintains economic sanctions on Russia and has been reported to have placed malware in its electrical grid's software! To achieve precisely what? Where to from here? The essential problem in U.S.–Russia relations is that neither side's desires, nor either's calculus of ends and means, is clear to the other, or perhaps even to itself.

Russia's Reconquista

In this century, Vladimir Putin rebuilt the Russian state into a major European power with worldwide influence. Poverty and a resource-based economy notwithstanding, the Russian state is on a sounder financial basis than any in the West. The country is under a firm, united leadership appreciated by the vast majority, whose national pride and solidarity dwarf those of Western publics. Nearly all Russians approve strongly of the absorption of Crimea. Russia effectively controls Ukraine's eastern end and has exposed the West's incapacity to interfere militarily in the former Soviet Empire.

Vladimir Putin famously said that the USSR's demise had been a tragedy. But no one suspects that he would re-create it if he could. Certainly, he wants to re-create the empire of the tsars. But to what extent? He certainly has expanded Russia's influence beyond what it had been in about 1995, encountering little opposition. More than most, Putin is painfully aware of Russia's limits. What then are his—and what can be any modern Russian leader's—national objectives?

As always, Ukraine is where Russia's domestic and foreign policy intersect. With Ukraine (and the Baltic states), Russia is potentially a world power. Without it, much less. Post-Soviet Russia's horizons have shrunk because the twentieth century's events forever severed Ukraine's and the Baltic states' peoples from Russia. Even Belarus has become less compatible with Russia. Modern Russia is reluctantly recognizing Belarus's independence, even as the Soviet Union, at the height of its power, effectively recognized Finland's.

In sum, post-Soviet Russia is a major European power, exposed to events in the Far East that it cannot control.

This Russia has no sane alternative than to live within that reality. Russian writing on international affairs focuses exclusively on the country's role as a member of the European state system. By the 2030s, if not sooner, the Russian government will have filled such space and established such influence as comport with its own people's and its neighbors' realities, and will be occupied keeping it. Its conquest of Ukraine east of the Don signifies much less the acquisition of a base for further conquest than the achievement of modern Russia's natural territorial limit in Europe.

As the Russian Federation's own demographic weight shifts southeastward and Islamism continues to gain favor there, the Russian government will have to consider whether to keep the Muslim regions within the Federation or to expel them and build fences against them. As in decades past, post-Soviet Russia will have to work harder and harder to cut the sort of figure in Europe that it did under the tsars.

Russia has always been a Western country by virtue of its Christianity. Indeed, it has believed itself "The Third Rome," and has acted as protector of Eurasia's Christians against Islam. Today's demographic and economic weakness has made it more Western than ever. No sooner had the USSR died than Russia restored the name Saint Petersburg to Peter the Great's "window on the West." As Moscow rebuilt its massive Christ the Savior cathedral to original specifications, it let countless priorities languish. As the Russian Orthodox Church resumed its place as a pillar of the Russia that had been Christianity's bastion against the Mongol Horde as well as the Muslim Ottomans, golden domes soon shone throughout the land. Whatever anyone might think of the Russian Orthodox Church, it anchors the country to its Christian roots. Even under Soviet rule, Russians had gone out of their way to outdo the West in Western cultural matters. To call someone *nekulturny* (uncultured) was and remains a heavy insult in Russia.

Adams knew from personal experience, and would remind us, that Russia's Westernism is not and never was imitation or love of the West. Rather, it is the assertion that Russia is an indispensable part of it. The Russians saved Europe from Napoleon. They are proud of having saved it from Hitler too. Their having done the latter tyrannically, as Soviets, does not, in their minds disqualify them from their rightful place in Europe or justify Europeans, much less Americans, trying to limit Russia's rightful stature. Adams would recognize that today's Russian rulers are not gentler or nicer than the emperor who shook off the Mongol yoke—who was not known as "Ivan the Nice Guy." Today's Russians, like their forebears, are calculating Russia's stature in terms of the limits—primarily in Europe—set by their own present power as well as by that of their immediate neighbors. Today's Russia is all about working the edges of limits it knows too well.

This Russia is no more willing to conquer Europe than it is able. Willingness and ability had stemmed from the communist political apparatus that ruled the USSR and projected itself throughout the world. Sister communist parties and front groups made significant portions of foreign countries—especially European ones—positively eager for Soviet domination. The Soviet armed forces, already in control of Eastern and Central Europe, were well equipped to take, if not to hold, the rest. Now, the political infrastructure—the Party that decided things in Moscow and the communist-friendly apparatus in Europe—is gone. Nobody in the West envies Russia. Russian influence in Europe now stems from Europe's reliance on Russian natural gas and from the opportunities for corruption that this entails.

Nor do Europeans fear Russia enough to reduce their reliance on Russian gas. In addition, West European diplomats lobby Americans consistently against America's imposition of sanctions on Russia for its seizure of Crimea and the Donbass. This is not the case with Poland and the Baltic states, and of course Ukraine, who view enmity between the U.S. and Russia as some kind of insurance for their own independence. But America cannot possibly guarantee it.

Russia's armed forces, for their part, are now configured for area-denial rather than for projection of power. The Russian military establishment, unlike that of the tsars and of the Soviets, emphasizes technology to economize manpower that, for the first time, is scarce and precious in Russia. Russia's reliance on nuclear weapons recalls nothing so much as the 1950s Eisenhower doctrine of "more bang for the buck."

The Russian military's prospective areas of operation are, not incidentally, the ones where the U.S. military envisions conflict: the area around the Niemen river on the borders between Poland, Lithuania, Ukraine, and Russia; and the area north of Crimea. Both are places where Russian armies have won historic victories. Though Russia's military posture has ever been and remains strategically defensive, its operational doctrine since World War II calls for taking the initiative in a preemptive, massive, decisive manner. In these prospective conflicts, the Russians would use the S-400 air/missile defense system to isolate U.S./NATO forces by air, as well as strikes (or threat thereof) by the nuclear-capable Iskander missile to cut them off on the ground. Their ground forces, led by Armata tanks, the world's best, would then press to make them prisoners.

Russia is confident that it can safely conduct military operations on its borders, even with nukes, because it possesses missile and anti-missile weapons superior in number and quality to those of America and China combined. As regards strategic offense, suffice it to say that the 2011 START treaty's aggregate limits of "800 deployed and non-deployed ICBM launchers, SLBM launchers, and heavy bombers equipped for nuclear armaments" refer to "launchers." In Russia, these are mobile, invulnerable platforms, which almost certainly contain a larger but unknown number of missiles.

On the defensive side—beyond the sixty-eight underground-reloadable launchers protecting Moscow—Russia's strategic defenses rest on the connection between its peripheral radars and some three hundred of the S-400 systems (to be replaced by S-500s beginning in 2021) deployed near every population center and other important points throughout Russia. Unlike U.S. systems like Patriot, Aegis, and THAAD, the S-400s are programmed and launched before they come into view of the local radars, on data provided by the early warning radars. They carry nuclear warheads to minimize the need for extreme accuracy. In short, Russia has a viable missile defense. Russia's nuclear submarines are deployed in defensive positions for denial of naval access to Russia itself, as well as to the deployment areas of Russian ballistic missile subs on the edges of the Arctic ice cap. The U.S. military has no way of dealing with this.

Russia's 2015–18 intervention in Syria, and its adroit management of Turkey, achieved the tsars' historic desire for a warm water port. But while its hold on its Mediterranean naval and air bases is firm, keeping Turkey friendly to Russia must ever be troublesome. Absent a securely friendly Turkey, Russia's renewed control of the Crimea, and even the Mediterranean bases, will be of limited worth. Whatever else might be said of Russia's role in the Middle East, Adams would acknowledge that Russia has brought more stable balance to local forces than ever in this young century. Along with most Americans Adams would not envy Russia's new responsibilities for the region.

The U.S. Side

John Quincy Adams would ground U.S. policy toward Russia on the facts of Russia's interest as regards America, and America's as regards Russia. Since any and all U.S. missile defenses are our supreme interest, and supremely our business, Adams would not listen to, never mind accommodate in any way, Russia's objections to them. But he would not regard Russia either as a grave geopolitical challenge to the United States or as a particularly difficult diplomatic problem.

While agreeing that Russia's sales of advanced arms to China and alignment with it against America in the UN are serious matters, Adams would reject the notion that today's triangular United States–Russia–China calculus is comparable to what it had been between 1949 and the early 1960s, when the Soviet Union directed a common long-term enterprise, and ideology covered somewhat China's and Russia's racial antagonism; nor what it was during the Soviet–Chinese military confrontation of the 1970s and '80s when China feared Russia, and the United States was in the position of relieving China's worries. Today, a weak Russia sells arms to strong China just for money, which hardly relieves its growing fear of "yellow hordes" that are more numerous and richer than ever. Unlike in the '70s and '80s, the problems between the two stem from basic disparities. Adams would judge that the best that America can do for itself is to do nothing that obscures those disparities. He would bet that without backhanded U.S. support for current Russo–Chinese relations, the two countries would be each other's principal enemies within a decade.

Ukraine is the greatest practical limitation on Russia's ambitions. Its independence is very much a U.S. interest, but it is beyond our capacity to secure. Adams would see U.S. relations with Russia with regard to Ukraine as resembling U.S. relations with Europe and Latin America two hundred years ago. Then, Adams knew that the Europeans realized (or that experience would force them to realize) that they could not control any part of the Western Hemisphere. By stating America's intention to guard its hemispheric interests while forswearing meddling in European affairs, he encouraged the Europeans to think and act reasonably. Today, he would be confident that Russia realizes it cannot control Ukraine except for its Russian part, nor the Baltics, never mind the states of Eastern Europe. He would reassure Russia that the United States will not interfere with Russia joining the mainstream of European affairs and will not use normal relations with Ukraine or any of Russia's neighbors to inconvenience Russia. Adams would not engage in any hostilities to try defining Russia's limits in Europe, knowing full well that this is beyond America's capacity and that it undercuts the basis for fruitful relations.

Adams would not hide the fact that U.S. policy, implemented by ordinary diplomacy, is to foster the Baltic States', and especially Ukraine's, independence. But he would know and sincerely convey to Russia that their independence depends on themselves, and that he regards it as counterproductive to try making them into American pawns or even to give the impression that they may be. He would trust in a Ukraine that had stopped longing for the borders that Stalin had fixed for it in 1927 and Khrushchev augmented in 1954, in a Ukraine retrenching into its Western identity (as, for example, by asserting its Orthodox church's independence from Russia's), and that is standing firmly on its own feet. He would trust in Russia's actual acceptance of its inability ever again to control this Ukraine. This would be Adams's Ukraine policy.

Since fruitless strife was the result of the sanctions that other administrations had placed on Russia to punish it for taking Crimea and the Donbass, Adams would remove them. The sanctions had done nothing to move Russia but emboldened Ukraine to suppose it has U.S. support for acting as if it had the same right to navigation in the Sea of Azov, passing under a Russian bridge, as it does in the Atlantic Ocean. Adams never much trusted in formalities.

But Adams, the Monroe Doctrine's author, would be willing to wage outright, destructive, economic war on Russia were the Russians to continue support of anti-U.S. regimes in the Western Hemisphere. If you want economic peace with America, he would say, stop interfering in our backyard. We Americans, for our part, are perfectly willing to reciprocate, regarding your backyard.

In sum, nothing would be geopolitically clearer to Adams than that natural policy for both America and Russia is not to go looking for opportunities to get in each other's way.

CHINA AND THE PACIFIC BALANCE

Prior to the 1949 Communist takeover, which, ironically, American officials fostered, the history of U.S.–China relations was one of friendship. Americans have never ceased being fascinated by China. Many of the traders, missionaries, scholars, and officials who have dealt with China have been captivated by its people—hard working, intelligent, and curious, with a civilization as deep as it is foreign. Chinese who are aware of the outside world have a soft spot in their hearts for America, which they call *mei guo*, the "beautiful country." China's historic geopolitical focus on itself and its surroundings, its racial distinctiveness, and its lack of transferable ideology, mesh well with America's maritime orientation and original commitment to independence for all.

The tyrannical dynasty that has ruled China since 1949 draws identity and legitimacy from having won a civil war with Stalin's massive help, under the label "Communist," against forces supported nominally by the United States. Communist China jointly sponsored and fought the Korean war of 1950–53 against America and continues to celebrate its victory and America's humiliation. Chinese communist ideology has always been Marxist gobbledygook, the only intelligible aspect of which is to justify the Party's rule. The Party's chosen path to glory lies across the geopolitical order established by America's victory in the Pacific War of 1941–45. But America is also China's main market and source of technology. Chinese leaders have paid for unfettered access to American markets, schools, corporations, and political systems with money from their people's cut-rate labor.

They have intelligently designed and are deploying armed forces to control the Western Pacific ever farther from their shores, with increasing boldness. Somewhat like the Soviet Union's, China's challenge is worldwide. Unlike the Soviets', it is wholly national, entirely nonideological. Unlike the Soviet Union, China does not mean merely to steal and surpass American technology for military purposes but to use it to subordinate America by outright economic warfare, the objective of which is to reduce America to the role of supplier of certain commodities into a universal system of production centered on and controlled by China—the most thoroughgoing mercantilism ever conceived. China's military, economic, and political successes have been so great and have come so quickly, America's internal decline has been so precipitous, that today's Chinese leadership may be unable to imagine any limits.

China's Limits

Other factors being equal, however, the shadow that China casts over the Western Pacific is likely to shrink over the next generations. By 2050, there will still be about 1.4 billion Chinese living in an area a bit larger than that ruled by the Qin dynasty between 221 and 206 BC. But only about a fourth will be in the prime working–military age between twenty and forty—roughly half of the proportion today. In the following twenty years, that proportion is now set to shrink by another third. That will still be a lot of hard-working, hard-studying, disciplined Chinese. But they will be more occupied than ever taking care of their elders—the importance of which has always been part of Chinese culture.

The ruling Communist Party fears that other cultural changes may also diminish its ability to marshal the people's energies and is taking steps to suppress what it deems inherently dangerous cultural influences. Between 1990 and about 2010, the Party had sponsored Christian scholars in order to discover the cultural "secrets" of Western success, while at the same time turning a blind eye to the unobtrusive practice of Christianity. No more. Since then, it has suppressed the huge (Protestant) House Church movement, de-legitimized the traditional Catholic Church via a deal with the Vatican that confers legitimacy on the "patriotic" Catholic Church that it controls through whose bishops it names. These success or failure of these moves will have a lot to say about what China's government can ask of its people.

But cultural change in China is not limited to religion. Modernity itself is something of a cult to which the Chinese people have been turning since the turn of the twentieth century, when the elite turned away from Confucian traditions. In the twenty-first century, the United States of America is the main source from which modernity's seductive light shines. So subversive is that light that untold thousands of elite Chinese are stashing their wealth in the United States or Canada and preparing havens there for their families. In sum, as years and decades pass, motivating the Chinese body politic against America will become more difficult.

China's regime is also conscious of the historic tendency of regime barons to lead revolts against the center, and that any number of events may trigger the devastating loss of "the Mandate of Heaven." But it is useless to speculate about when or how these congenital weaknesses may manifest themselves.

The Challenge

John Quincy Adams, who dealt with his era's superpower, Britain, which was at once America's primary trade partner and its chief threat, would stress the China challenge's uniqueness. Nineteenth-century Britain's concerns in the Western Hemisphere were counterbalanced by others in Europe and Asia. China's economic challenge, however, is far greater than Britain's had been. But today, China's geopolitical challenge is intensely regional to the Western Pacific. China's larger challenge also differs from what had been the Soviet Union's. The racially distinctive Chinese lack the attractiveness that the Soviets had exercised over the world's progressives of all races via communism's universal claims. Money and military power are no substitute for these. Whatever universal ambitions the Chinese leadership may have rest on the emperors' traditional view that China's rulers' Mandate of Heaven extends over *tianxia*, all under heaven—something that emphasizes rather than transcends China's particularity and foreignness.

In this century, the Chinese government has worked hard and

paid much to make the uniqueness of its country attractive—or at least nonthreatening—to the rest of the world. Its embodiment of large-scale efficiency in the service of an orderly way of life anchored in Confucian civilization may have peaked at the time of the 2008 Beijing Olympics. Since then, its heavy-handedness in Hong Kong and against its Muslim population, its authoritarianism, and especially its mendacious handling of the Wuhan COVID-19 pandemic, has tarnished its brand. In the 2020s, the rest of the world, America especially, is warier of China than at any time in a generation.

That endangers what is surely China's most precious nonmilitary asset, namely the large share of the world's industrial production that its hard work has won for itself. Yes, many of the world's industrial goods now include key China-made components, including pharmaceuticals and electronics. In the short run, this gives China leverage over other nations. But that share's permanence depends on other nations' good will, which China has been wasting. China's political leverage over the United States flows less from generalized good will than from prominent American businesses being literally in business with China. The Chinese Communist Party need not remind corporate executives and news organizations that their prosperity depends on Chinese good will, and hence to act as a potent lobby. Self-interest is enough, and it is a lot. But, with good will waning, China's vast but increasingly naked capacity to bribe is a fragile asset. In the final analysis, bought Americans are even more subject to pressures by their fellows. China can buy them, but it can't make them stay bought.

The rest of the power that China has gathered and is gathering to itself through its technical–commercial prowess is similarly fragile, because it is also dependent on good will. Yes, when Chinese officials and businessmen establish their presence abroad, they, unlike the Soviets, bring substantial money and expertise. Still, Adams would advise against undue worry that the Chinese can establish long-term influence in countries from the Silk Road regions to Africa and Latin America, never mind Europe, through business and technical projects as well as by promoting indebtedness. Today's Chinese are even more foreign in these countries than troops of the Holy Alliance would have been in South America in the 1820s. And of course, Chinese railroad builders, oil refiners, port builders, and businessmen from Tanzania to Tajikistan are unarmed. Adams would judge this facet of China's challenge to be self-limiting.

What Now?

That is why Adams would stress the need to focus on China's straightforward military–geopolitical challenge in the Western Pacific. China has claimed sovereignty over 1.3 million square miles of ocean and has built major bases on the Spratly Islands' Mischief Reef, Subi Reef, and Fiery Cross Reef. Their harbors, airfields, barracks, and repair facilities can support the full gamut of Chinese military equipment. They have launched all manner of missiles from there. Their radars reach out. This occupation of international waters that effectively controls access to East Asia from the Atlantic and Indian Oceans as well as from the Americas has been *a slow-moving, borderline act of war, now largely completed.*

U.S. policymakers would like nothing better than for the U.S. role in the Western Pacific to be as it was between 1945 and about 2010, and for China and Japan to be for us over the next half century more or less what they had been for the previous one. But our unquestioned primacy in that region was an artifact of World War II. It could not last. Sooner or later, the local powers would reassert themselves. They did. The reasons notwithstanding, the United States reduced its own military capacity as China was increasing its own dramatically. In short, China already has largely displaced the United States from its post–World War II control of the Pacific. *Round one has gone to China.*

Consequently, trying to reassert the previous level of American dominance in the region would take a major war. America does not want that. Since the 1990s, the U.S. establishment had counted on China's leaders becoming nicer as they got richer. But, since the opposite has happened, all must ask, what now? Adams would advise us that our natural role in the region is set by our need to secure our freedom to move and trade there, by the local powers' willingness to resist China, as well as by the balance between these powers themselves. For example, containing China would be far simpler were it possible for Japanese and Koreans to trust each other, or for people in the Philippines to forget their experience with the Japanese during World War II.

China's Strategy

China's long-term strategy is familiar to readers of Chinese military classics. That strategy and its operational doctrine are defensive: success is to be achieved by maneuvering the enemy into a position that is itself a defeat and that invites foredoomed attack. *China has done that successfully in the South China Sea.* Its strategists deserve that worthy label. America's overpaid lot do not.

Chinese strategy's essence is to choose and prepare the ground on which battles must take place. That ground will be familiar. It will be ground that the enemy must struggle to reach, but onto which China can bring maximum force to bear. China's operational objective is to defeat attempts to penetrate defenses. The military tactics that support these operations strike at those things that enable the enemy to fight on unfamiliar ground. The political tactics, prominently including deception, aim at controlling the times and circumstances of the conflict's development. This is a time-tested, coherent conception of conflict.

China's long-term objective is to dominate the Western Pacific eastward, and nearby Eurasia to the West, with power that radiates out from *Zung Guo*, the center country. Interior lines of communication. No foreign deployments. From the east, the American enemy, one-fifth China's size, must send a tiny number of its most irreplaceable people, with precious, vulnerable assets, to fight across the world's biggest ocean on ground onto which China can pour abundant force.

Therefore, China's military tactics in the Pacific—the ones that can prejudge the victory with little or no fighting—must aim at countering the high-tech equipment that makes it even conceivable for American armed forces to think of trying to break through China's locally numerically overwhelming layers of missiles, aircraft, submarines, etc.

Since that U.S. equipment relies so heavily on intelligence, command, control, and communications from and through satellites, since that space-based information architecture is the weakest link in the U.S. operations that must work perfectly to stand a chance, the execution of China's military tactics probably hinges on its capacity to control orbital space or at least to deprive the United States of reliable use thereof. That means gaining the capacity to destroy U.S. military satellites while protecting its own, and it means preventing the Americans from protecting themselves against Chinese ballistic missiles. In short, China's space program will arguably play the key military role.

The character of China's space program became unmistakable when China placed an unmanned probe on the moon's far side. By minimizing reporting on a feat on the scale of the U.S. Apollo program, China made clear that, unlike the Cold War Soviet and American space programs, its own program has no *political* dimension, and that its *military* purpose is best served by the Americans paying as little attention as possible to the fact that, *going forward, China can do anything in space that America can do—and that it may do or have already done or may be doing things that America has chosen not to do.*

Particularly, repeatedly since the 1980s, U.S. officials have chosen not to assemble a high-energy, orbit-based laser weapon. There is nothing exotic about this weapon's elements. Manufacturing such weapons has long since ceased to be a technical challenge. In 1994, the United States finally rejected testing a prototype.

As a result, it may be useful to consider that Chinese technical publications have discussed the development of a laser device to be placed in orbit for the reported purpose of destroying the debris that resulted from the testing of a direct-ascent Chinese antisatellite weapon in 2007. U.S. officials may take comfort in the Chinese project's advertised purpose. But that supposed purpose does not change the fact that an orbit-based laser powerful enough to destroy debris can even more easily destroy or disable working U.S. satellites and protect China's own. By so using such a device at the outset of a crisis, China might so boost its defensive operations as to significantly influence the outcome of that crisis.

Dealing with China's Challenge

Given the China challenge's near-comprehensiveness, conscious that China has not crossed the line into war, keen that the line not be crossed, and yet determined to put America in the position to reassert some control of the Western Pacific by defensive means, Adams would recommend building U.S. bases on Taiwan and fortifying them with the wherewithal to neutralize the Russo–Chinese S-400 (eventual S-500) as well as ballistic missiles on China's coast, plus whatever might be necessary to win an eventual battle for the place.

Taiwan is the geographic (hence the military) as well as the political key to U.S.–China relations. The Republic of China on Taiwan is a nation of some 23 million Chinese that lies 110 miles from the Chinese coast, in the middle of the first chain of islands along the Western Pacific rim. Capturing Taiwan is China's foremost symbolic political–military objective. Isolating it from international support—primarily America's—is Beijing's proximate political objective. They see this as an indispensable first step in the conquest of the island nation and as a measurement of China's influence in the world. Taiwan's people, with per capita GDP 250 percent of mainland China's, fiercely guard their independence from Beijing. Their mountains are ideal for placing modern sensors, as well as missiles, defensive and offensive.

The United States' 1979 choice officially to de-recognize the Republic of China on Taiwan was a gross breach of the Adamsian principle of recognition *de facto*—as well as a gesture of geopolitical surrender. De-recognition and the limited relationship that exists with the island under the Taiwan Relations Act were intended to appease Beijing. They have only whetted its appetite. They have also foreclosed using Taiwan as the natural centerpiece of U.S. resistance to China's attempt geopolitically to appropriate the Western Pacific. *Placing Taiwan in its proper geopolitical context is prerequisite for any serious U.S. resistance to China.*

Military deployments that prove—not promise—that Taiwan is beyond China's reach would go a long way to convincing China that it would gain nothing from greater military assertiveness. Making Taiwan impregnable, far from inciting war, may be the key to persuading Beijing that it has no sane alternative to peace.

For America successfully to resist China's expansion, the United States would also have to reverse its current policy of placing no obstacles in the way of Chinese or Russian missiles headed for America itself. That would send a message of seriousness that has been so obviously lacking.

Whatever else China is doing, it is also bidding for control of the seas, in part by trying to control the port of Djibouti on the Horn of Africa's tip, dominating the Red Sea (hence Suez) and the Arabian Sea. Ensuring freedom of the sea requires preventing hostile powers from controlling major transit points, and especially islands on the oceans' edges. That is particularly important in the Pacific. That is why Japan's, Taiwan's, the Philippines', and Indonesia's independence is important to America. These vital interests cannot be served merely by adding ships to the U.S. Pacific fleet, by "freedom of navigation" patrols, and by making encouraging gestures to traditional allies—more of what we have been doing.

Land-based sea control has the advantage. Chinese military preparations already in place to control the Pacific approaches to the Straits of Malacca can defeat substantially greater numbers of ships. The occasional, protested, pro-forma sail-by or fly-by of the deserted Scarborough Shoal only confirms tacit U.S. acceptance of Chinese control of what it has chosen to occupy. Devaluing China's militarization of the islets and reefs without war would require other nations in the region to similarly fortify their land approaches to the straits. Adams would encourage and aid that. But Adams would not try to substitute for locals' commitment.

Adams would not abide China's pretense that North Korea is anything but its pawn. North Korea's missile threat to America is an extension of China's threat. As sanctions have squeezed

North Korea, China's support for it has risen, thus discrediting the pretense of North Korean independence. Adams would remove doubt about who is responsible for what by collapsing North Korea's regime through the total application of secondary sanctions on everything. He would be confident that China would then rule the North directly. That would not change reality—only clarify it. This clarity would solve a host of U.S. diplomatic problems throughout East Asia—problems (notably China's diplomatic effort to detach South Korea from the U.S.–Japan alliance) that are becoming self-fulfilling expectations.

Thus, by making clear that America will not allow China simply to own the Western Pacific, America will have set a concrete limit to China's maximal expectations. Having reestablished America's credibility in the region, Adams would engage China and the rest diplomatically to discover and adjust who would be content with what. Thus would he serve America's interests in peace and in free international relations.

The Japan Factor

Japan's hostility is the price that China must naturally pay for displacing America's influence in the Western Pacific.

A Chinese–Japanese crisis may have become inevitable after 2018, when the United States effectively accepted North Korea's status as a nuclear missile power. That is because the Japanese fear North Korea's possession of nuclear-tipped missiles more than they do China's. Hence it is a safe bet that, if North Korea retains its nominal independence from China and retains its missiles as well, Japan will acquire nukes. Japan as a nuclear power would remind the Chinese people forcefully why they fear the Japanese. That would increase China's bellicosity as nothing else would.

The Japanese have been pacifist in general and particularly careful not to stir Chinese animosity. But Japan's pacifism has been mere policy. Japan's major cultural feature, unchanged, is neither pacifism nor bellicosity. Consciousness of its own uniqueness is Japan's culture. Superiority over—or at least avoiding subjection to—neighboring races, especially China, is Japan's baseline policy.

While reduction in America's role in the region is a certainty, the degree of it—*the range of choices*—available to the United States depends on decisions that the U.S. government will make in the 2020s. Will the United States be able to defend itself—or anyone else—against missiles from China and North Korea, or not? Will the U.S. be able to defend anyone against Chinese attack, or not? Will the U.S. be militarily able to defend Taiwan, or not? What will happen to the alliances among the U.S., South Korea, and Japan? Who will dominate orbital space? The range of choices available to the United States in the 2030s and beyond depends on the near-term answers to these questions.

Since, regardless of circumstances, Japan will still be tied into U.S. command, control connectivity, and intelligence systems in orbit, any serious Chinese military action against Japan would have to involve attacks on those systems. Even the prospect of such attacks presses U.S. policy to choose between entering the conflict on Japan's side, or limiting itself to protecting orbital assets and retaliating strictly in kind, or remaining neutral. This choice is not entirely unlike that faced by the United States in 1916–17 with regard to World War I. Perhaps in the 2030s, American statesmen will recall that, had the United States either stayed out of the Great War entirely or limited its actions and objectives therein, the Central Powers and the Entente would have worked out some arrangement among themselves, which would not have caused the rest of the twentieth century's catastrophes.

America's interest in the 2030s will be, as it was during the Great War, not in any local power's triumph over the other, but in the kind of balance between them that would allow Americans to live in peace and fruitful cooperation with both.

WHAT IS POSSIBLE?

Reality is forcing us to acknowledge that U.S. foreign policy as practiced over the last hundred years is unsustainable. Hence, a default Left–Right consensus exists for reexamining the relevance of the Founders' statecraft to today's problems.

Since today's international environment, and America itself, differ so much from what they had been between 1790 and 1910, returning to America First statecraft can only consist of practicing the principles of the presidents from George Washington to Theodore Roosevelt. There is nothing new or sophisticated about them. They are on the homey level of "early to bed, early to rise," "don't get into debt," "eat your veggies," and so forth. They boil down to minding our own business and minding it well.

Having learned the hard way the truth of J. Q. Adams's 1821 warning that "by once enlisting under other banners than her own ... [America] would involve herself beyond the power of extrication, in all the wars of interest and intrigue, of individual avarice, envy, and ambition, which assume the colors and usurp the standard of freedom," let us consider what it means forcefully to refocus on the primary objective: securing America's own peace.

But transitioning to that is not simple and can't be wholly peaceful. Current engagements and century-old bad habits of heart and mind are first-order obstacles to safely resetting America's place among nations. In chapters 11–18 we considered some concrete steps by which to deal with current problems. Now let us consider what it would take to reset the underlying priorities.

Transition

When war-weary Athenians regretted having built the empire that got them involved in the Peloponnesian War, Pericles told them: "To recede is no longer possible ... for what you hold is, to speak somewhat plainly, a tyranny ... to let it go is unsafe." Athenians, he said, could not escape paying the price of the comforts and honors which they enjoyed because of the empire. The safest course now, because of "the animosities incurred" in running that empire, would be "to pay attention to the navy, to attempt no new conquests, and to expose the city to no hazards," in other words, to stick to defensive fundamentals. In short, said Pericles, if the Athenians really wanted peace and quiet, they would have to earn them by working through their current troubles while using as much as possible the principles that had made possible their earlier peace.

Pericles gave no new insights and made no promises. He reminded Athenians of the truths immanent in who they were and where they were, of what had made the city of Athens great in the first place under Miltiades at Marathon and Themistocles at Salamis. But Periclean Athens was no longer that city. Soon, under the influence of constant war, the citizens would no longer be able even to listen to arguments such as Pericles' in favor of the old Athenian way of doing things.

Thus, during the Mytilenean Debate the following year, one citizen, Diodotus, began by telling his countrymen: "The advocate of the most monstrous measures is not more obliged to use deceit to gain the people, than the best counselor is to lie in order to be believed. The city, owing to these refinements, can never be served openly and without disguise." This is to say that, in a corrupt city such as Athens then and America now, arguments have to be made less in terms of principles than in terms of consequences. People who no longer care about doing the right things may still fear the consequences of doing the wrong ones.

By the same token, if presidents from Washington to Teddy Roosevelt were to be asked for the "secret" to their foreign policies' success they, like Pericles, would tell us to pay attention to state-craft's fundamentals, as they did, and to apply them in our time. Would they be listened to any more than Pericles was? Like Diodotus, let us be clear that reaffirming the fundamentals is essential because we can't avoid the consequences of not doing so. Like Diodotus, we must argue for doing the right thing because to do otherwise simply multiplies our troubles.

Regardless of the reasons, the choice for Americans now, as it was for Athenians then, is to do what it takes to reestablish peace, or to suffer unending war. The "secret," then and now, is to deal with our wars' problems in ways that reaffirm peaceful fundamentals.

George Washington had advised his successors to "observe good faith and justice towards all nations; cultivate peace and harmony with all," because "religion and morality enjoin this conduct." Today, we are reduced to noting that if we don't orient what we do to cultivating peace and harmony with all, endless wars will consume us from within.

Washington and his successors tried to give foreign nations no cause for hostility. Wanting them to stay out of our business, he advised staying out of theirs. Even by 1909, Theodore Roosevelt could write: "Throughout the seven and a half years that I was President ... the weakest nations knew that they, no less than the strongest, were safe from insult and injury at our hands; and the strong and the weak alike also knew that we possessed both the will and the ability to guard ourselves from wrong or insult at the hands of any one." That mutual political forbearance built a reputation, engendered respect, and, along with growing power, made for peace.

Progressive foreign policy, however, built a set of U.S. involvements, left a trail of resentments, and engendered a reputation for offensiveness combined with vulnerability that preclude peace. Leaving those wars, that trail, those reputations, without stimulating deadly contempt is problematic.

Millions of Americans have invested lives, treasure, and honor during the past century, serving causes which they were led to believe were America's and that would lead to peace. They, not our establishment, have concluded that something was amiss in these commitments. They want to refocus on America, not to give up on it. For this reason, it is not inherently hard to show them, or any reasonable person, how separating from current engagements serves securing the mutual respect between nations that had been the basis of America's original peace. But what we must do to secure respect as we separate from current engagements and how much or how little violence, if any, this must involve depends as well on the other parties.

Though the America of George Washington, J. Q. Adams, Andrew Jackson, Abraham Lincoln, and Theodore Roosevelt was no shrinking violet, there is no doubt that for us now to return to its ways would be something of a retreat. In international affairs as in military ones, retreats are the most difficult and dangerous of all maneuvers—inherently complex and unsafe. By nature, retreats are maneuvers like any others. They are dangerous primarily because they risk being misunderstood—internally as well as internationally—as abandonment of purpose and honor rather than as other paths to their affirmation. Western statecraft does not pay due attention to retreats and regroupments. Not so Russia, whose military gives a prize for successful retreats, the Order of Kutuzov, commemorating the commander whose 1812 retreats defeated Napoleon. Much of Chinese military writing has always been about redeployments to more advantageous places and circumstances—offense by retreat.

Surrender may bring others' versions of peace. But even peace-by-surrender happens only when the winners retain respect for the losers and the losers respect for themselves. Honor and mutual respect are the universal keys to national existence as well as to peace. As Charles de Gaulle's experience shows, a nation may continue to exist, though all else be lost, so long as its honor is not lost. But if and when a regime loses its own self-respect, it has forfeited the respect of others and ceases to exist. That is why wise statesmen guard national honor at all costs. But our establishment, having banished the very concept of honor from its vocabulary, has further advertised its incompetence. Guarding one's honor is especially important in the course of retreats, given the natural tendency to mistake them for acceptance of defeat and internal collapse.

Honor and Respect

The importance that America's founding generation placed on national honor may be seen in Alexander Hamilton's 1790 memo to President Washington regarding the choices facing the United States if Britain where to choose to transit its troops from Canada to the Mississippi across U.S. territory to attack Spanish New Orleans. For the U.S. government explicitly to have permitted such transit would have dishonorably violated America's peace with Spain. To have opposed the transit verbally but done nothing to stop it would have been doubly dishonorable. To oppose it by force would have meant a war with Britain, which the new nation would lose, possibly along with its independence. Perhaps, wrote Hamilton, Britain might spare America the cruel choice between war and dishonor by transiting in a way that the U.S. government could pretend to ignore? But, if British troops crossed blatantly, said Hamilton, America would have to "redeem its honor by the sword"—to fight a war that would likely finish the United States of America, rather than suffer a loss of honor that would have finished it for sure.

As America tries to return to minding its own business as much as possible, what is it to do about current commitments? The following suggest some of the relationships between commitments and honor. Keep in mind that any international commitment is, above all, a commitment of American lives, treasure, and honor, and that betrayal or cavalier attitude about commitments is, above all, betrayal and cavalier attitude toward the lives, treasure, and honor of Americans; and that U.S. officials have made a habit of promiscuous commitments halfheartedly engaged, and then dropped for new, similarly halfhearted ones. Reversing this habit, were it possible, would take a lot of doing.

In short: Progressive foreign policy having led America into some of the world's toughest saloons, today's statesmen would be well advised to back out of them without lingering at the doors, with guns pointing at enemies preferably dead.

Object Lessons

Presidents from Washington to Teddy Roosevelt would remind us that exiting commitments is more consequential than making them.

Nothing that America did in Vietnam was as consequential as how America left Vietnam in 1975. As a North Vietnamese tank pushed through the U.S. embassy compound's gate and as U.S. Marine rifle butts were smashing the fingers of doomed Vietnamese allies clinging to the last U.S. helicopter departing from its roof, millions of other Vietnamese were throwing themselves into the sea on anything that would float to get away from the vengeance that North Vietnam would wreak upon those who had worked with Americans during the previous two decades. America had given solemn promises to these people. Then, it abandoned them to cruel deaths. As well, because the U.S. government tried to pretend that it had made "peace with honor," it refused to pay the ransom that North Vietnam demanded for some 311 of our own POWs. The U.S. government tried hiding the dishonor of feckless defeat by committing the greater dishonor of abandoning its own. Then, the government officially lied about it.

Months after being awarded half of the controversial 1973 Nobel Peace Prize (he donated the prize money), Henry Kissinger led the U.S. government's bureaucratic silencing of concern for the fates of our soldiers. (North Vietnam's Le Duc Tho refused his half of the Prize, along with the pretense that he had made peace). America has never recovered from calling peace with honor something that was neither peaceful nor honorable.

Exiting Our Wars

Today, America wants out of the Middle East as much as it ever wanted out of Vietnam. How to leave this longest of our wars without engendering worse ones is by no means clear.

The following examination of what it might take to exit some of the wars that we wish did not exist shows that observing the principles of statecraft is at least as important in exiting wars as it is in entering and waging them.

Who started the U.S.–Iran War is disputable and irrelevant. In 1979, Iran's new Islamic Republic had seized the U.S. embassy and held its personnel hostage for 444 days. Arguably, that classic act of war and the subsequent train of events would not have taken place had the U.S. government not abetted one Iranian faction's overthrow of another's government in 1953, as part of the Cold War against the Soviets, and then identified itself with the winners. In 1979, when Iran's 1953 losers became the winners, their enmity to America was not to be wondered at. Anyone may regard another's interference in his affairs as an act of war. What is important is how wars end. But the U.S. government has made no attempt to end it.

Its attempt to avoid the reality that wars end only when one side wins and the other acknowledges defeat has led—among other things—to the Islamic Republic perpetrating other acts of war against the United States. With every one, the U.S. has tried to evade the question of how to establish peace—whether by surrender to whatever demands the Islamic Republic might impose, by crushing it, or by true agreement on a way to move forward. Nothing cancels out the basic choice between war and peace.

As the Islamic Republic murdered U.S. Marines in Lebanon (1983), killed U.S. troops during the U.S. occupation of Iraq (2003–9), and captured and humiliated a boatload of U.S. sailors (2016), the U.S. government complained loudly and retaliated weakly. Dumb. If you are going to absorb a beating, crying about it advertises your impotence. America's responses—unserious sanctions—have been mindless attempts to split the difference between trying to defeat Iran in war and merely bearing the conflict. All administrations judged that confrontation with Iran must not get in the way of their priorities. All have wanted out of this quandary. Nevertheless, all have acted to stay in it—with one partial exception.

President Obama tried to transcend the quandary by surrender. Choosing peace largely on Iran's terms, he gave up U.S. claims on Iran, dropped economic sanctions, released some $150 billion in frozen Iranian assets, and paid ransom for prisoners amounting to nearly $1.4 billion in U.S. hundred-dollar bills. He hoped that Iran, appeased and strengthened, would balance other forces in the Middle East and allow America to "pivot" away. It was a coherent approach. But it did not secure peace because, for the Islamic Republic's own reasons, it chose to continue and even to increase its subcritical war on America. Perhaps Iran did not accept Obama's surrender in good faith because it had lost all respect for America. But in the end, the reasons don't matter.

President Trump, even more determined than Obama to leave the Middle East to its own devices, tried to exit the quandary by forcing Iran to give up its war against America. He intended to force Iran into peace by restoring and tightening U.S. sanctions and by backing Iran's Sunni Arab opponents even more strongly. He returned bigger tits for Iran's tats. But Iran was sure to raise the stakes. At what point would Trump "raise and call"? What would Trump do to force Iran to be peaceable? The multiplication of harsh words was sure to become counterproductive: every time you remind an enemy of your power, you reassure him that, once again, you have chosen not to use it. Similarly, the ease with which Iran's ally, Qatar, lobbied Trump to relieve the pressure that the Saudis had put on that alliance helped reassure Iran that Trump's bark was worse than his bite.

In 2019, the Iranians bet that continually raising the stakes, including attacks on ships in the Strait of Hormuz, would make America's quandary increasingly untenable. Trump had been elected, promising to withdraw from the Middle East's wars *and* to be tougher on Iran. Iran's 2019 attacks surely meant to force Trump to choose between two potentially incompatible promises. Trump's initial reaction was more bombing: bigger tits for tats. Then he countermanded his order, perhaps conscious that the American people rightly fear that the bombs would eventually be followed by U.S. soldiers kicking down doors to try pacifying yet another country. Then, after Iranian attacks on the U.S. embassy in Baghdad killed an American contractor, Trump authorized killing Iran's second-ranking personage, General Qasem Soleimani and followed up with yet more sanctions. This, being bigger than any previous tit or tat, discomfited the Islamic Republic and showed its people its weakness. A little, for a while.

The Biden administration's announced intention to return to Obama's "Iran deal" shifted the focus to how much U.S. pressures would decline. The Biden team used Iran's announcement that it had increased enrichment of uranium as an argument for easing sanctions. The war continues at Iran's discretion.

What Does Peace Take?

But tits for tats cannot secure peace because they do not settle wars one way or the other. Nor do they establish mutual respect.

The public despises U.S. officials as weak if they fail to respond to provocations, and it accuses them of incompetent warmongering if they respond militarily. It could hardly be otherwise, since few alive have experienced U.S. military action as anything but incompetent sacrifice of blood and treasure for gauzy goals. The U.S. establishment knows only sanctions, bombings, invasions, and occupations without end. It does not ask: how do we end this war? How do we reestablish the respect and fear that had previously made peace possible? And if we don't do it now, how do we do it after Iran acquires nuclear weapons?

Here is one possibility. There may be others. Because America is the world's primary economic power, American *secondary sanctions*—meaning "we will not trade with anyone who trades with" the target country—are potentially deadlier than atom bombs. Trump added secondary financial sanctions as part of his revocation of the "Iran deal," reducing Iran's oil sales to a trickle. Compared to that measure of war, bombing a few ports is nothing. Were the United States to place secondary sanctions on all manner of goods, especially food, the effect would be far greater than an invasion by the entire U.S. army. How the Iranian people would deal with the choice between starving and ending their government's war on America would be their business.

Backing out of our military ventures in the Middle East into peace requires reestablishing unambiguous fear for what happens to whoever crosses America. That depends on the U.S. government re-earning a reputation for respecting its own commitments. Given our establishment's record, that will take some doing.

The Kurds

In 1975, as Kissinger was masterminding the U.S. exit from Vietnam, he also withdrew the United States from a war between Iraq and its Kurdish population. To relieve the pressure that Iraq was putting on America's then-ally Iran, Kissinger had armed Iraq's Kurds and blown their smoldering resentment into war. Then, Iraq having agreed to back off its pressure against Iran, Kissinger withdrew support from the Kurds, leaving them to face the Iraqi government's genocidal vengeance, disarmed. Asked to explain, he replied: "Covert action should not be confused with missionary work." Earlier, he had quipped that while "it may be dangerous to be America's enemy... to be America's friend is fatal." Such retail Machiavellism and wholesale naïveté can only undermine respect at home as well as abroad.

In 2014, after nearly all U.S. ground troops had left the Middle East, and as the Islamic State sect was ritually slaughtering Americans, the U.S. government saw in the Kurds the only local force willing and able to fight ISIS on the ground. In exchange for helping America, these Kurds were given some arms, barely sufficient to secure themselves for a time in the mountainous strip that runs westward from Iran along the border between Syria and Turkey. The U.S. government knew that the governments of Turkey, Iraq, Iran, and Syria, are dead set against the Kurds ever having a home of their own. Nevertheless, the U.S. government committed to the Kurds without plans to deal with a matter of honor that, eventually, it could not escape.

By 2019, with ISIS dead, Turkey's President Recep Erdoğan, having made no secret of his commitment to crush the Kurds, nearly convinced President Trump to leave them in his tender care. The U.S. public "wants out" of the Middle East. But, how America exits the Middle East is more important to our honor—that is, to our interest in the respect that makes for our own peace—than why we engaged in the first place.

As Plato shows, doing good to those who have done good to you, and harming those who have harmed you, is far from all there is to justice and political competence. But the opposite, doing harm to those who do good to you, is obviously stupid, as well as unjust and dishonorable. *Morality enjoins the positive side of simple justice; self-interest the negative.* History records few instances of durable peace built on betrayals.

Through a half century of U.S. involvement in the Middle East, the Kurds have been the only group that has never shot at Americans, indeed on whom America has called for help, repeatedly and fruitfully. America is under no obligation to deliver a Kurdish state. But, as America withdraws from the region, a Kurdish state's existence would be in America's interest because, in our time, America's enemies are the ones who benefit from its absence— specifically, Erdoğan's Turkey, an Iraq increasingly in thrall to Iran, Iran itself, and Bashar Assad's Syria. Nothing could quite so surely put the brakes on these bad actors' ill designs as would the existence in their midst of a state composed of the region's incomparable fighters, well-armed by America. Think of it as America's parting gift to the region, or an object lesson on the beneficent power of smart, peaceful retreats.

What Makes for Honor and Respect?

What, then, are the principles by which statesmen may earn the respect that permits peace? This question does not call for another of the countless "mirrors of princes," guides for the behavior of statesmen (religious but mostly secular) written since St. Augustine's fifth-century *City of God*, the best known of which is Machiavelli's *Prince*. That is because, in the American tradition, these principles, elaborated and practiced by John Quincy Adams and his successors, follow from George Washington's simple observation that "the foundation of our national policy will be laid in the pure and immutable principles of private morality." He did not need to elaborate.

Respect from others presupposes respect for one's self. That is why the U.S. ruling class's disdain for at least half its people and for America's history, its canceling of heretofore iconic names and symbols, the toppling of statues, makes it impossible for foreign nations to respect it.

We have no choice but to point out, embarrassing as it might be, that honesty and plain dealing really are the best policy. It is as necessary for us to do that as Diodotus once did for the Athenians, because the past century's U.S. statesmen and academics, following European traditions and pseudo-scientific ideologies, have scoffed at Washington's, Adams's, and others' simplicities. They have done so because the very "principles of private morality" are becoming foreign to America.

PRACTICING THE PRINCIPLES

We began by stating that any country's foreign policy is less a choice than it is another expression of the character of the nation itself, and of the persons who set its tone. As we try to resume the foreign policy that once made for America's peace with the world, let us keep in mind the timeless principles that made possible that peace. Plato, Aristotle, and Cicero led classical philosophy in understanding how very difficult it is for any individual properly to establish order in his own soul, thereby achieving peace within himself, and consequently on what it takes to achieve the proper order of families and society. Jesus and his followers deepened that understanding: giving what is due to each is justice's simplest definition. That understanding of justice presupposes that each soul's parts have their proper claims, which must be satisfied in proper order. By the same token, justice within families and countries means maintaining proper order among their parts' just claims. Establishing proper order within one's own nation may be literally the most necessary and most difficult task on earth. International relations complicate it.

Consequently, the order and welfare of one's own nation is international statecraft's paramount concern. Minding America's business must be American statesmen's primary objective—an objective for which the highest human talents are scarcely sufficient. America First must be American statesmen's primary goal and compass. Seeking any other nation's order, or the world's order, is sheer madness.

From these general assumptions there follow a few practical principles applicable to personal as well as to international life. Let us see how they might apply to our time.

Plain Truth

Because words are thought's raw material, precision of speech is a precondition for responsible thought. *In all languages, matching words to the realities with which they deal anchors minds to reality.* As we have seen, Progressive statecraft is built on the opposite, on euphemisms—synthetic intellectual drugs that make unpleasant facts of life seem pleasant, impossible things seem possible, and unmanageable ones manageable. From these come fantasies: e.g., that foreigners value what Americans value, that respect is unmixed with fear, that wealth is everyone's overriding goal, and that the diplomatic process is powerful all by itself and can be a substitute for purpose backed by force.

In fact, shedding euphemisms, calling things by their proper names, and removing excess language are all preconditions for sober statecraft. The biblical injunction to "let your communication be, Yea, yea; Nay, nay: for whatsoever is more than these cometh of evil" is as valid for nations as for individuals. Using words correctly, as did Americans of an earlier age, would help us deal with reality as they did.

A firm understanding of what the Declaration of Independence says are self-evident truths—the universality of "certain inalienable rights" as well as the absolute right of each and every people to rule itself—would enable American statesmen in our time, as it did in earlier ones, to deal without pretense with diverse foreign regimes regardless of their differences with ourselves. It would allow Americans today to practice moral judgment together with respect, as much as Lincoln did when professing friendship with Russia's tsar, or Seward did as he cozied up to China's Qing dynasty.

Teddy Roosevelt's injunction to say (only) what you mean and to mean what you say might have been a paraphrase of Confucius's "If what is said is not what is meant, then what ought to be done remains undone ... hence there must be no arbitrariness in what is said." Or it might have been a paraphrase of Jesus. Perhaps it was simply the American people's common sense. Anyhow, Adams's and TR's clarity makes for fewer misunderstandings than Kissinger's "creative ambiguity."

The American people as a whole have few views about foreign matters; to speak as if they did is a lie that possibly endangers peace. Since no government is obliged to pay attention to events outside its own jurisdiction, when it "takes note" of an event, it signals that it may do something about it. But to speak and not to act, or to act at variance with one's words, is as irresponsible as it was when TR called that practice the combination of "the unbridled tongue with the unready hand."

If we want foreigners to respect our words, we ourselves must be the first to respect those words. Boasting, manufacturing a charade of power à la the Wizard of Oz, threatening, demanding, deeming "unacceptable," drawing "red lines"—and then acting as if such words had never been spoken—has become so normal for U.S. statesmen that much of mankind has ceased to take America seriously. Worse, Americans are ceasing to take America seriously. Far better to shut up. As TR said, "Unreadiness for war is merely rendered more disastrous by readiness to bluster; to talk defiance and advocate a vigorous policy in words, while refusing to back up these words by deeds." Neglecting the dictionary definitions of peace and war, making half-baked war, and perverting peace, is how Progressive statesmen have squandered America's respect.

In 1954, merely conveying the hint that America might be supporting the shadow of a (non-existent) guerrilla army was enough to convince Guatemala's dictator to flee. But by 1961, when the United States mounted a massive show of force to convince Fidel Castro that it would ensure the success of the substantial rebel force that landed on the Bay of Pigs, Castro had already learned by experience that American officials did not have it in them to do what they advertise. Since then, the odds have been with those who bet against American seriousness. The fact is, the U.S. government can be counted on to back off, perhaps to make an expensive show, but ultimately to let others have their way. Re-earning squandered respect requires saying less, promising much less, and making sure that America's word is its bond.

Thinking of the people who run the Muslim world's oil states as "producers"—though they produce nothing—is contrary to reality. That word's granting of rights and privileges to them is unjustified. Understanding them as did American statesmen of an earlier age—in terms of their real weakness, moral squalor, and dependence—would make it possible to have from them the peace that those Americans enjoyed rather than the troubles we get.

The U.S. government's 2018–19 attempt to remove the regime of Nicolas Maduro from Venezuela tracks its anti-Castro debacle of 1961 all too closely: massive resources and power, local allies encouraged to put themselves in vulnerable positions and basically abandoned to their fates. Given the plan's lack of an efficient cause—that which actually forces the thing to happen—it would have been better had U.S. officials left bad enough alone. As it is, they let Maduro and his Russian, Iranian, and Chinese supporters make a ridiculous example of America. Making an even livelier example of those countries and ones like them is indispensable to America's interest.

The discrepancy between America's words and deeds is a moral problem, not an intellectual one. It has gone on for so long, so obviously, that it is a wonder why some president (recognizing that failure to back up one's words is the equivalent of lying) does not do away with all the confusion and impose on himself and his administration the discipline of silence, truth, clarity, and integrity. That is because there is nothing clever about lying or pretending, because lies and pretenses have short legs, and because agreement between words and deeds is as essential to the nation's peace as it is to any individual's moral order and social interactions.

Mind Our Own Business

Statecraft's primary question is: what exactly are we after? Intelligence professionals and diplomats who ask rhetorically: "How can we know what we are to do unless we understand others?" have it backward. Knowledge of others is secondary. We may understand others only to the extent that we understand ourselves. Indeed, what we need to know about others is how they may relate to what we ourselves are about. Knowing ourselves is the primary necessity. Only by knowing ourselves can we know what we need and what we should fear from others.

Our own defense—of our borders and of the ocean, air, and orbital space approaches to our country—is our primary business. What do we want from other nations, and what are we willing and able to do to get it? Woodrow Wilson said that "the interests of all nations are our own also. We are partners with the rest." No. On the contrary, American statesmen must regard whatever may be happening in Ruritania from the American people's perspective. What, if anything, is what happens elsewhere to the American people? Why should any American invest attention, honor, money, and blood in it? The answers had better be good—and presented in good English.

Peace is what we want from and with others. Refraining from meddling in others' business helps. But Americans can control only half of the equation of peace. Peace requires mutually sorting out with each what each regards as its own business. In 1783–1830, no peace was possible with North Africa's sheikdoms, whose business was to seize American ships and sell their crews. Nor was any peace other than forbearance and formalities possible with the Ottoman Empire that enslaved Christians—which most Americans were.

The Soviet Union made itself our business in the biggest of ways. Its hostile intentions toward America and Americans were tempered only by the limited means at its command and by the United States' capacity to resist. Its Cold War on America mixed peace with war. To a far more limited extent, so has Iran's government made itself our business. What sense does it make to consider ourselves at peace with a regime that shouts "Death to America!" while building nuclear weapons? North Korea is in the same category. China neither shouts nor commits acts of war, and it is a major trading partner. Yet its military, diplomatic, and commercial policies are as hostile as any of the Soviets' ever were. Its interference in our internal affairs, though of a different kind, may be even more serious.

Such confrontations have confused the categories of peace and war in the minds of U.S. statesmen and led them mistakenly to suppose that we live in Thomas Hobbes's world of permanent war of all against all. Ironically and ignorantly, they also concluded that peace itself is an illusion and that war need not be taken seriously.

But war is deadly serious, and peace is not an illusion. Pursuing peace in the context of other peoples' or governments' character, sentiments, and intentions regarding ourselves requires constant attention to the distinction between what is and is not our business.

Iraq's Saddam Hussein did not become America's business by behaving in a beastly manner toward his own people or by displeasing Saudi Arabia. He made himself our enemy when he became involved with anti-American terrorism. The U.S. government chose not to mind our business. Syria's Assad dynasty also made itself our business by injuring America over a half century. The U.S. government paid insufficient attention to that business, choosing instead to join the war that Syria's Sunnis are making on its current ruler, fighting on their behalf, not ours. But identifying America's business with that of Syria's Sunnis cannot be justified to the American people, since the Sunnis would oppress Syria's Christian minority, which the Assad dynasty protects. In short, our statesmen have not been minding our business as the American people understand it. They should.

While the distinction between peace and war, drawn as it is by willingness to kill and die, is clear and bright, the character of any peace depends on assessing correctly what the constantly shifting balance of foreigners' affections and interests mean for the American people.

By definition, any foreign government's "unfriendly acts" intrude upon our business, though not in as compelling a manner as acts of war. "NATO ally" Turkey's purchase of Russia's potent S-400 air defense system is such an act. The Qatari government's hosting of the al Jazeera TV network is another, one that borders on war. Securing our peace means minding our business in such cases in ways that command respect. In the case of Turkey that should mean, in the short run, less reticence on our part in supporting the Kurds—something that we might do regardless of our relations with Turkey. With regard to Qatar, it would mean, at least, making its government choose between hosting al Jazeera and hosting the U.S. base at Al Udeid, as well as U.S. investments. But the U.S. government minds America's interest less than it does the interests of its components and officials.

No one disputes that the Qatari government sponsors anti-American groups and causes, that it is Iran's only ally in the Gulf, that al Jazeera is the Muslim world's foremost anti-Western megaphone, and hence that a substantial part of what its government does results in dead Americans. But Qatar's money bought deep influence in the State Department and U.S. politics, while its hosting of the base secures a consistent friendly voice within the Defense Department. Its willingness to pay top dollar for U.S. military equipment secures the U.S. defense industry's support. In June 2017, President Trump, citing Qatar's various nefarious activities, supported Saudi Arabia's, Egypt's, and the Emirates' boycott and blockade of the country. By 2019, after much lobbying, Trump gave its Sheik al-Thani red carpet treatment at the White House and said how happy he was that he had brought America so much good business.

What is America's proper business with Qatar? Surely, examining that question from the standpoint of America rather than from the interests of corporations and its officials would point to one item of business that overrides all others: stopping its government from doing things that end up killing Americans.

A hundred years ago, this priority would have been crystal clear. It should be no less clear today.

Take Responsibility

Sound foreign policy depends on unity of conception, expression, and execution. But no government, including monarchies, has ever been immune to equivocation or corruption. Beginning in 1670, English royal officials—including King Charles II and later James II—were being paid secretly by Louis XIV to skew policy France's way. Much of George Washington's Farewell Address was a rebuke to Thomas Jefferson and Alexander Hamilton for their policy partisanship. The current U.S. establishment's size, diversity, and disjointed bureaucracies encourages

presidents to shed their appropriate responsibilities by defer-
ring—or pretending to defer—to the diplomats, the intelligence
agencies, and the military that, in turn, have not been shy about
claiming monopoly of legitimacy over policy—although denying
responsibility for it. Reestablishing the responsibility of presidents, and their responsibility to the voters, is prerequisite to
sound policy.

Too many people performing too many functions physically
prevent presidents from exercising control as they did a century
ago. Mere imposition of bureaucratic discipline cannot overcome
this. Drastically reducing the foreign policy bureaucracy's size is
prerequisite to responsibility. But irresponsibility itself flows from
the top.

The role of U.S. intelligence agencies is a prime example of how
foreign policy has succumbed to the ways of the administrative
state. Prior to World War II, American statesmen made decisions
on the basis of their own understanding of foreign situations,
augmented by reports from diplomats and from a press that actually reported facts. But the wartime Office of Strategic Services
(OSS, 1942) and the CIA that succeeded it, composed as they were
and are of academics, promoted the novel notion that statecraft
had to be informed by deep research leavened by spying's secret
tidbits—that is, by specialized "intelligence" (by which they meant
their own opinions), not intelligence of the ordinary kind. This is
part and parcel of Progressivism's core proposition that the correct path in human affairs is to be discovered through specialized
knowledge rather than by politically responsible common sense.

The CIA has long contended that intelligence, properly done,
would leave the president only command's ceremonial function.
Thus, President Kennedy felt that he would be on politically firm
ground confronting the Soviets in 1962 only after he had close-ups
of Soviet missiles in Cuba, and President George W. Bush invaded
Iraq in 2003 only according to the rationale that the CIA was willing publicly to support—saving the world from "Weapons of Mass
Destruction." During the subsequent occupation, Bush defended
his actions by saying that they were what the generals advised.
From the outset of Donald Trump's presidency, the intelligence

agencies, backed vociferously by the media, argued that he acted irresponsibly because his decisions sometimes were in opposition to their own or other bureaucracies' "professional" views.

The point here is not that presidents are likelier to make better judgments than bureaucrats, but to reiterate that the logic of operations requires unity of conception and consistency of execution, while the logic of representative government demands that the persons responsible for conception and execution be answerable to the people. Like everything else, U.S. foreign policy is the sovereign American people's business. That means decisions about what ought or ought not to be done must be made by persons who must explain them to the satisfaction of those who can throw them out of office.

Explaining things to ordinary persons immersed in their ordinary reality requires abandoning the make-believe language of Progressivism in favor of ordinary language. But ordinary language itself may be used to obscure reality, through boasting or common allusions. Politicians are just as drawn to escapism as bureaucrats. Political accountability guarantees only that, under pressure to explain things to others, those responsible for decisions may explain them to themselves.

For this reason, the discipline that is most essential to good policy is the intellectual one by which we think, speak, and act in terms of plain truth and distinguish our business from that of others—the important from the trivial—as well as the moral discipline by which we act. It is also the discipline to make today's choices *today* rather than to protract studies and arguments, or simply to kick cans down the road.

Match Ends and Means

Solvency is the basis of business. Ensuring that you have sufficient means to accomplish the goal is required when considering any proposed enterprise. The range of what we might try to accomplish with regard to the Pacific Ocean, for example, runs all the way from 1) trying to crush China and establish hegemony as never before, to 2) reestablishing the primacy that we enjoyed for the half century after 1945, to 3) fostering the capacity of Western Pacific nations from Japan to the Straits of Malacca to maintain their independence, to 4) merely maintaining freedom of navigation throughout, to 5) just safeguarding Hawaii and eastward. Which option we choose is arguably less important than that there be no confusion in our minds or in anybody else's that the U.S. government and the American people are ready, willing, and able to use all the means, do all the things necessary to accomplish the chosen goal, and absorb the costs.

Matching the means committed to any given objective, lowering the objective, or raising the level of means to ensure enough means to achieve the ends will henceforth be required of America because, given the U.S. government's consistent record of weak incompetence, any foreign government will assume that America can be pushed or pulled off whatever position it might take. Proving otherwise will be costly.

Jealous squaring of ends and means is difficult enough when the distinction between our business and others' business is accurate and when the matter is discussed in plain language. But when these vital categories are confused and matters are framed in allusive language, reason is rendered powerless.

What is "world order"? What is a "rules-based environment"? What are "international democratic values"? What is "international comity"? What are "international norms"? Who or what stands in the way of mankind's enjoyment of these goods? Who would have to be killed to remove these obstacles? Who would do the killing? At what point would it stop?

The point is that trying to fulfill Progressive dreams would require far more power, knowledge, and virtue than is available to human beings. If such efforts were to be approached honestly, they would not get past the initial planning phases. But the past century's foreign policy of semi-forceful global meliorism has been based on pretense. It is time to get back to reality, to America First.

TWENTY

America's Peace

In the *Federalist Papers*, No. 1, Alexander Hamilton wrote: "It seems to have been reserved to the people of this country, by their conduct and example, to decide the important question, whether societies of men are really capable or not of establishing good government from reflection and choice, or whether they are forever destined to depend for their political constitutions on accident and force." The eighty-five *Federalist Papers*, by Hamilton, James Madison, and John Jay, argue that fostering the people's reflection and choice is the Constitution's whole purpose. Reflection and choice are all that may turn a merely popular government into a virtuous republic. The first eleven papers concern primarily America's relations with foreign nations. But they leave no doubt that peace with foreigners and peace among Americans—they might also have said the safety of individuals—depend equally on cool reflection and choice, and that what happens in each realm impacts the other.

The United States Constitution, especially as the *Federalist Papers* describe it, is much about procedure, checks, and balances. Yet its authors were under no illusions about what Madison called "parchment barriers." They saw discussion and mutual persuasion as means to "refine" the "deliberate sense" of the people. In the final analysis, they placed their trust in a good people's capacity to reason about better and worse.

Beginning in the 1820s, as the American people, North and South, began to regard each other as enemies, their passions tore through the Constitution's parchment barriers. But even as the Civil War raged, both sides retained among themselves the constitutional habits of procedure and internal peace. All revered their American-ness. Surely the most surprising thing about the Civil War is that something like national unity returned within a mere half century.

In our time, the enmities among Americans that Progressivism has fostered pose challenges to peace at home and abroad potentially greater and longer-lasting than those that underlay the Civil War. From Progressivism's outset in the 1880s, its adherents—

a distinct social class from the beginning—have disdained the limits that the Constitution places on government, precisely because these limits require the public's consent for anything significant to be done. Obvious contempt for the general run of humanity is the Progressive class's distinguishing feature. They suppose that most Americans are not good, and neither is America. As a result, Progressives are unshakably certain of their own right and duty to have their way. In Progressive minds, persuasion by reason is not for opponents any more than it is for animals.

This has meant endless, ill-considered strife abroad. At home, it has meant peremptory demands that the general public bend to the Progressive class's evolving mores and judgments. Since war abroad has helped endow the government with ever greater powers at home, Progressives have been eager to use them against domestic resistance. A cold civil war at home has been the result. Nineteenth-century American society's split had been merely political and had occurred along geographic lines. That limited the Civil War's horrors. But today's warming civil conflict is religious and social even more than it is political—and the contending sides are intermingled. If this century's American civil war turns hot, it is difficult to imagine its end. Preventing or mitigating that conflict's inflammation, maintaining peace among ourselves, is our paramount task.

Foreign policy, the defense of the Republic, is the one undeniable interest that all Americans share, whether they like it or not. It should not be difficult, even for Americans who hate one another, to agree that the consequences of foreign wars, especially of wars unsupported by the public, are not good for anyone. For this reason, "reflection and choice" about George Washington's commandment to place policy on morality's "immutable foundations" may be as good a cornerstone as any on which to put America First.

A NOTE ON THE TYPE

AMERICA'S RISE AND FALL AMONG NATIONS has been set in Fontsmith's Sally types. *A crisp, contemporary take on transitional types* (*think Baskerville and Bulmer*), Sally's *elegant letterforms make for pleasurable reading, even at small sizes and over long texts. The types' slightly narrow proportions and vertical emphasis make it an economical choice for compositors, allowing large amounts of text to be set tightly without sacrificing legibility.*

DESIGN & COMPOSITION BY CARL W. SCARBROUGH